PRAISE FOR *NEW YORK MINUTE*

"These revelatory pages prove that New York's public clocks are more than just keepers of time; they are, with their ceaseless determination and perpetual swirl of activity, reflections of the city itself. With the eye of a designer, the mind of a historian, and the heart of a true New Yorker, Matthew White shows us how these timepieces have shaped our urban landscape—and the rhythm of our daily lives—in ways both practical and profound."

—David Rockwell, architect,
designer, and founder and president
of the Rockwell Group

"Matthew White captures the very soul of New York through the beauty of its hidden-in-plain-sight timekeepers, as they quietly and insistently mark the pulse of a city that never sleeps. Father Time has never felt so omnipresent nor so wonderfully life-affirming."

—Joel Grey, award-winning
actor and photographer

"Matthew White adroitly relates with what generosity the city was endowed with so many clocks, beautifully made and in great variety. He carefully documents both those which survive and others long lost. My assessment of his fine book is the highest praise possible to give: Oh how I wish I had written it myself!"

—Michael Henry Adams, Harlem-based
preservationist, historian, and author

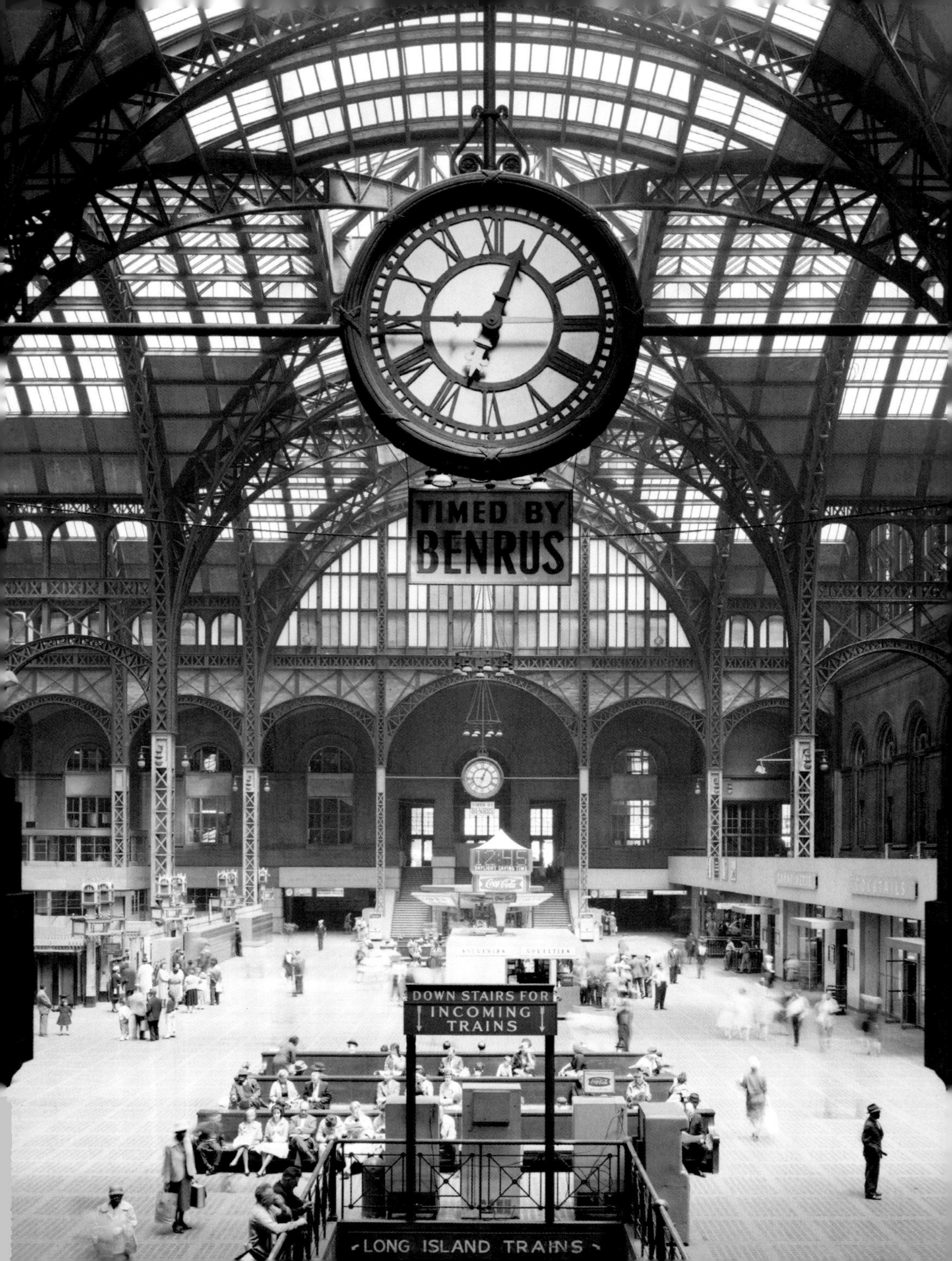

TIMED BY
BENRUS
SOUVENIRS
DOWN STAIRS FOR
INCOMING
TRAINS
· LONG ISLAND TRAINS ·

MATTHEW WHITE

NEW YORK MINUTE

PUBLIC CLOCKS THAT MAKE THE CITY TICK

ABBEVILLE PRESS

NEW YORK   LONDON

FRONT COVER: The *Sun* Newspaper clock; see p. 70.
PAGE 2: Old Penn Station clock; see p. 178.
Clock drawings by Matthew White

PROJECT EDITOR: Lauren Orthey
COPY EDITOR: Stephanie Baker
DESIGN: Misha Beletsky
PRODUCTION MANAGER: Louise Kurtz

First edition
10 9 8 7 6 5 4 3 2 1
ISBN 978-0-7892-1517-8

Library of Congress Cataloging-in-Publication Data available upon request
For bulk and premium sales and for text adoption procedures, write to Customer Service Manager, Abbeville Press, 655 Third Avenue, New York, NY 10017, or call 1-800-ARTBOOK.
Visit Abbeville Press online at www.abbeville.com.

CONTENTS

FOREWORD

BY WENDY GOODMAN

Matthew White's *New York Minute: Public Clocks that Make the City Tick* opened my eyes to the amazing beauty hidden in plain sight on the streets and buildings of our urban landscape. These exquisite timepieces, many erected during the Beaux-Arts glamour of the Gilded Age, seem to be everywhere once you have been made aware of them. They originally served as a vital public service for most of the population, who could not afford personal timepieces, and in doing so became decorative elements within their immediate environment.

Matthew's book is a unique lens on the city's architectural history, illustrating what we have gained and what we have lost. The most grievous loss being the original Penn Station, where beneath the glass roofs and iron trusses, mighty clocks gave passengers a clear picture of the time. The photographs in Matthew's book remind us that the station was as beautiful as any world monument, and its demise in 1963 was an incomparable loss to the city.

And no surprise that it would be Matthew to bring all this to light, as he has always applied his curiosity, talent, and scholarship to the things he loves. When he arrived in New York City from Amarillo, Texas in 1977 to study ballet, he would walk the streets getting to know the different neighborhoods. He cofounded the interior design firm White Webb with designer

Frank Webb in 2004, and his preservationist and entrepreneur-
ial spirit took root, restoring the 1855 building where he opened
Hillsdale General Store in 2011.

I met Matthew shortly after he started White Webb, and we
discovered our mutual love of the ballet. Our friendship has en-
riched so many aspects of my life, ballet being but one of them.

Matthew is a gentleman in the truest sense of the word, with
an innate elegance that goes way beyond his impeccable sense
of style. He has an astute eye that never misses anything, and
that is why this unusual and highly valuable book adds so much
to the discourse about the design of the city we love and love to
hate sometimes. The city keeps reinventing itself for better and
for worse—and leave it to Matthew to show us how beautiful it
can be.

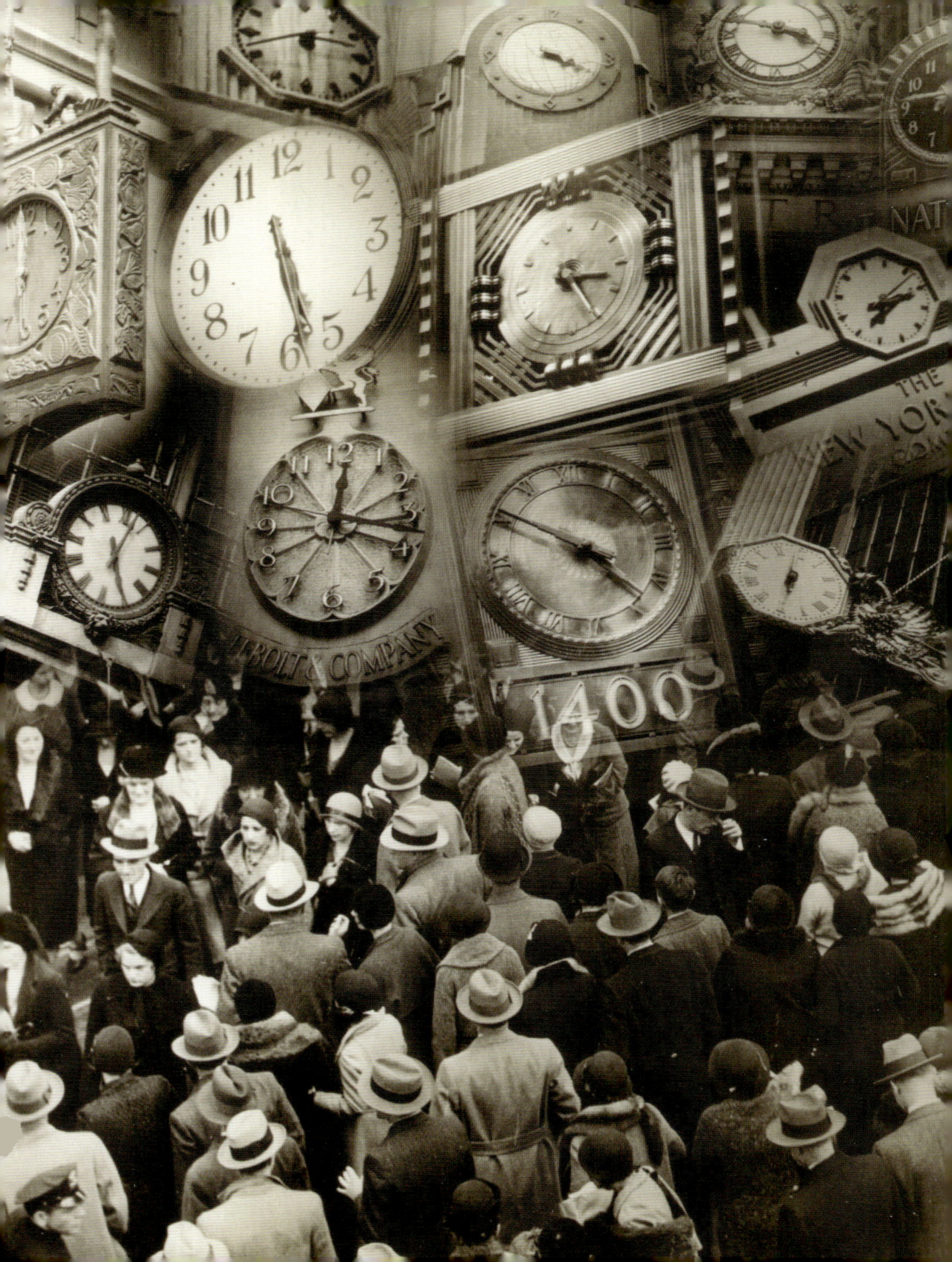
NAT
THE NEW YOR
BOLT & COMPANY
1400

INTRODUCTION

From its earliest days as a Dutch trading post in 1624 to becoming the largest city in the United States in 1790, New York attracted immigrants and refugees, movers and shakers, outcasts and wannabes. It still does. Those of us who came to the big city in pursuit of big dreams left places that, by definition, were smaller and certainly slower. Many sacrificed everything to come here in the late nineteenth and early twentieth centuries, filtering through Ellis Island and passing the Statue of Liberty to see a city like no other. Others, like me, arrived not as an immigrant, but as a sort of domestic refugee, escaping places that weren't just slow but, more critically, held no room for us. For many, escape to New York meant a chance for survival.

On August 15, 1958, at 9:51 p.m., I was born in Amarillo, Texas, a place where time wasn't just slow but seemed to have stopped. Texans from the panhandle often speak at a glacial pace, stretching out their words and even adding syllables where they don't exist. This speech can be enormously charming and hats off for the ability to take one's own time to express a thought, but I never had the patience to sit still while waiting for folks to finish a story whose punchline I already knew.

As in most small towns in those pre-internet days, our social circle was limited with little hope for diversity or expansion. In the 1960s, my world was confined by religion and race. If my large extended family mixed with outsiders, I was not aware of it. Perhaps those boundaries brought comfort to some, but for

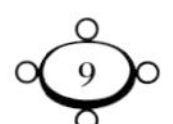

This photomontage was perhaps created to illustrate a story in a metropolitan publication.

me it brought both clarity and concern as I started to understand such differences and realized I was an outsider in my own hometown. I was a gay kid in an enthusiastically religious family and as I watched and listened, I saw every concept outside the family's belief system quickly debunked and dismissed. I began to wonder whether I could survive if, and when, my truth was known.

As usual, I am getting ahead of myself. Let's go back to the topic of time.

Timepieces are among the earliest inventions created by humans. Designed to measure dimensions of time shorter than years, seasons, or days, they allowed the user to divide their waking hours in an organized way. Sundials, water clocks, and hourglasses are among the oldest known timepieces. Centuries later, in the 1300s, mechanical clocks were invented in Europe. Once those early clocks were created, people lucky enough to have them had to learn how to read time. It wasn't until the late nineteenth century and well into the twentieth that personal timepieces were used by the average person, making the reading of clocks an essential part of every child's education.

Following the typical American school curriculum, my elementary school teacher attempted to teach our class how to tell time. Numbers were never my thing. I understood the big hand and little hand part, but the rest required math I found confusing. I missed the point of the hidden numbers—the idea that between each numeral on the clock was five minutes. My undiagnosed dyslexia and escapist daydreaming didn't help me learn a skill that was clearly in my interest as a future New Yorker. My teachers never revisited the subject, and I meticulously avoided it due to my profound embarrassment and fear of being seen as stupid.

Fast-forward to freshman year in high school, where Mrs. Douglass (ironically my math teacher) asked me what time it was in front of the entire class. There was no clock in our classroom, and

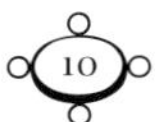

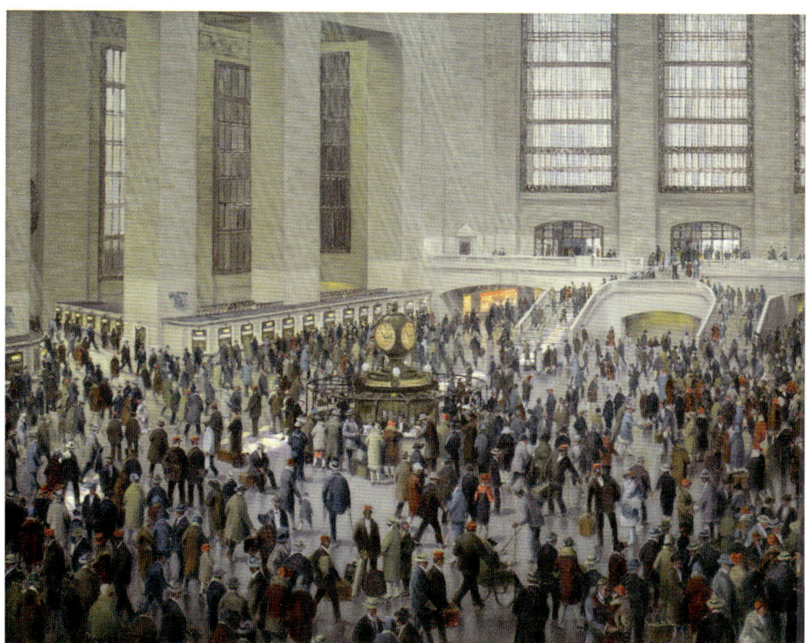

Howard Thain (1891–1959)
Grand Central Station, NYC, 1927
Oil on canvas, 30 × 36 in. (76.2 × 91.4 cm)
New York Historical, New York

Howard Thain moved from Texas to New
York in 1919, and his own travels perhaps
inspired this scene of a busy Grand Central.

she had forgotten to wind her watch that morning. The wall of
the classroom abutting the hallway was plate glass and in that
hallway was a clock perfectly positioned for me to see from my
desk, so she naturally called on me.

Under pressure, I panicked. I was a painfully shy kid trying
my best to remain invisible, but there I was, forced into the un-
wanted spotlight by Mrs. Douglass. Exposed, with my head spin-
ning, I was at a loss. My heartbeat counted off the seconds as it
pounded deafeningly in my ears. Had I been the class clown I
could've made a joke to escape my predicament, but that wasn't

me. Instead, I slinked up to Mrs. Douglass and came clean by whispering in her ear: "I don't know how to tell time." Red-faced, I quickly returned to my seat as she didn't miss a beat to ask the girl behind me the fated question. Asked and answered.

That Christmas, after hinting for months, I received a digital watch, the hot new accessory for stylish gentlemen, which I aspired to one day be. Gold-toned with a plain garnet-colored glass face, it required the pushing of a button to illuminate the concealed numbers. I loved it, mostly because I no longer had a panic attack if asked for the time.

At long last the day arrived for me to leave Texas and seek my future. At eighteen, I boarded a flight to New York City to attend the School of American Ballet and pursue my dream of becoming a classical dancer (plot twist!). A bit of time and experience led me to this moment, and finally I was leaving Texas to go to a place where people moved and shook as fast as I hoped to do. (It was a miracle I even made it to the airport in time, given my family's habit of being notoriously late to absolutely everything.)

Thrown into a city throbbing with energy that sweltering summer of 1977, I dipped a pointed toe into the adventure of making my way in the world. For the first time in my life, I felt I belonged. In New York, there was no time for chitchat with store clerks. Here people were not necessarily nice, but I immediately found New Yorkers to be enormously kind. The opposite was true back home, at least in my experience. Outsiders in Texas were looked on with mistrust, at best, but in my new city I shared sidewalks and subway cars with outsiders of every possible stripe. New Yorkers had places to be and things to do; talking endlessly on topics everyone agreed on was not one of them.

When I wasn't in the ballet studio, I indulged my passion for historic architecture by simply walking through my adopted, centuries-old city. These walks allowed me to time travel. That's how I experienced New York then, and how I still experience it today. Besides the astonishing buildings and sidewalks crowded with people from every walk of life, I was attracted to Manhattan's extravagant public timepieces, most created in an age when the regular New Yorker did not carry a watch. These clocks performed a public service while beautifying the urban landscape. Towers, pediments, skyscrapers, building lobbies, and even sidewalks featured beautiful clocks that functioned as metronomes counting out the pulse of a great metropolis.

The surprising and often glorious public timepieces in this book are some of my favorites. Each has a story to tell. I've organized these clocks into categories, one for each chapter, ordered in a way one might move through the city, from workday to weekend. We begin this "tour" at Grand Central Terminal, a monumental structure with perhaps the largest concentration of recognizable clocks in the city, among them one that is a perfect expression of Gilded Age exuberance. As we move through the city and toward the weekend, time slows a bit during our visit to iconic New York clocks while shopping, going to church, and taking in the delights of automaton clocks.

The final chapter highlights a group of phantom clocks that live in the memory of a dwindling number of New Yorkers—the timepieces of one of the world's greatest train stations, the tragically lost Pennsylvania Station. *New York Minute* closes with a lone contemporary clock, an excellent example at the new Moynihan Train Hall. This clock joins scores of others from centuries past that still make New Yorkers proud while keeping the city running on time for generations. Each one was created, and remains, for all New Yorkers—ex-Texans and every possible variety of urban refugee joyfully included. These glorious timepieces tick for us all, telling the story of not just any city, but of New York City, where there isn't a moment to waste.

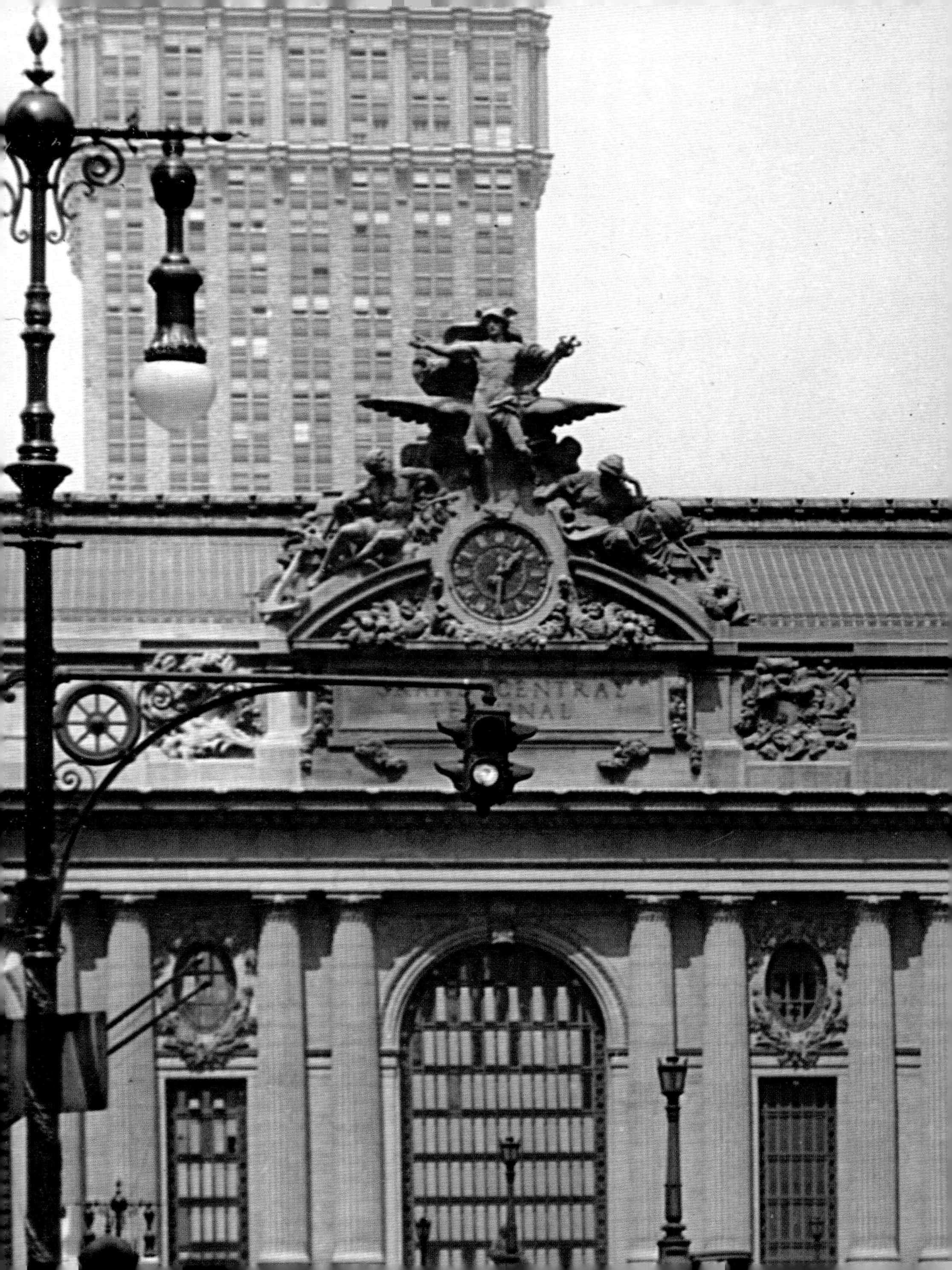

THE TRAIN'S ON TIME

GRAND CENTRAL
TERMINAL CLOCKS

When I arrive at Grand Central Terminal and enter the main concourse, I feel the whole of New York open, as if just for me. This is a private pleasure, shared by millions. The city's history, aspirations, brilliance, and even hospitality hover in this room. My heart lifts every time, and as I watch the faces of those around me, I recognize in them the same wonder of the sheer magnitude and thoughtful beauty of it all. The zodiac ceiling seems as expansive as the sky itself, and on the ground level a human-scaled brass kiosk rests, surmounted by the famous globe clock. This isn't simply a singular, historic room; it is a living space filled with a constant flow of energy. And smack dab in the middle of the organized chaos of humanity: a calm and steady reminder of time.

Grand Central is a world landmark while being of practical daily use to New Yorkers for more than a century. Two architectural firms were engaged: Reed & Stem created the overall plan, while Warren & Wetmore designed the exterior. This Beaux-Arts masterpiece was erected between 1903 and 1913.

There were two prior versions of train depots on this spot before Grand Central Terminal was built. One might say these two previous buildings were practice runs for the star performance.

GRAND CENTRAL TERMINAL facade, built 1913, 89 East 42nd Street, 1932

This facade, this clock, and its forty-eight-foot surround is the largest sculptural grouping in the city.

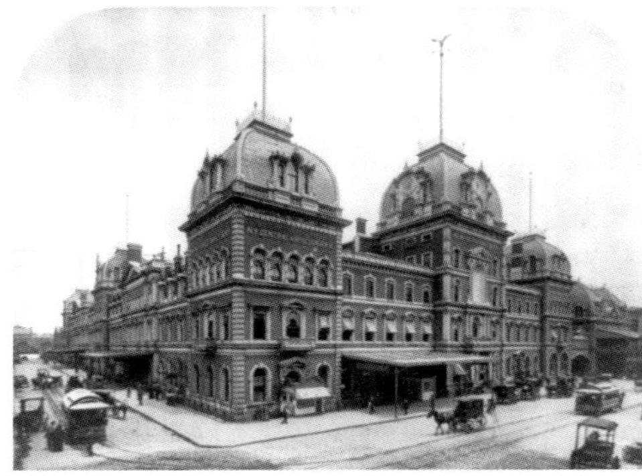

Three clocks adorned the central Second Empire–style dome of the old Grand Central Depot.

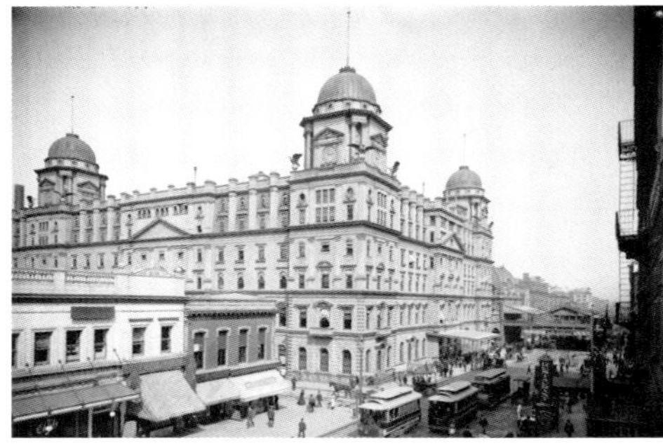

Multiple domes surrounded the updated Grand Central Station, each with a clock, or in the case of the corner domes, two clocks.

Grand Central Depot was built between 1869 and 1871, and keeping the clocks in tip-top working order was obviously important. The Self Winding Clock Company was brought in to help ensure accuracy with their automatic winding mechanisms. In 1886, J. M. Toucey, the general superintendent of the New York Central and Hudson River Railroad Company, wrote the Self Winding Clock Company to confirm a job well done: "Replying to your inquiry, would say that the large Self Winding Clock purchased from you … for our Incoming Passenger Station has never failed to wind, and has proven entirely satisfactory." Like most New Yorkers, he got right to the point.

In 1895 and again in 1900, the depot was redesigned and dramatically expanded to keep up with increased traffic, and as the

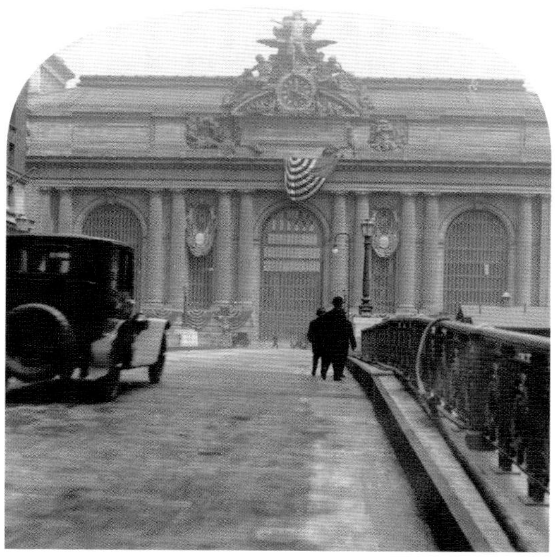

century turned, the name changed to Grand Central Station. Train stations of the nineteenth century were a dirty business, with steam power creating heavy black smoke. The Park Avenue we know today, north of the terminal, simply did not exist. Instead, a sprawling open train yard, unpleasant and unlivable, scarred the Upper East Side landscape. Smoke filled the tunnels that fed into the old Grand Central, resulting in horrific explosions and, finally, a deadly crash. This last straw made a redesign urgent. The major element of the bold, new design was to take the web of exposed train tracks and tunnels and reorganize them underground, some tracks even ten stories beneath the surface. New smokeless, electric-powered locomotives allowed for this reengineering of the unsightly industrial landscape, making it possible to transform the ground level to the north from a dangerous death trap into an elegant avenue planted with gardens and framed by luxurious buildings. Like the Erie Canal and the Brooklyn Bridge before it, Grand Central Terminal was proof that New Yorkers did not think small.

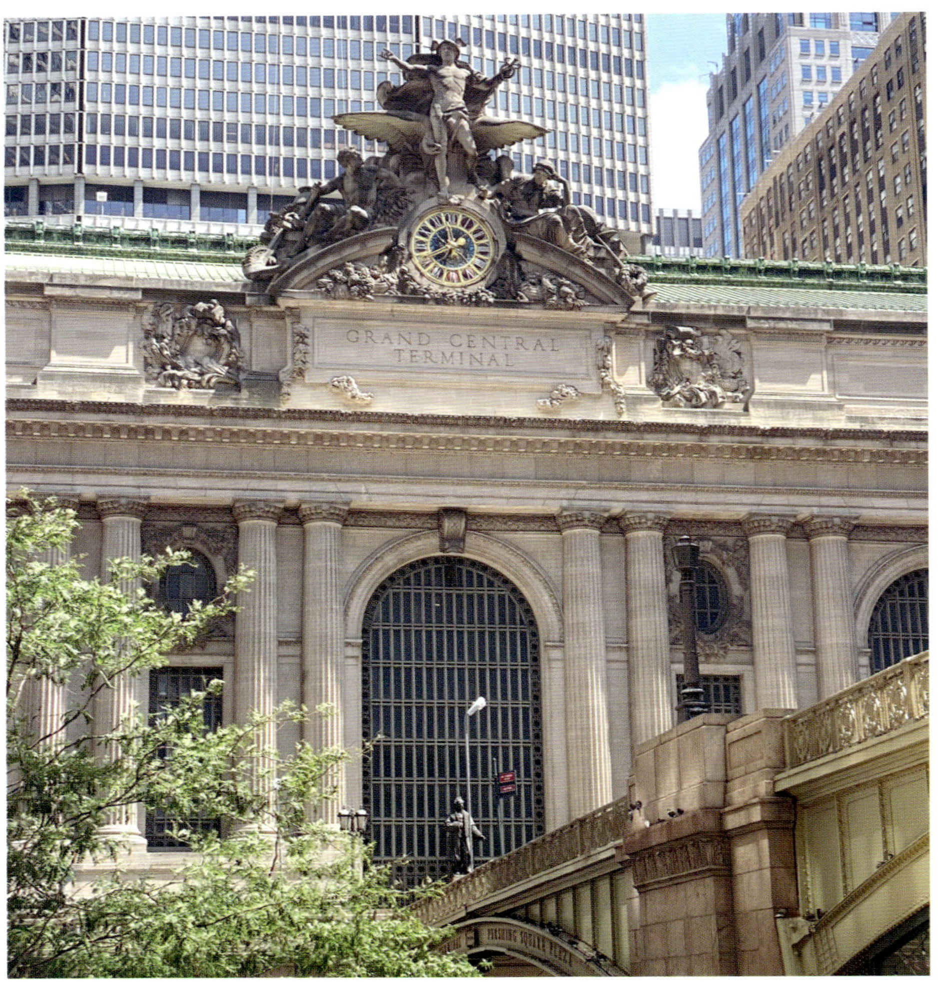

Grand Central Terminal, facade

The south facade, crowned by the city's most
spectacular clock, provides daily pleasure to
New Yorkers and tourists alike.

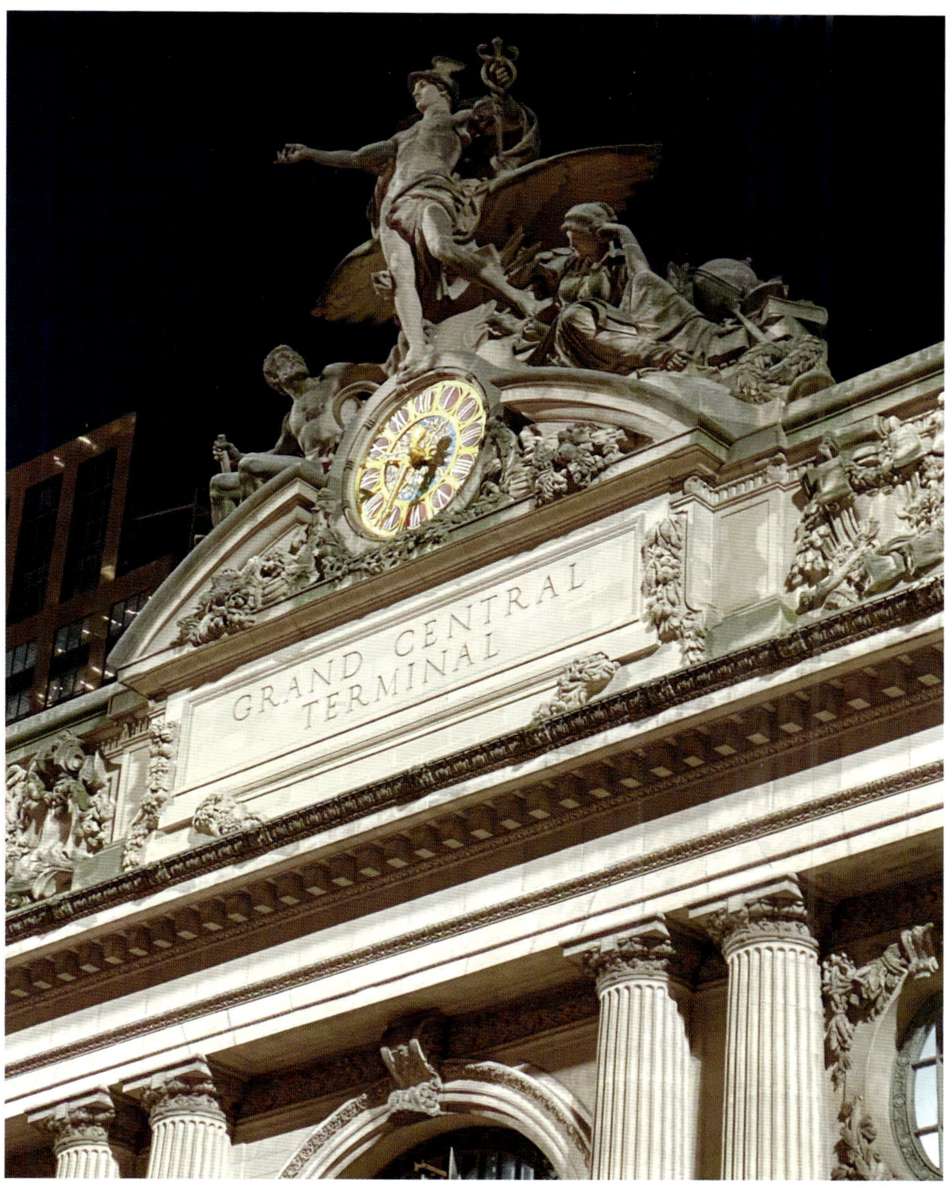

GRAND CENTRAL TERMINAL, facade clock

Day and night, the god Mercury presides above
Grand Central's gilded clockface, which is inset
with Tiffany glass panels.

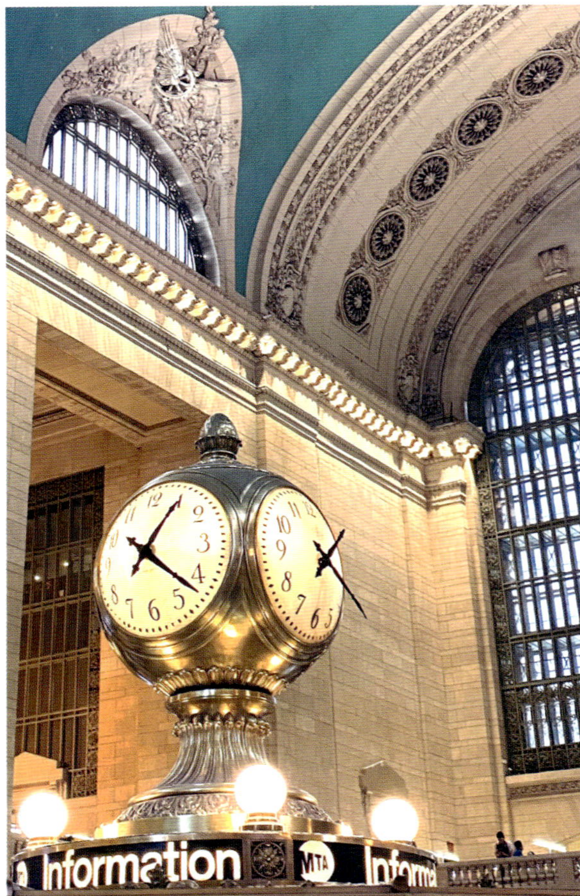

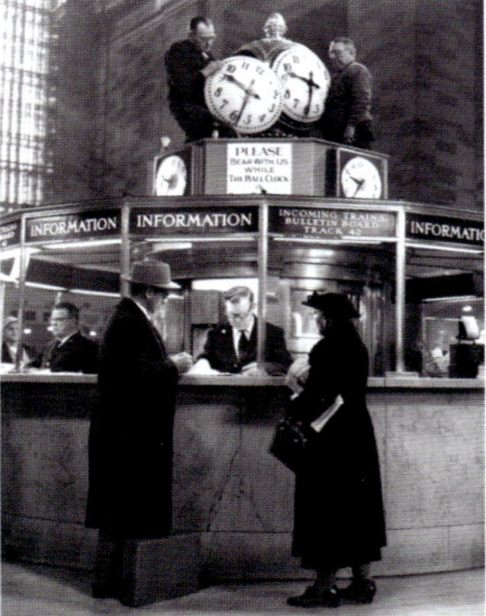

Above
Neal Boenzi (1925–2023). "Workers reinstall the clock at the information booth at Grand Central Terminal, in New York" *New York Times*, March 4, 1954

When one of the city's most-used clocks needed repairs, it made news, as captured here by the *New York Times*.

Left
Grand Central Terminal, interior clock

The four-faced concourse globe clock beneath the famous zodiac ceiling has long marked a meeting place for travelers.

An essential part of any proper train station is a clock program with strategically placed timepieces throughout the structure for the use and convenience of travelers and, if budget allows, as symbols of company status and civic pride. The most iconic clock of Grand Central Terminal, and perhaps of the entire city, crowns the south facade. The clock boasts the world's largest Tiffany

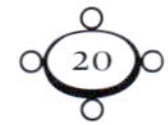

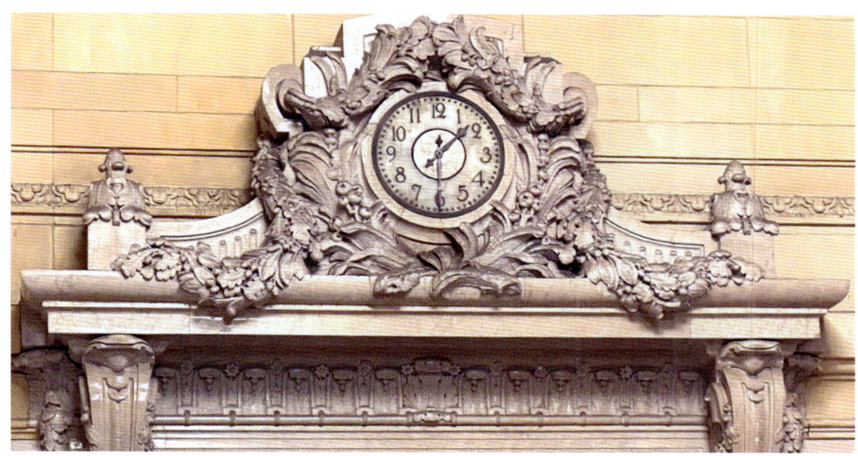

GRAND CENTRAL TERMINAL, interior clock

This clock is typical of the station's elegant style.

glass installation, measuring fifteen feet in diameter. This regal clockface has red glass Roman numerals with a central starburst, surrounding framework, and hands rendered in gilded metal. A larger frame for the clock is the monumental limestone sculptural group towering forty-eight feet tall, designed by Jules-Félix Coutan and carved by the John Donnelly Company. The heroic central figure is Mercury, to the right is Minerva, and on the left, a reclining Hercules gazes up at the young god. The primary symbolism of these three figures is commerce, with additional attributes of strength (Hercules), speed (Mercury), and wisdom (Minerva), all good things to be associated with a railroad station and a growing city.

Inside the building, at the center of the magnificent main concourse is the aforementioned information kiosk with its four-faced clock of opaline glass set into a spherical brass case topped by an artichoke finial—the well-known phrase "meet me at the clock" made this iconic timepiece *the* meeting point for millions from the moment it was installed. This clock was designed by Henry Edward Bedford, a sculptor and executive of the Self Winding Clock Company, the enterprise that built the clock with assistance from the Seth Thomas Clock Company, maker of the movements. Seth Thomas was born in 1785 and founded his clock business in 1813. The company survived his death in 1859 when his son, Aaron, took over and added new styles and innovations. The nearly-two-centuries-old business closed its doors in 2009.

Scattered throughout the terminal are smaller clocks, some elaborately carved in stone, while simpler versions repeat the clockfaces on the globe in the main concourse. Almost all these timepieces are luxuriously appointed with gilded bronze or brass frames and numerals mounted onto stone faces. However, there are two simple but notable outlier clocks in Grand Central that I find interesting (not pictured). One is a large square double-faced oak clock typical of older railway stations. This workaday clock was once tucked inside Track 21 but was relocated to a more practical position outside the lower-level tracks. It looks out of place amid the elevated elegance of the stone and plasterwork of ceilings and walls here. The other is an exterior clock on the west side of the building sheltered by the porte cochere at street level. This is where carriages and motorcars once tucked in out of the weather for drop-offs. This simple but elegant clock near the entry doors is handsomely framed in the same pink granite of the exterior walls. A narrow frame of brass holds the glass protecting a creamy stone face mounted with cast bronze Roman numerals. It is easy to picture stylish travelers observing this clock as they entered or exited their coaches when the terminal opened in 1913.

Among the more elaborate interior clocks that I particularly love is inside the central vestibule on 42nd Street. Well placed, of course, but more touchingly it is a monument honoring everyone

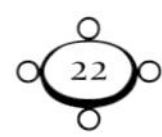

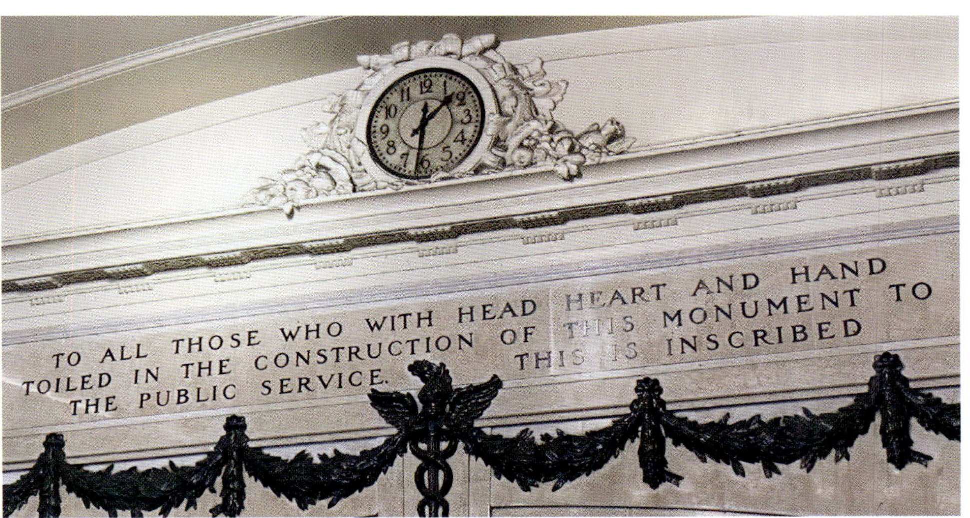

GRAND CENTRAL TERMINAL, interior clock

This clock is accompanied by a memorial to
those who built the terminal.

who created the terminal building. Beneath the cornucopia-festooned clock is an inscription that reads: "To all those who with head[,] heart[,] and hand toiled in the construction of this monument to the public service. This is inscribed." Thanking not only the truly groundbreaking engineers and splendid architects but also those who dug the deepest tunnel or carved the highest stone is a very New York thing. Like the building itself, the inscription ennobles all, especially the passersby who gaze up in gratitude for what was built for them.

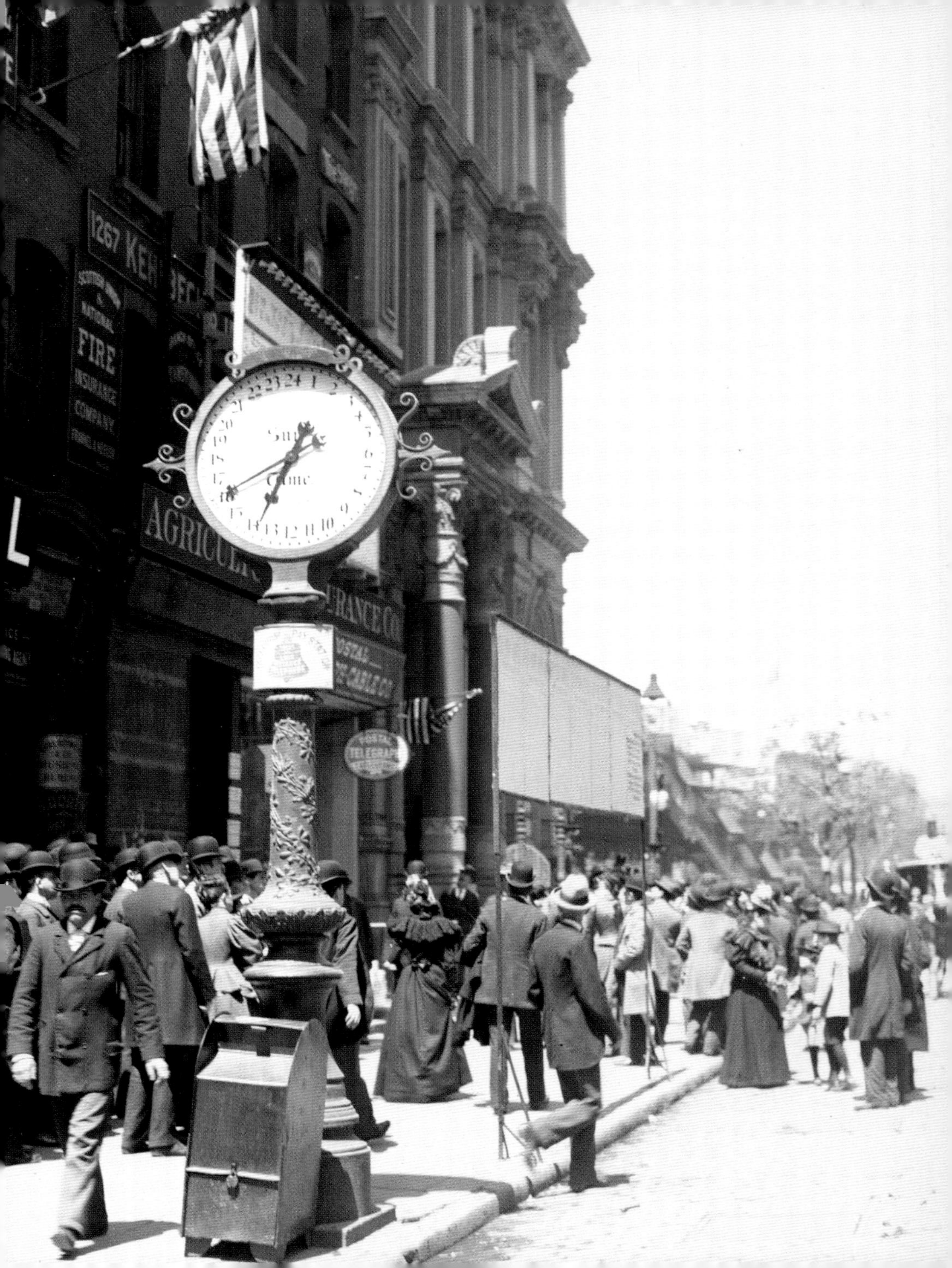

1267 KEN
SCOTTISH UNION & NATIONAL FIRE INSURANCE COMPANY
AGRICUL
RANCE CO
POSTAL
CABLE CO
POSTAL TELEGRAPH
Sun
Come

PASSING TIME
SIDEWALK CLOCKS

Timepieces not physically attached to buildings but planted in sidewalks popped up like daffodils all over the city in the late nineteenth and early twentieth centuries. Ornamental and functional, these clocks told a story of the neighborhood and the people or entities that commissioned them. Business promotion and civic pride were the shared purposes of these timepieces, usually in that order. Shaped like lollypops and installed close to the curb, they were considered urban "street furniture," adding attractive visual landmarks to the paths of everyday New Yorkers while reminding them that this was a city on the move.

Sidewalk clocks are primarily two-sided, creating easy visibility for passing pedestrians and vehicles. Four-sided post clocks exist but are more often found in parks or plazas of smaller cities and towns. An unusual and long-gone example of a four-sided clock that broke conventions is seen in the 1907 photograph on the next page.

This elaborate four-faced version was mounted onto an iron archway, but because it was close to the corner of 60th Street and Fifth Avenue, across from Central Park, it was more visible in the round than the standard two-sided sidewalk clock would be.

SIDEWALK CLOCK, 32nd Street
and Broadway, 1898.

This post clock illustrates the prevalence of
such timepieces on crowded sidewalks.

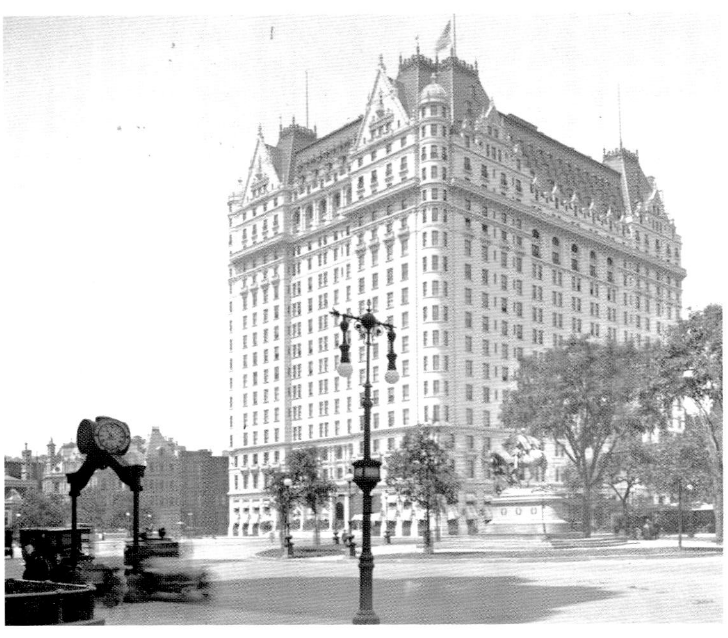

Above
FOUR-SIDED CLOCK,
60th Street and
Fifth Avenue, 1907

At the left-hand side of this
photo, an unusual four-sided
clock surmounts an arch centered on the entrance to a
glamorous apartment building. The Plaza Hotel and the
Vanderbilt mansion loom in
the background.

Left
SIDEWALK CLOCK, 42nd
Street (between Seventh and
Eighth Avenues), c. 1900

Across the street from the
American Theatre, a long-lost
sidewalk clock towers over
pedestrians (pictured left).

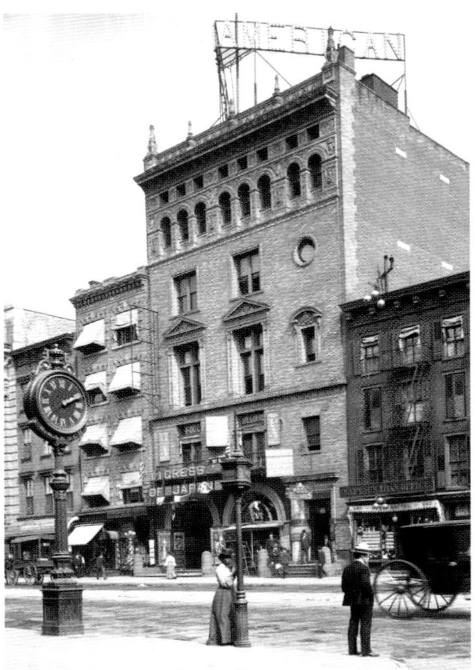

Plus, this was a period and a neighborhood where excess was appreciated, so why not gild the daffodil? This clock arch was centered on the portico entrance of 787 Fifth Avenue, known then as the Fifth Avenue Estates Building. This ten-story apartment building was designed by Henry J. Hardenbergh, who later designed the Plaza Hotel, shown looming in the background.

The Fifth Avenue Estates building was part of a new trend on the mansion-lined Fifth Avenue—apartments for the well-heeled instead of stand-alone homes or townhouses. This was no typical apartment building, as every floor held only one residence, each inhabited by some of the most golden names of the Gilded Age. The apartments included everything one needed to live a grand life amid the celestial heights of New York society. Elegant reception rooms and bedroom suites made these apartments function as spacious houses. To properly run them, each dwelling was inhabited by servants, and included multiple maids' rooms, while various butlers and valets lived on the top floor tucked beneath the mansard roof. It was apparently important to separate the sexes of staff in those days, honoring tradition. The building was destroyed in the 1960s to make way for a functional, and frankly yawn-worthy, one that still sits on this corner. What became of the unusual sidewalk clock remains a mystery.

New York City streets were filled with clocks like the ones pictured in this chapter. The street scene in the bottom image opposite was photographed around 1900 on 42nd Street between Seventh and Eighth Avenues and shows an impressive sidewalk clock, easily three times the height of the young woman to the right of it. Another example nearby was on Broadway and 22nd Street, only a short ten blocks away. As seen on the next page, the clock is visible to the right of a shop selling Regina's Music Boxes, beneath the Hotel Gazette.

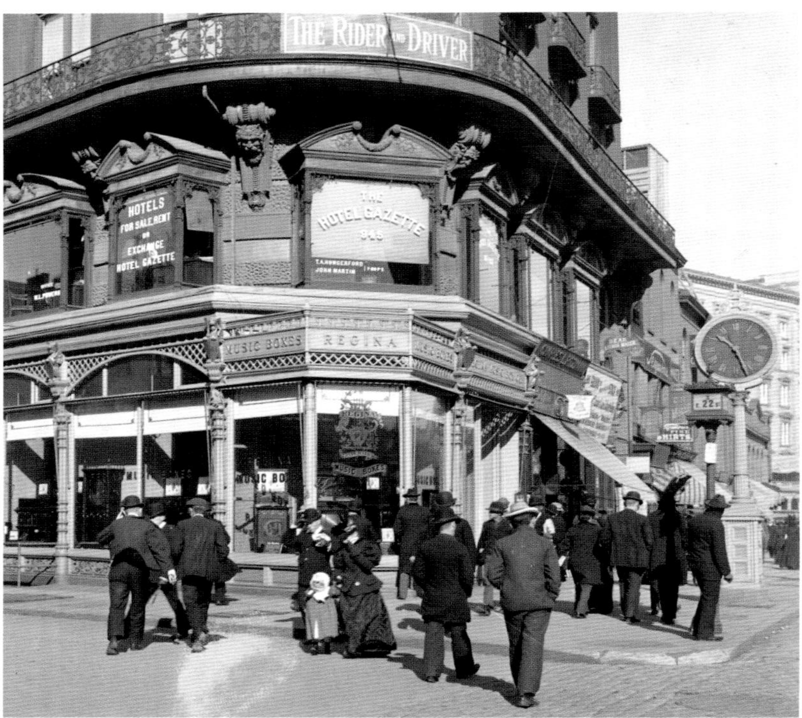

Sidewalk clock, 22nd Street and
Broadway, 1898

This image shows the bustle of pedestrians near a post clock facing north, just
steps away from where the Flatiron Building would be erected a few years later.

While a good number of New York's sidewalk clocks survive,
most became victims of careless drivers or expedient development. A small number have been restored and in some cases
relocated. While the basic forms of these sidewalk clocks, commonly called "post clocks," are somewhat similar, the sizes and
designs vary from simple and human-scaled to monumental

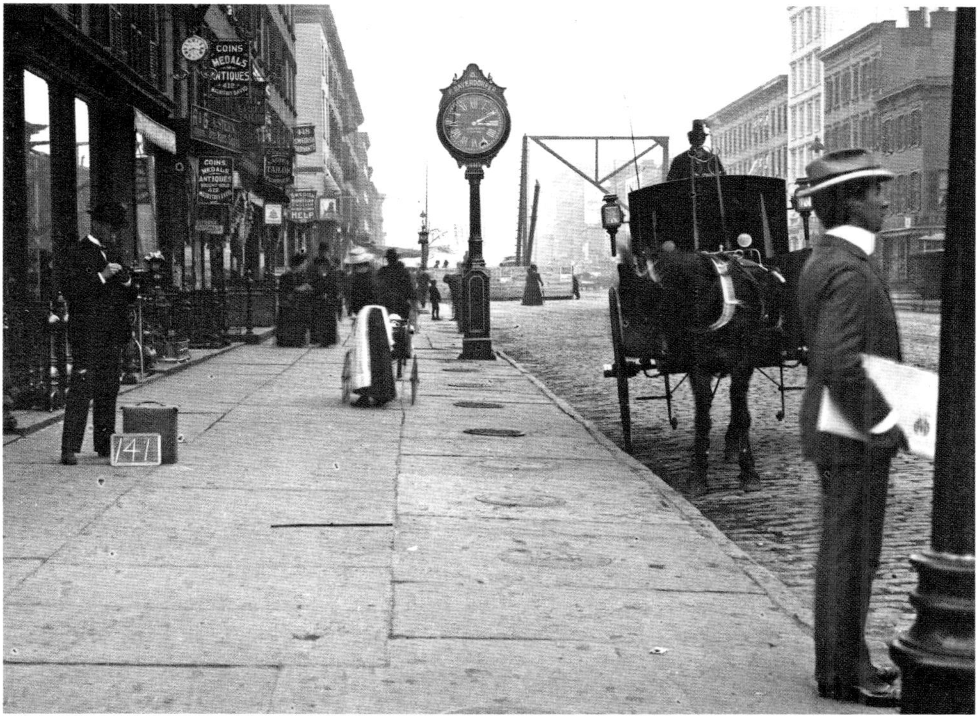

SIDEWALK CLOCK, Fourth Avenue
(near East 28th Street), 1900

Taken soon after the turn of the century, this photo
shows the clock standing between two eras: the
past, with a horse and carriage, and the future, with
subway construction in the background.

and highly ornamental depending on the patron's purse, purpose, and prevailing styles of the era. The surviving examples
that follow are just a handful that top my list, including the
much-beloved Barthman clock seen at the end of this chapter,
a quite atypical version that redefines the meaning of the term
"sidewalk clock."

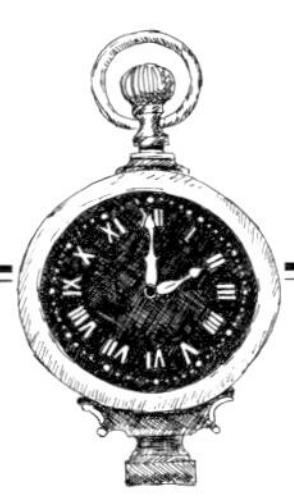

SIDEWALK CLOCK

1501 THIRD AVENUE
C. 1898

This delightfully witty pocket watch–shaped clock was designed by the E. Howard Clock Company and stands in front of a building that once held the Adolph Stern jewelry store. It was doubtless intended as an advertisement for that business, since pocket watches were typically pawned or purchased at jewelry stores. In many ways, it is a standard form for a sidewalk clock, the main difference being that this clock is crowned with a giant thumb-turn and loop depicting the winder and watch fob ring of a nineteenth-century pocket watch. Known to some as the "Yorkville Clock" (named after its neighborhood), curiously, it was sold in 1985 and ended up in the garden of a private home in Long Island, only to be tracked down, reclaimed, restored, and maintained by generous and concerned citizens.

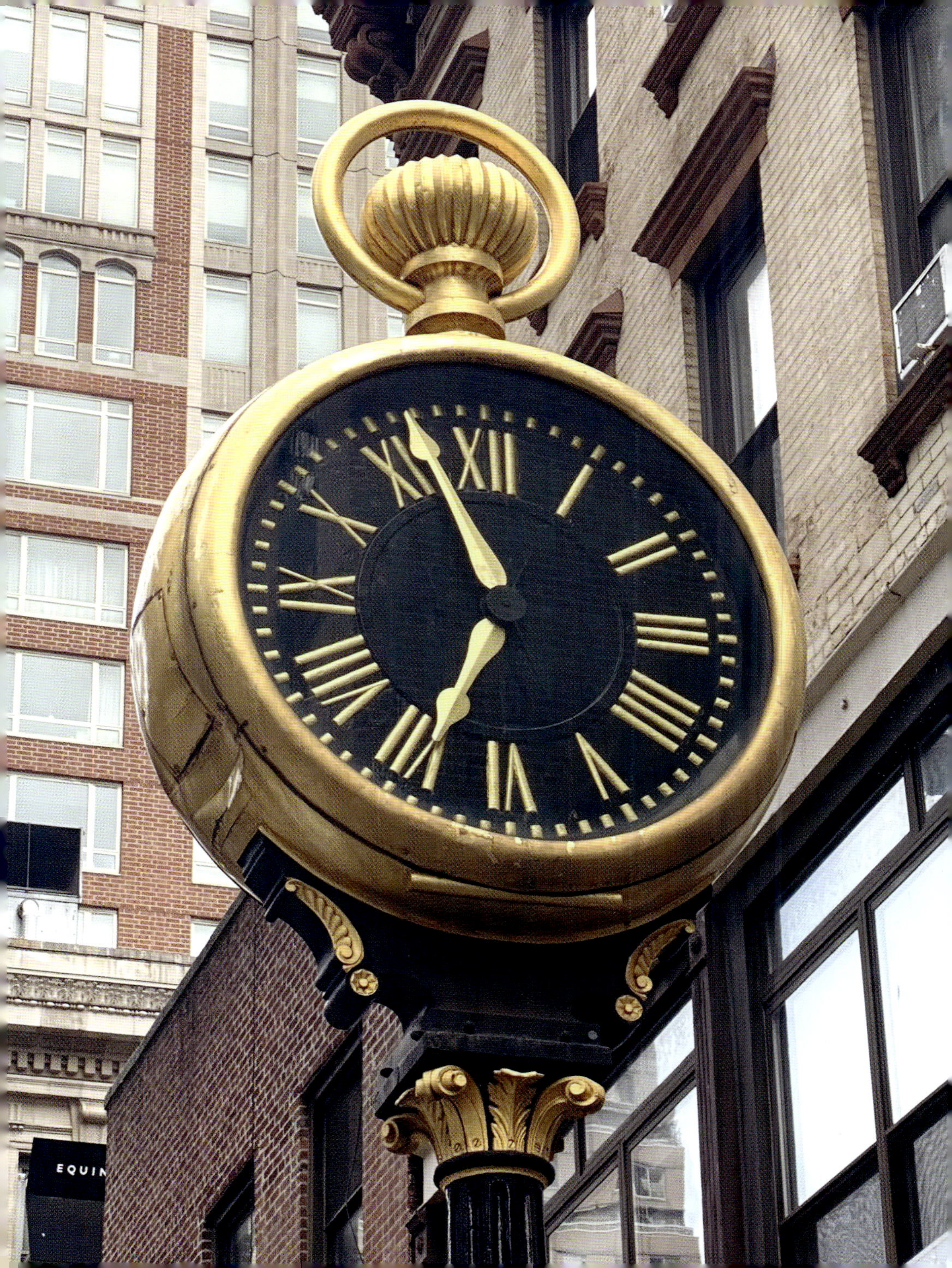

XII
EQUIN

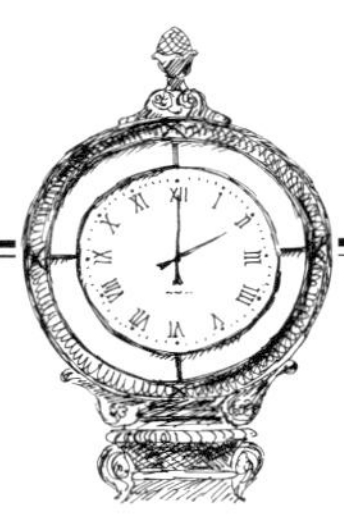

SIDEWALK CLOCK

522 FIFTH AVENUE
1907

The largest surviving post clock in Manhattan towers over pedestrians at 522 Fifth Avenue and remains one of the city's most beautiful. This imposing cast-iron clock was manufactured by the Seth Thomas Clock Company in 1907 and was originally located a block away at the southwest corner of 43rd Street. Roman numerals grace the dial, but more than the numerals reflect the classical style of Rome. The entire effect—including most of the decorative details on this otherwise rather sober post clock—recalls motifs of the ancient western world. The double-faced clock is supported by a fluted square column lifting the finial-crowned clock to nearly twenty feet tall.

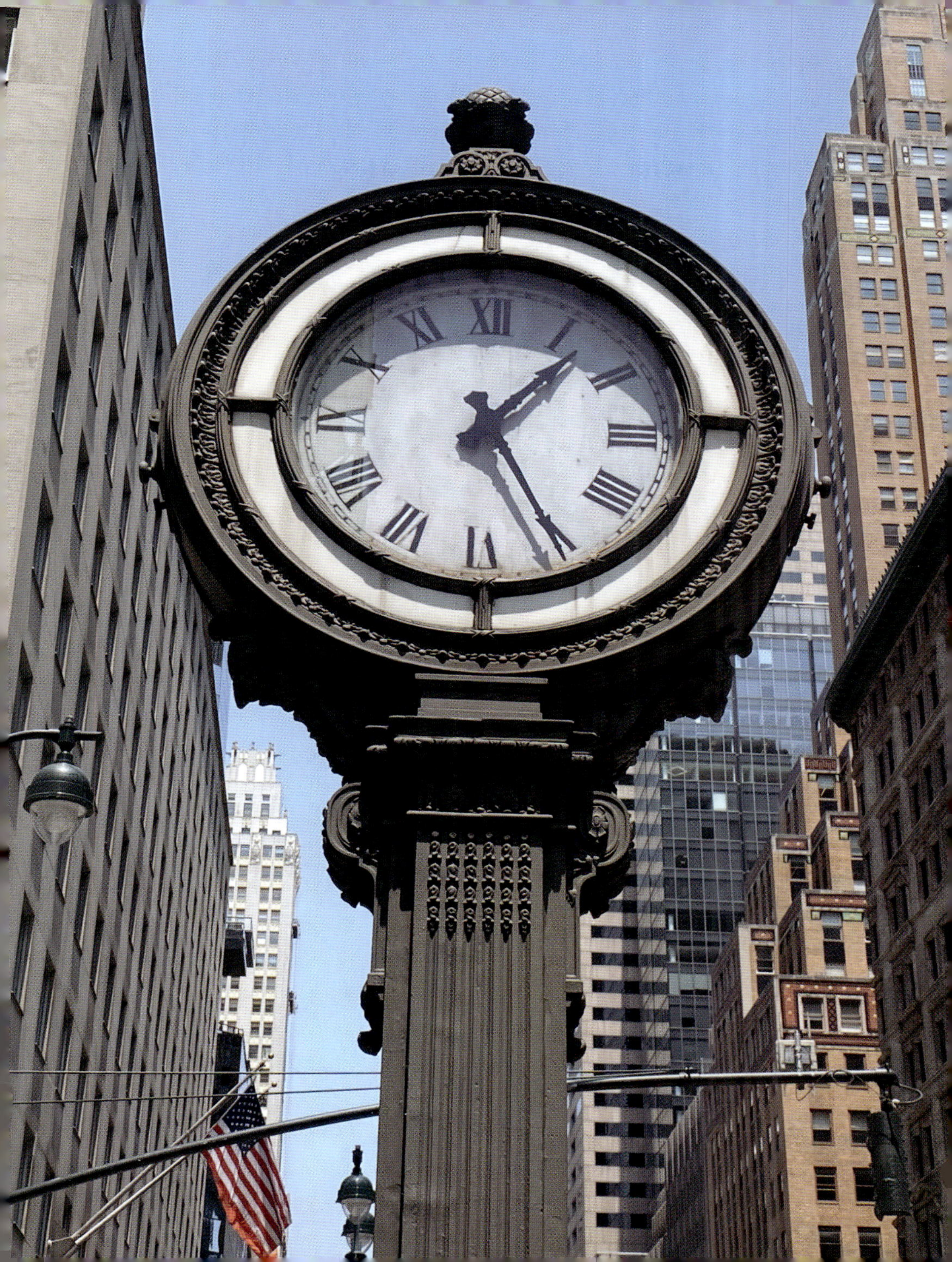

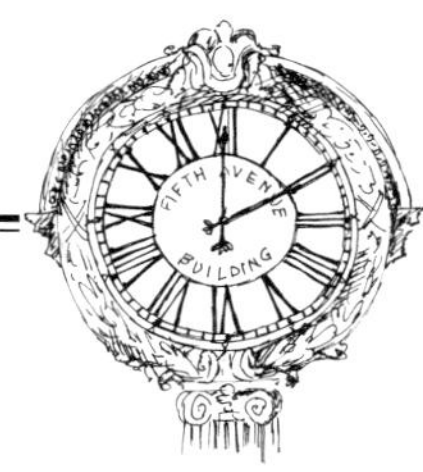

SIDEWALK CLOCK
200 FIFTH AVENUE
1909

The owners of the early twentieth-century building at 200 Fifth Avenue commissioned an impressive sidewalk clock that visually enhanced their edifice, which still faces Madison Square Park in the Flatiron District. Hecla Iron Works of Brooklyn won the commission to produce this striking gilded cast-iron clock case—perhaps because of their city enhancements of over a hundred iron subway kiosks, and their high style cast-iron building facades, including B. Altman's on Sixth Avenue. Of the many street clocks gracing the sidewalks of New York City, this one still stands apart. The fluted Ionic column rises to a capital in a suitably Gilded Age neoclassic style, and the two large dials are framed by oak leaf wreaths. The Landmarks Preservation Commission called this "a gilded cast-iron masterpiece" when it was landmarked in 1981.

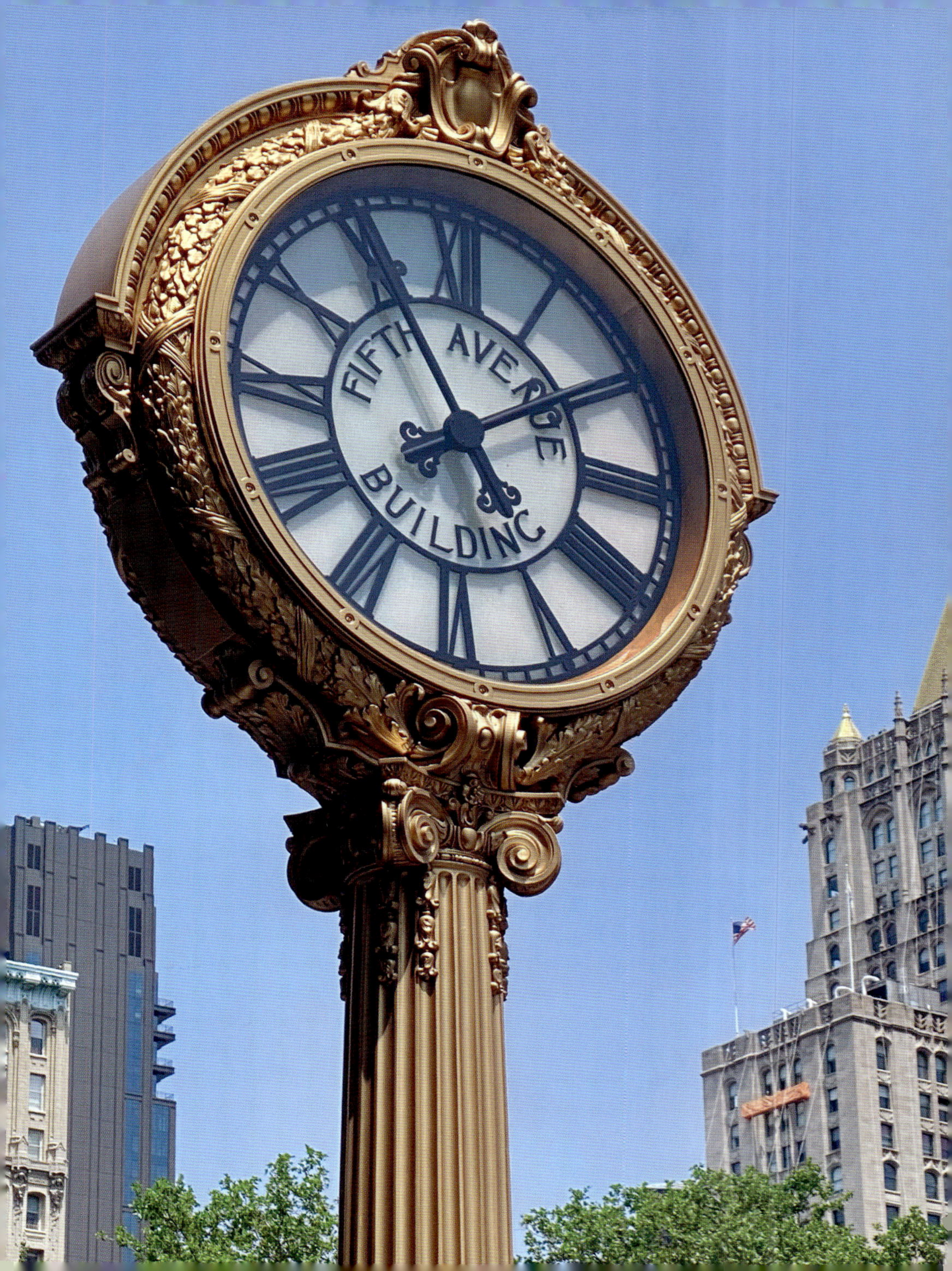

FIFTH AVENUE
BUILDING

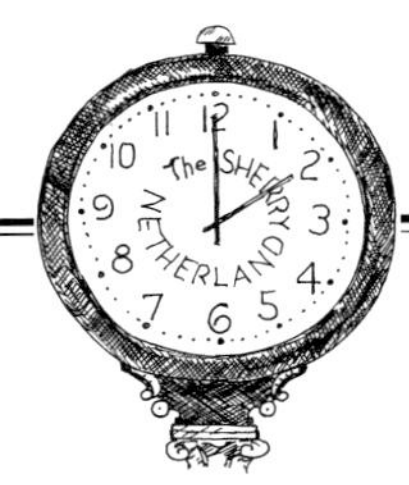

SHERRY NETHERLAND
SIDEWALK CLOCK
781 FIFTH AVENUE
C. 1927

At the southeast corner of Central Park, in front of the Sherry Netherland Hotel on Fifth Avenue, stands a sidewalk clock likely installed when the hotel was completed in 1927. Made by the E. Howard Clock Company, the clock's gilded lettering promotes the hotel to each passerby in true 1920s fashion. Instead of the highly detailed neoclassical surface ornamentation seen on the previous two clocks, this one embraces an elegant but more minimally modern aesthetic. With only a few gilded details, this post clock reminds us of the prosperous, devil-may-care attitude of the decade just before the stock market crash of 1929.

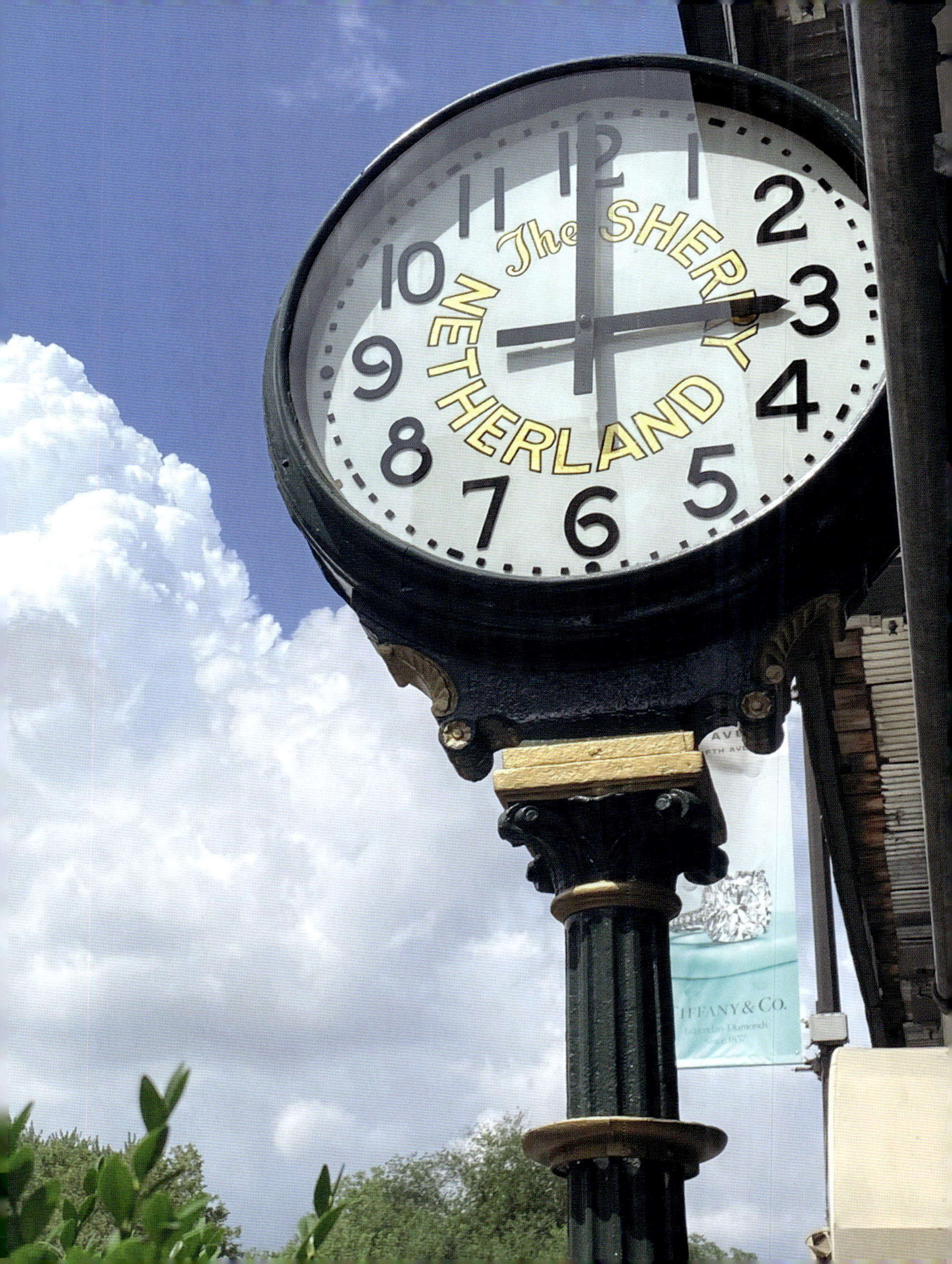
The SHERRY
NETHERLAND
TIFFANY & CO.

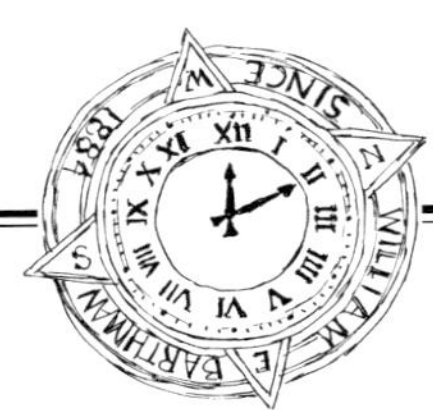

BARTHMAN SIDEWALK CLOCK

CORNER OF BROADWAY
AND MAIDEN LANE
C. 1899

Probably installed in 1899 by William Barthman Jeweler, a company founded in 1884, this beloved clock is perhaps New York's most curious public timepiece. Embedded in the sidewalk at the corner of Broadway and Maiden Lane, the Barthman clock has been stepped over—or stepped on—by millions of people. You, too, could intentionally stumble over its old clockface, but you won't find Barthman's jewelry shop nearby, as it has moved on, leaving this delightful relic behind. In addition to telling the time, the clock will also point you in the right direction, as its surround was cast in brass in an attractive compass rose design. As I walk in New York, I try to focus my gaze upward, but in this rare case, looking down reveals a lovely surprise.

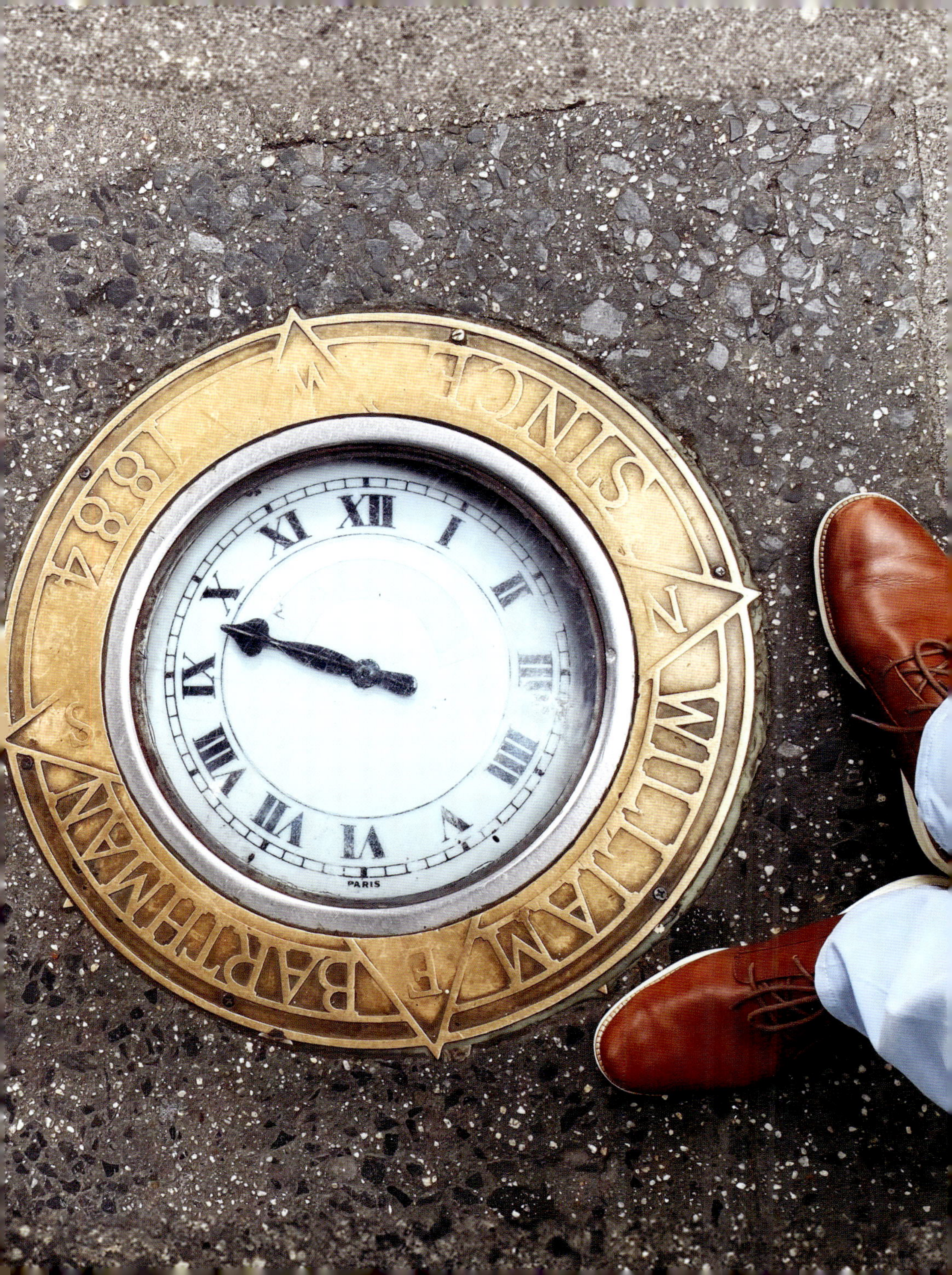

SINCE
1884
WILLIAM
BARTHMAN
PARIS

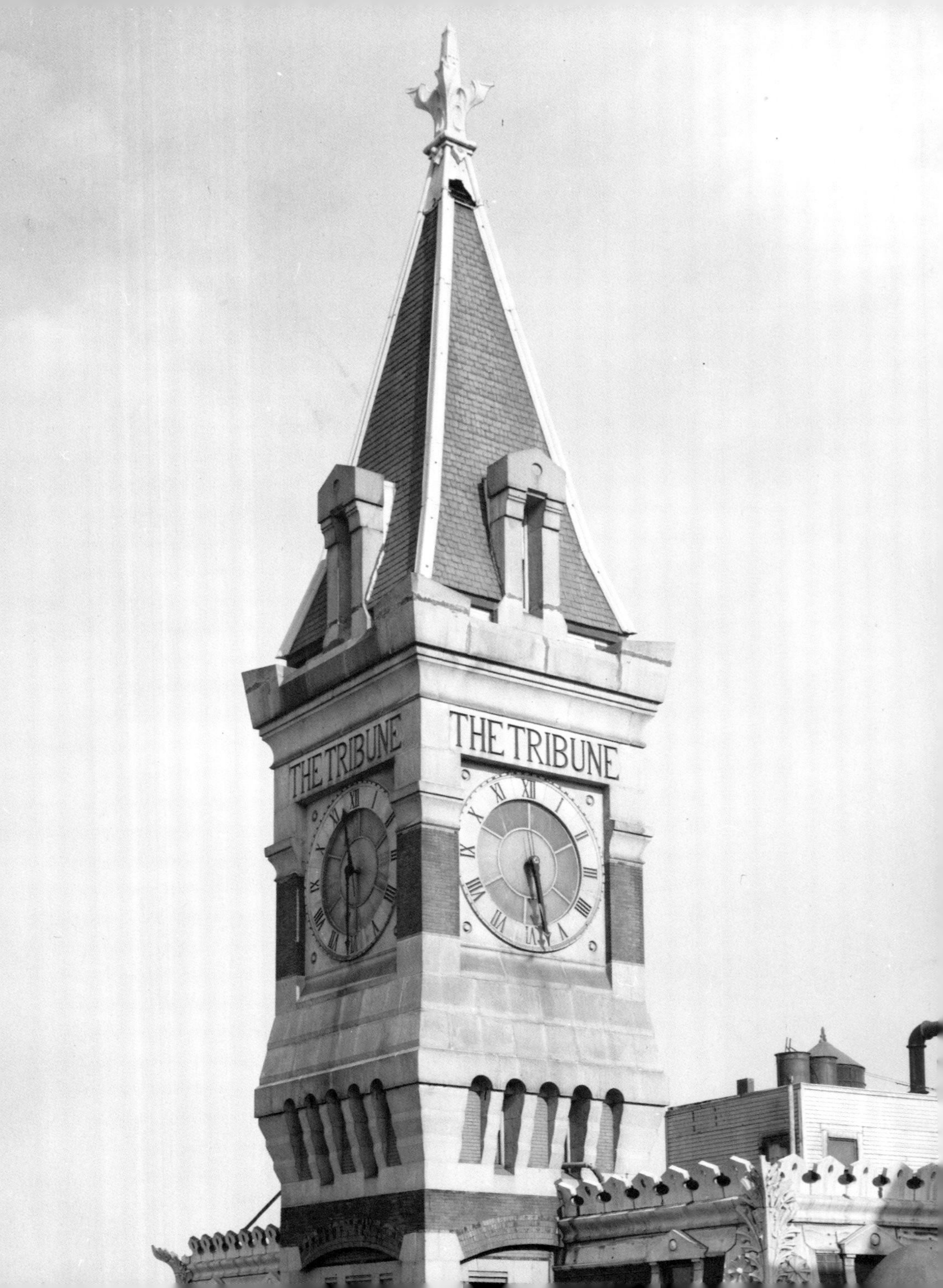
THE TRIBUNE
THE TRIBUNE

A POINT IN TIME
TOWER AND
PEDIMENT CLOCKS

Before skyscrapers were architecturally possible, towers both small and large sprouted across New York City. As the city grew, so did its towers—some even with clocks. Many of New York's towers were designed with a sense of nostalgia, recalling antique structures of Europe through revivals of Gothic, Renaissance, Romanesque, and other architectural styles. Shorter buildings with classical pediments made a desirable architectural statement as well, particularly for architects wanting to provide their clients with a connection to antiquity and the nobility that the style implied. Some of these buildings sported clocks, too. Towers and pediments were sprinkled among buildings with spires and domes (covered in chapter 7), all which gave the city dweller a sense of visual variety and civic pride. This assemblage of buildings was especially pleasing when viewed from a distance, creating a sort of pre-skyscraper skyline. When New Yorkers experienced the man-made landscape by walking the boulevards, the clocks offered both an attraction and useful convenience, a sense of place and purpose.

Among the city's nineteenth-century clock towers was the New York Produce Exchange Building in Lower Manhattan, completed in 1884. This massive building housed stores, offices,

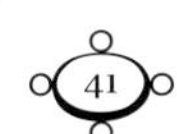

The Tribune's four-faced clock, once the largest in the city, ornamented an astonishing 335–foot tower.

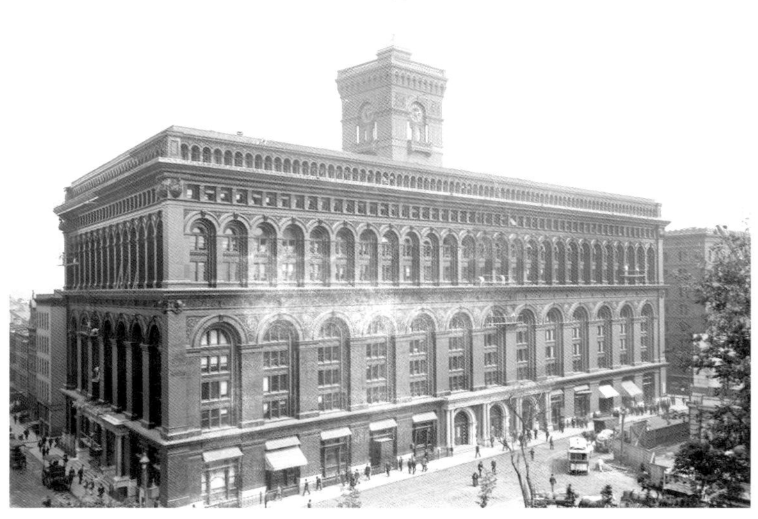

New York Produce Exchange Building,
built 1884, 2 Broadway, c. 1904

Demolished in 1957, this lost building erected east
of Bowling Green had a tower clock that was one
of the two largest timepieces in the city.

and a trading floor for its three thousand members. Designed by George B. Post in the Italian Renaissance style, it was the first building in the world with an iron superstructure combined with masonry. The 224-foot-tall clock tower rose above the ten-story building, which was entirely ornamented in terra-cotta relief. The *New York Times* published a story on May 4, 1884, about the building-in-progress, saying, "The clock tower at the east end of the Stone-street front covers a plot of ground 40 by 75 feet and is about 200 feet high. . . . Special pains are to be taken to make the clock an accurate timepiece."

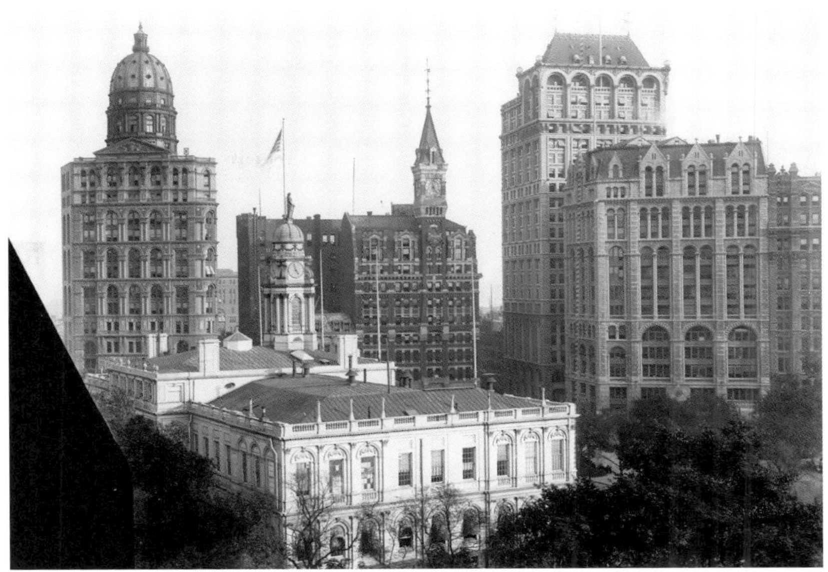

NEW YORK TRIBUNE BUILDING

The New York Tribune Building on Newspaper Row (center background) was derided by some contemporary architectural critics as "unsatisfactory," while the *New York Times* felt it resembled a "sugar refinery." City Hall and its clock, built 1803–11, are visible in the foreground.

The New York Tribune Building, built in 1875, was situated across from City Hall. The *New-York Tribune* mentioned the Produce Exchange tower clock in an article while it was being completed in November 1884 and, tellingly, they seemed somewhat competitive about the size of *their* clock, since they wrote: "The clock in the tower is—with the exception of that of THE TRIBUNE, which is the same size—the largest to be seen in the city. The diameter of the clock dial is 12 feet: length of hands, 6 feet, and length of figures on dial, 20 inches." Not surprisingly, size mattered among these men (and they were all men) when

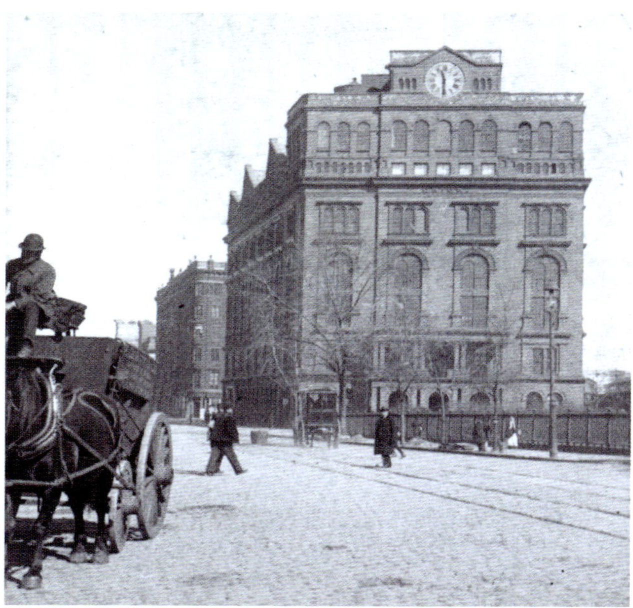

The sober Cooper Union building, with its
understated pediment clock, survives today,
as does the institution within.

it came to New York City clocks (and newspapers) of the nineteenth century. But money also mattered, and in 1900, when the Produce Exchange reached its zenith, it was taking in daily transactions of $15 million.

Sadly, both the New York Tribune and New York Produce Exchange Buildings and their famous clock towers were demolished. In his 1967 book *Lost New York*, Nathan Silver wrote: "The produce exchange, one of the best buildings in New York, was replaced after 1957 by one of the worst." Indeed, the best one might say about the regrettable mid-century replacement structure is that it's a perfect example of architectural banality.

Topping my list of most deeply admired pediment clocks is not one of the city's most beautiful or impressive, but one that represents what I believe to be the very best of New York—innovation and philanthropy. This pediment clock adorns the Cooper Union for the Advancement of Science and Art's Foundation Building, founded in 1859. Cooper Union was the brainchild of the brilliant New York innovator, industrialist, and philanthropist Peter Cooper, who founded a learning institution open to both men and women regardless of their race, financial background, or religious affiliation. And if that wasn't groundbreaking enough, Cooper Union offered free tuition to its wildly diverse students.

Since the nineteenth century, the Cooper Union clock ticked above some of the most important progressive minds in our history as they shared their views with audiences inside. Lincoln spoke here before he officially announced his candidacy for president. In the 1870s, noted Native American chiefs spoke on the plight of their people at the hands of new Americans. In 1909, the first meeting of the NAACP was held here, and Susan B. Anthony and other important women's rights leaders were also given a public voice within these rooms. One could easily say Cooper was ahead of the times while others, even today, barely seem to keep up with the belief in equality, basic human decency, and the greater good. Fortunately, both the Cooper Union's Foundation Building and its learning institution survives and thrives, so I've included it on the following pages, along with other surviving pediment and tower clocks greatly admired for their beauty and history.

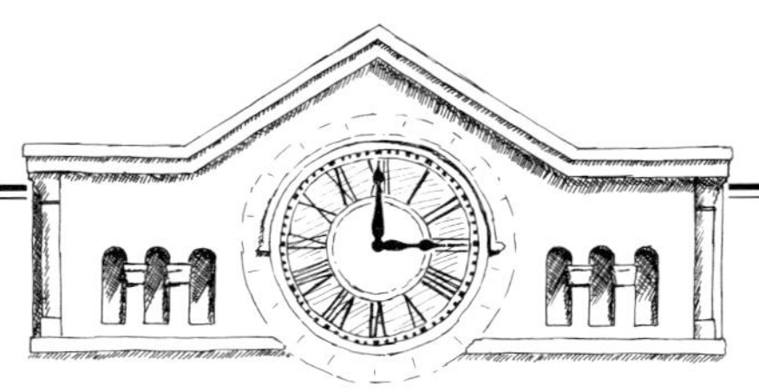

THE COOPER UNION
FOR THE ADVANCEMENT OF
SCIENCE AND ART'S
FOUNDATION BUILDING
7 EAST 7TH STREET
1859

Born in New York City in 1791, Peter Cooper was a self-taught engineer, industrialist, and politician who invented and built America's first locomotive steam engine that he named "Tom Thumb." Through Cooper's brilliance and hard work, he amassed a fortune that he shared with his fellow humans by founding the nation's first institution of higher education that was free to all students regardless of sex, class, or race. The Cooper Union clock, which was made by the E. Howard Clock Company, rests beneath an understated brownstone pediment of the Frederick Petersen–designed building. The architectural style of the building is not a showstopper, but is rather a sober testament of Cooper's modest goodness and enormous generosity.

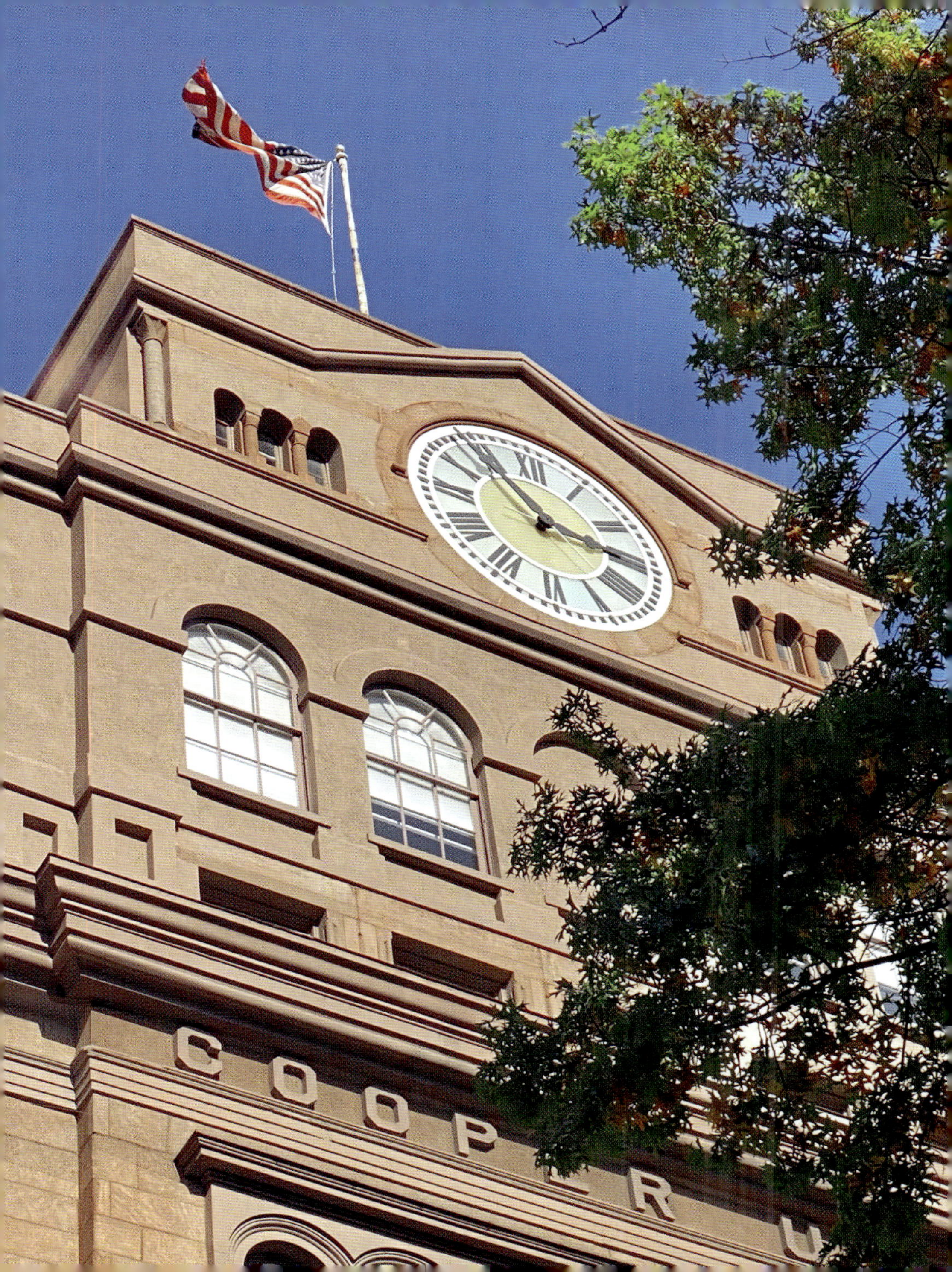

XII
COOP R U

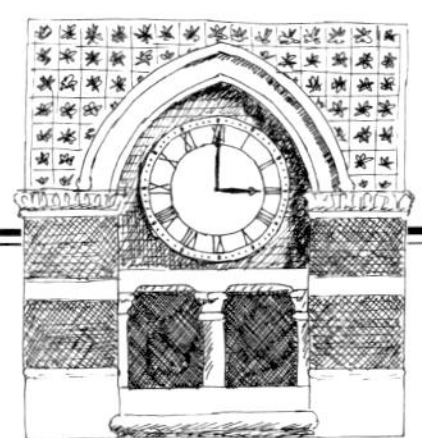

JEFFERSON MARKET
LIBRARY

425 AVENUE OF THE AMERICAS
1877

Built as the Jefferson Market Courthouse between 1874 and 1877, this highly detailed building with its impressive clock tower was designed by Frederick Clarke Withers of the architectural firm Vaux & Withers. Among its many historic moments, it held the trial of architect Stanford White's murderer, Harry Thaw. Like so many important nineteenth-century buildings in New York, this one faced demolition in the mid-twentieth century. Mercifully, it was saved thanks to public outcry and became a branch of the New York Public Library. Goodness knows what sort of hideous 1950s structure was planned to replace this beauty—thankfully we don't have to live with that mistake. The four-sided clock, affectionately called "Old Jeff," has a bell that still strikes on the hour from 9 a.m. to 10 p.m., while its fantastical tower continues to enhance the charm of Greenwich Village.

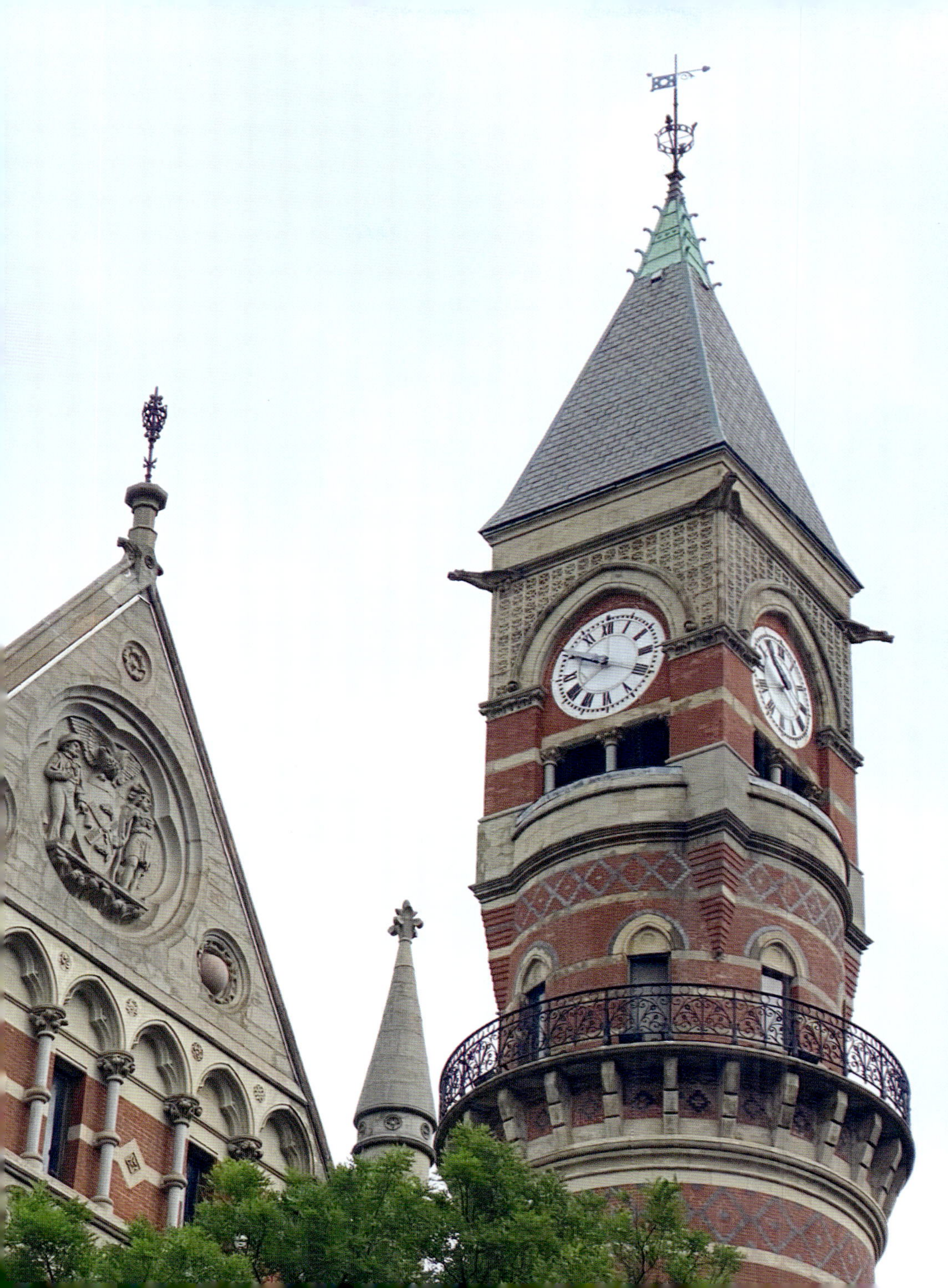

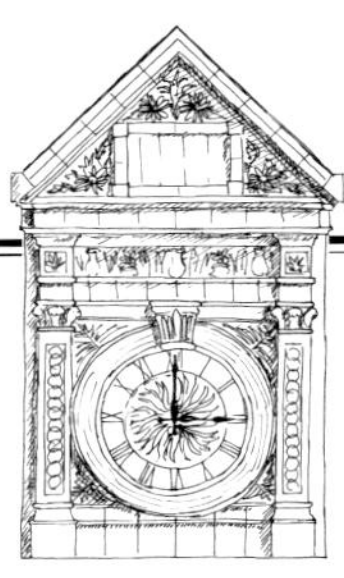

BROOKLYN
HISTORICAL SOCIETY
128 PIERREPONT STREET
1881

This little jewel of a terra-cotta-clad building was designed by George B. Post and built between 1878 and 1881; this was before the completion of his masterpiece, the massive New York Produce Exchange depicted earlier in this chapter. The exterior of the Renaissance Revival building is highly ornamented with reliefs, decorative architectural details, and busts by American sculptor Olin Levi Warner. The clockface, too, is made of terra-cotta with a sculpted sunburst and Roman numerals. The clock tower stands above the roofline over the main entrance and is crowned by a highly pitched, square, pointed roof typical of the late French Renaissance. This charming, human-scaled structure was landmarked in 1991, including its wonderfully intact interiors.

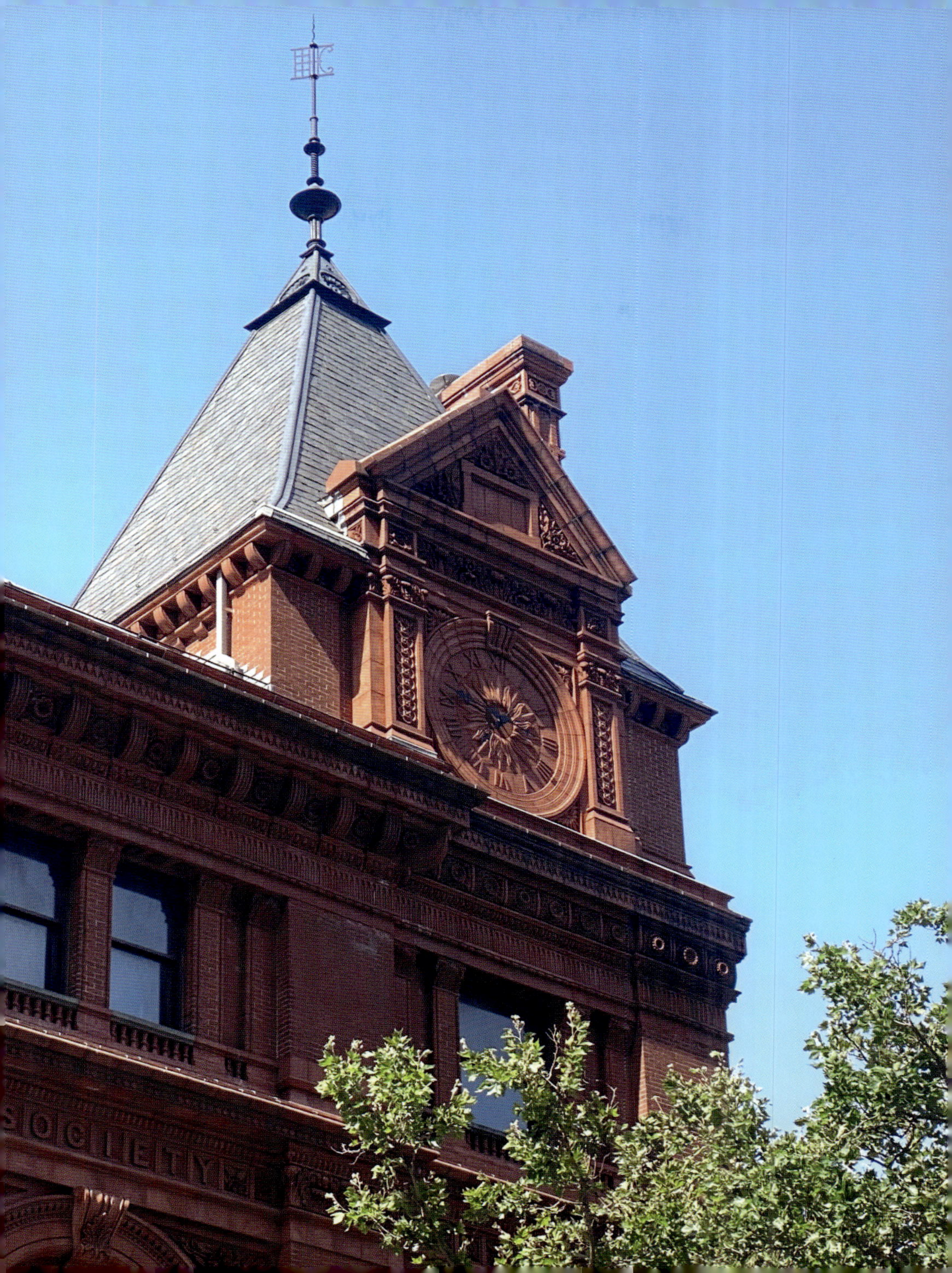
SOCIETY

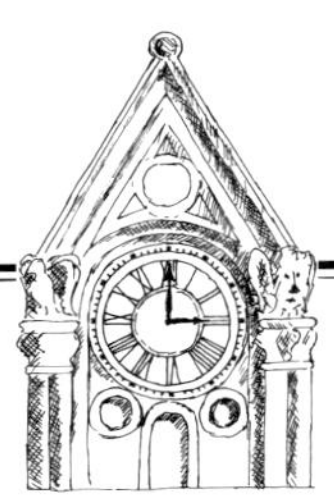

HARLEM COMMUNITY JUSTICE CENTER
170 EAST 121ST STREET
1893

At East 121st Street and Sylvan Place in Harlem stands a Romanesque Revival building designed by Thom & Wilson and built between 1891 and 1893. The elaborate corner tower is cylindrical on the lower floors, transitioning splendidly to octagonal at the roofline, where it boasts a four-faced clock by the Seth Thomas Clock Company. Originally a courthouse built to process and hold criminals, the building held forty functioning jail cells until 1940. It was restored in 2014 and is now a place where family, housing, and small claims civil cases are heard. The harmonious original exterior materials of brick, brownstone, granite, and terra-cotta remain intact. This beautiful structure is a New York City landmark that was added to the National Register of Historic Places in 1980.

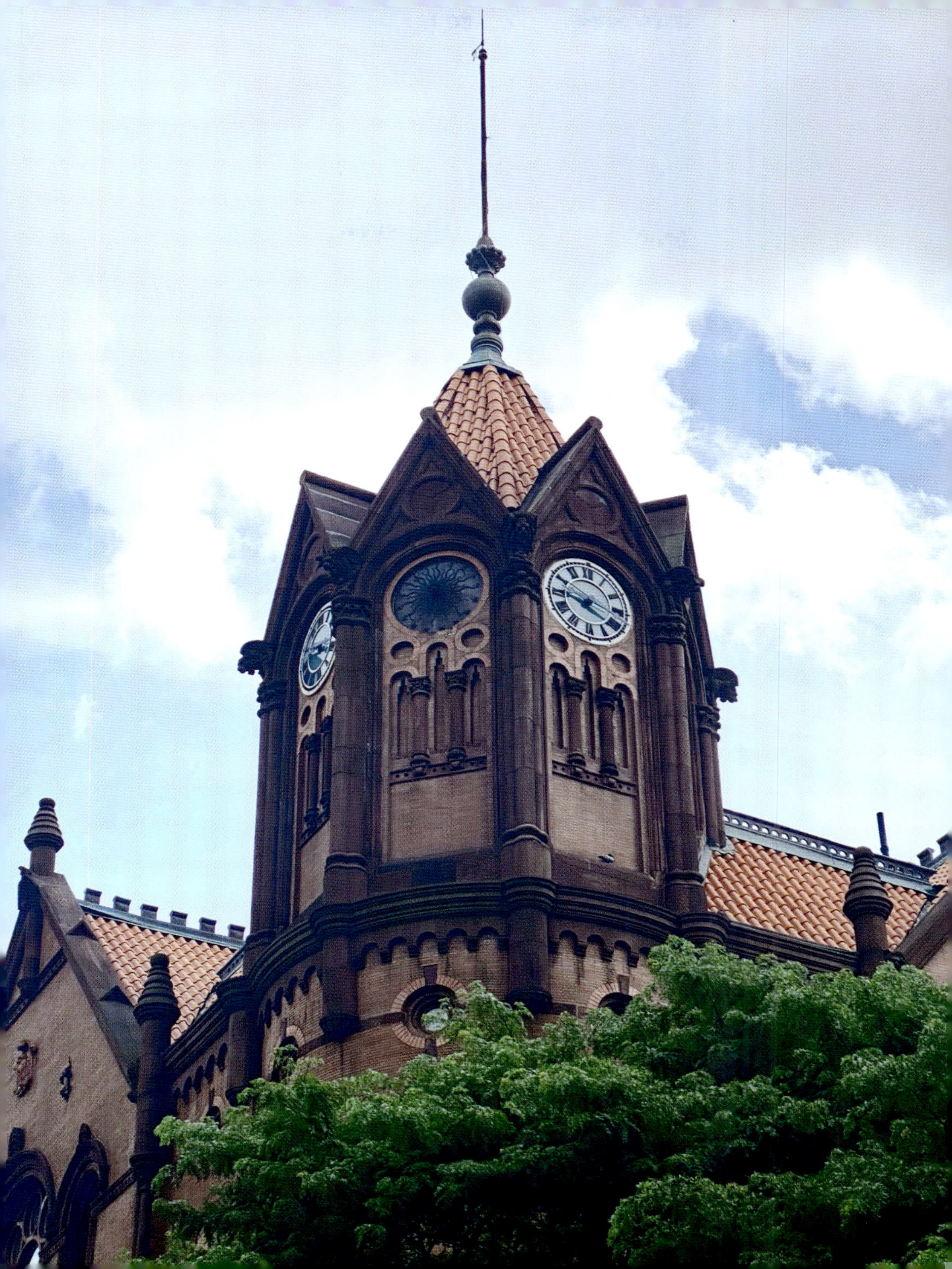

BOWERY
SAVINGS BANK
228 GRAND STREET
1895

Founded in the early nineteenth century, Bowery Savings Bank erected this Stanford White building in 1895. Inspired by ancient Rome, White created an architectural trend for temple-style American bank buildings that spread across New York and the country. The building is L-shaped, with two grand entrances, one at 130 Bowery and the other at 228 Grand Street. The two classical pediments at each entrance are by Brooklyn-born sculptor Frederick MacMonnies and feature clocks by E. Howard Clock Company, flanked by carved figures with lions—the Grand Street entrance with two women (pictured here) and the Bowery Street entrance with a man and a woman. The extravagantly carved stone pediments, Corinthian columns, and richly decorated interiors intentionally express substance and wealth. No longer a bank, this building, landmarked in 1966, now functions as an events space.

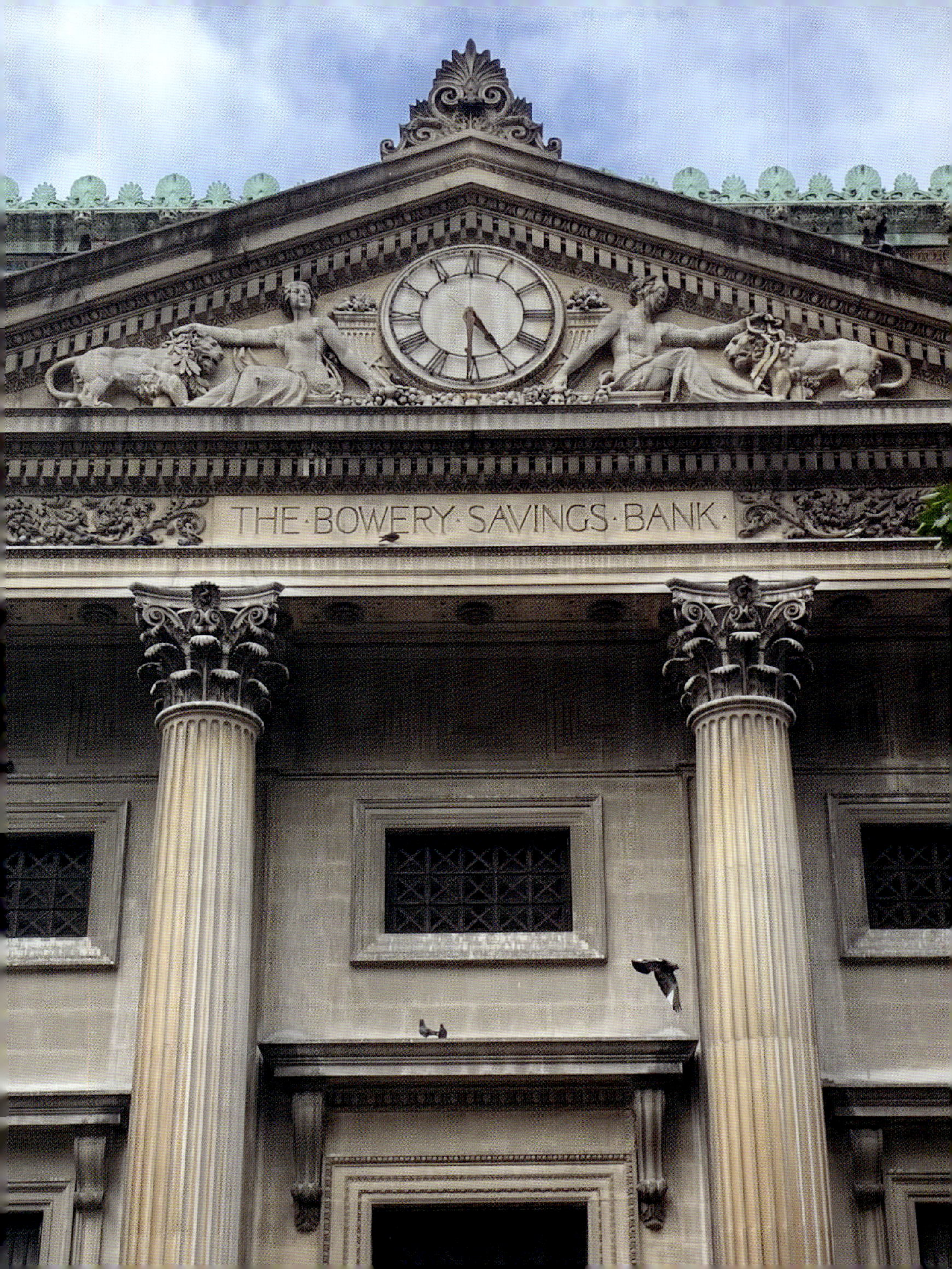

THE · BOWERY · SAVINGS · BANK ·

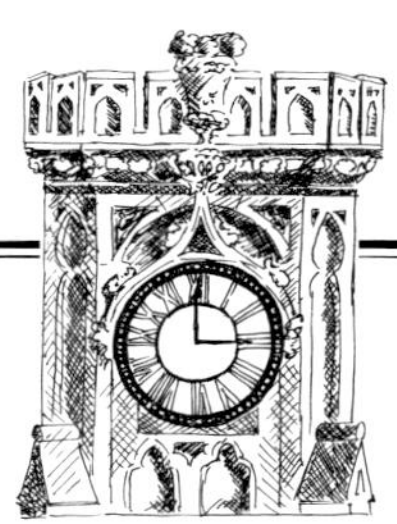

OCEAN VIEW CEMETERY
GATEHOUSE

3315 AMBOY ROAD, STATEN ISLAND
1905

At the entrance to this sprawling, 105-acre ceme-tery in Staten Island stands a handsome Gothic Revival gatehouse with a clock tower. Why a cemetery needs a clock—given its inhabitants have no place to be—is a curious question, but I'm glad that didn't stop landscape architect Daniel W. Langton from placing, to great advantage, this very pleasing gatehouse here in 1905. The clock has seemingly stopped, just as time has for those resting in this nonsectarian burial ground known for being as diversely populated as New York City itself. Perhaps the evocatively funereal Gothic-style tower and dormant clock are a reminder to those above ground that time is for the living.

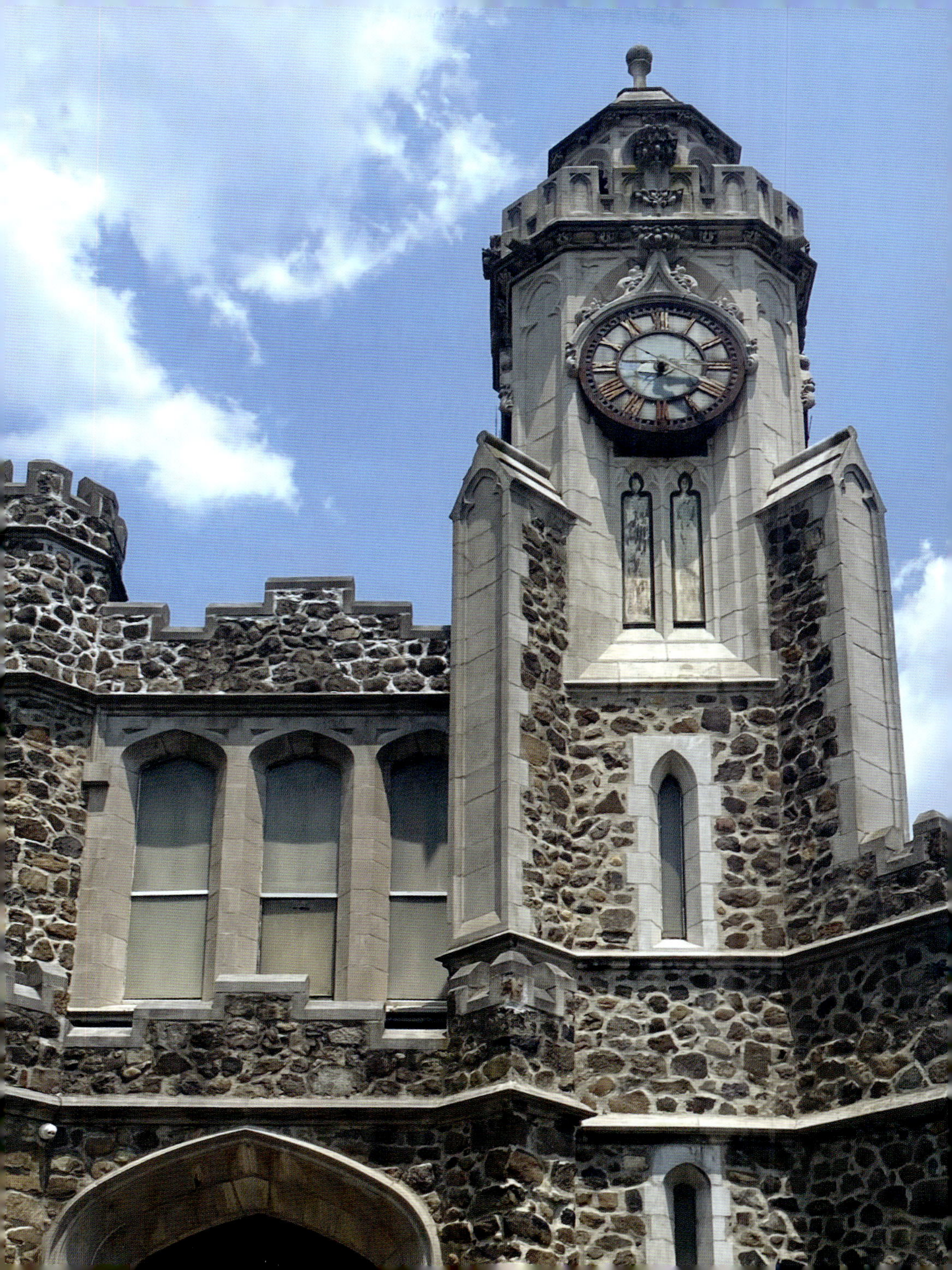

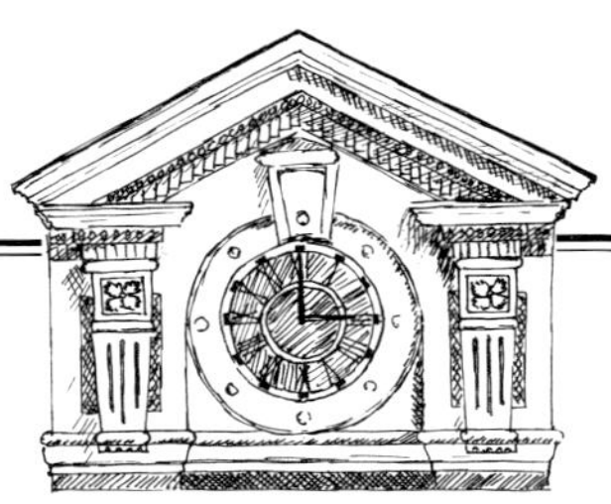

STATEN ISLAND
BOROUGH HALL
10 RICHMOND TERRACE
1906

In 1898, Staten Island was consolidated into New York City, and in 1906, this Carrère & Hastings–designed structure was completed. The late French Renaissance Revival brick-and-limestone building still holds its government offices. The tall tower is crowned by a two-sided clock, one facing the ferry terminal of the New York Harbor and the other visible from town. Each clockface is flanked by massive brackets supporting a soberly elegant pediment. John Carrère was born in Brazil but became a Staten Island resident and helped select the hilltop site for the Borough Hall. Along with his partner, Thomas S. Hastings, the firm also designed the splendid New York Public Library. They were both among America's most influential architects of their time.

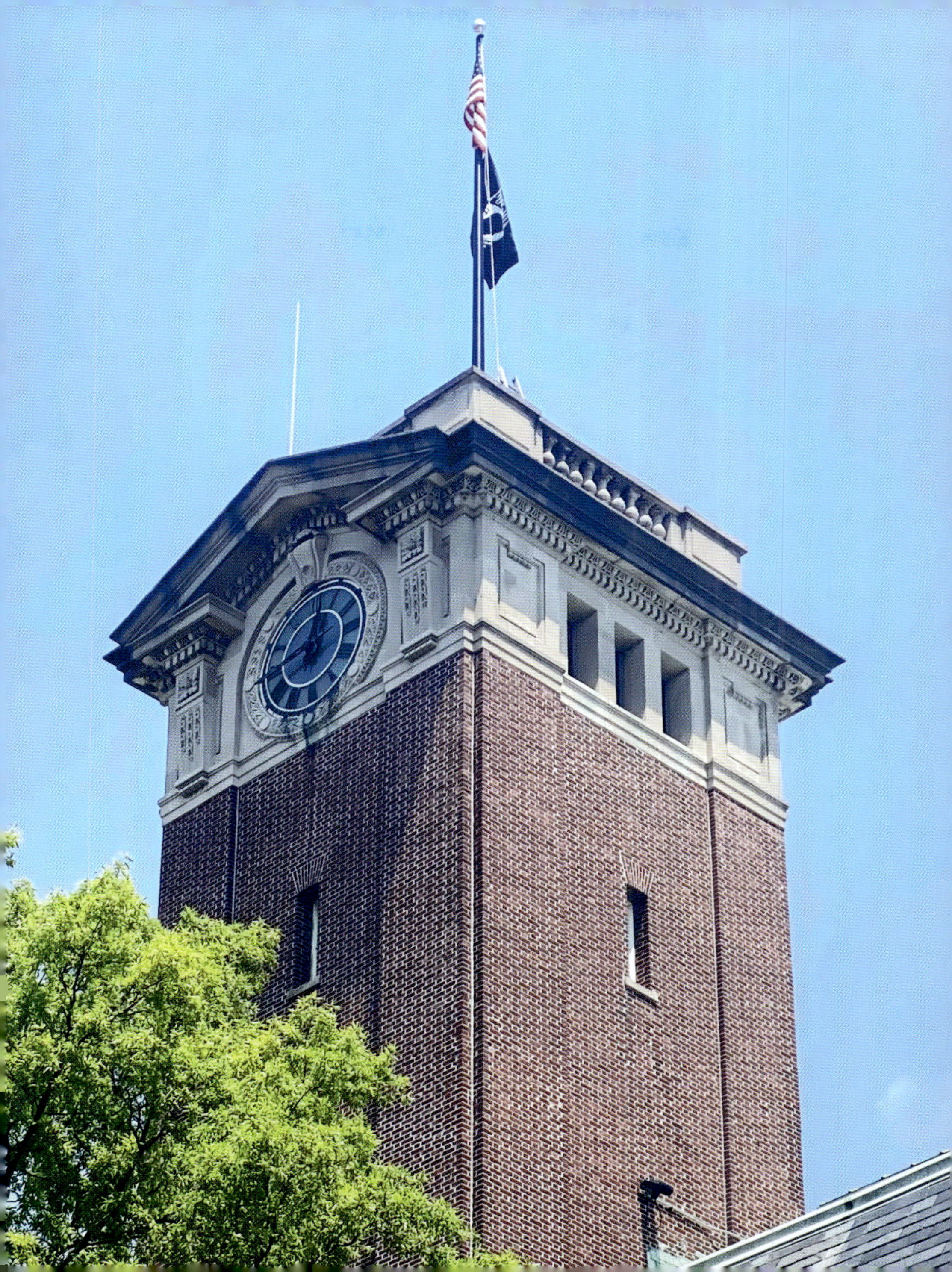

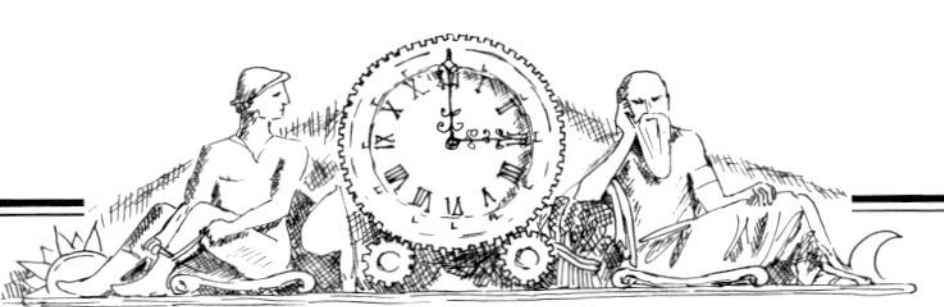

DIME SAVINGS BANK
9 DEKALB AVENUE, BROOKLYN
1932

The classical facade of the Dime Savings Bank of Brooklyn features a pediment supported by four Ionic columns with a central clock bordered by a ridged edge like a dime. Two male figures flank the clock: on the left, a seated youth ties his sandals, as if preparing for a day of labor, while on the right an older bearded man rests comfortably on his shafts of wheat. The grouping is both a metaphor for the passing of time and the reward of work. At the feet of the youth is the sun, while a crescent moon is near the feet of the old man. The building, landmarked in 1994, was originally designed by Mowbray & Uffinger but was dramatically redesigned by Halsey, McCormack & Helmer in 1931–32. It stylishly follows in the footsteps of the influential Stanford White Bowery Savings Bank.

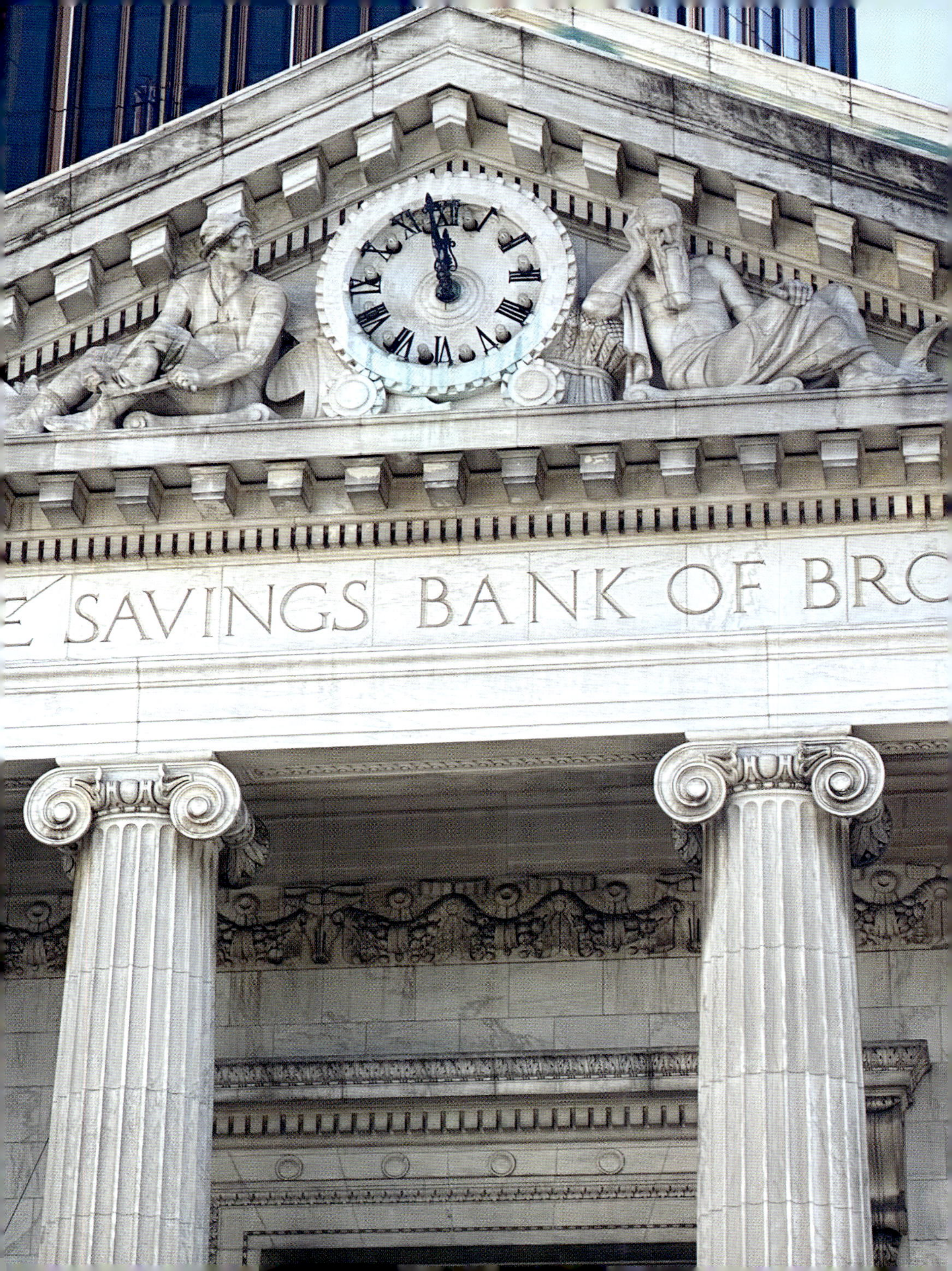
SAVINGS BANK OF BRO

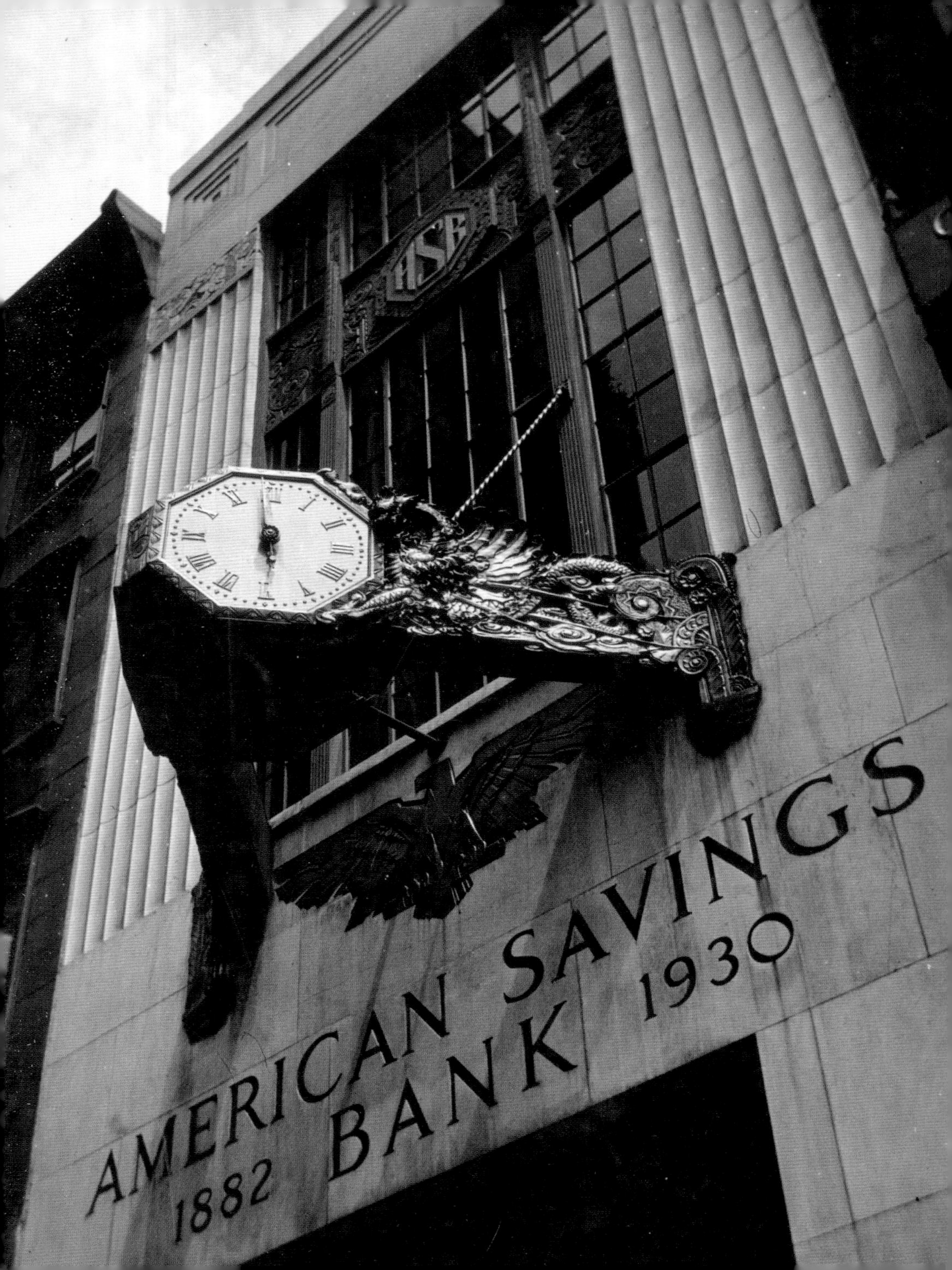
HSB
AMERICAN SAVINGS
BANK
1882
1930

4

HANG TIME

PROJECTING
AND CORNER CLOCKS

Walking through the streets of New York can be over-whelming, to the point where the pulse of the city drowns out one's capacity to take it in. If you are a visual person, as I am, the seeable noise can overpower the auditory. With businesses screaming out visual messages on every possible surface, one's overstimulated eyes may feel exhausted. When I left Texas for Manhattan in the 1970s, there was no such thing as video billboards. Still, my new city's visual noise was as shockingly loud as it was thrilling. In my attempt to not be overwhelmed, I focused my gaze on the beauty, not the bluster. Fortunately, there was plenty of beauty to carry me as I set out to discover the city. I found solace as I passed beautiful old buildings, some with clocks attached like a treasured pocket watch tucked elegantly into the waistcoat pocket of a distinguished gentleman.

Clocks projecting from buildings, unlike those that are part of the architecture, such as overdoor clocks or those that grace towers, can be delightful art pieces on their own. Often these clocks were promotional for businesses, but depending on the design, that aspect could feel secondary. The antecedents of these clocks were simple trade signs, created to promote the business by first

AMERICAN SAVINGS BANK,
115 West 42nd Street, c. 1930

This handsome projecting clock visually enhances a Manhattan bank facade.

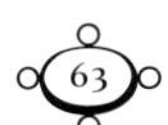

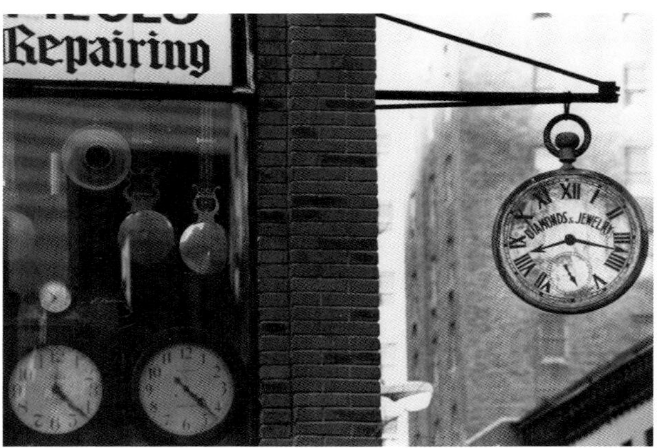

CLOCK REPAIR STORE, Manhattan, 1970

Trade signs have existed for centuries, and while this is a perfect example, it may have thrown off more than a few rushing New Yorkers who thought it was an actual clock.

charming, then communicating, with passersby. The twentieth-century image above of a historic New York City clock shop shows a classic example of a trade sign. This isn't a clock at all but a sign without words that clearly states what is within. One could see how the next step might be to upgrade such a sign to a functioning clock, giving the passerby a daily reason to look up.

Projecting clocks are a triple threat: business promotion, a sense of community, and visual enhancement. Typically made of metal, they commonly take a few different forms, such as two-faced clocks usually projected from walls and four-faced clocks mounted onto building corners. They could be simple or elaborate, making them attainable for smaller businesses or showpieces for those with more money to spend. The other advantage is they could be added to buildings years after they were constructed or when new buildings were purchased—just as a sign would be.

One wonders how many small public timepieces have been lost as businesses closed or buildings were razed to make room

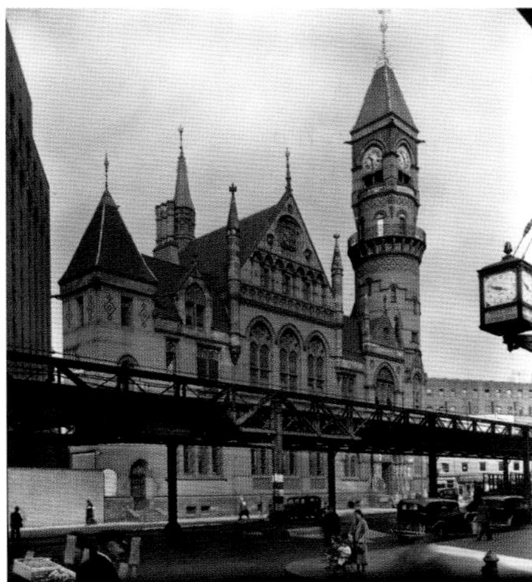

for larger, more modern structures. These vanished, unheralded clocks tell the story of how time has historically been valued by New Yorkers, even when the time-telling machines sometimes were not. They also tell us how even modest business proprietors felt compelled to spend their promotional dollars to be seen as a player in this very New York way. The early twentieth-century image above shows the heart of Greenwich Village with the Jefferson Market Courthouse behind the Sixth Avenue elevated train tracks. Projecting just into the photograph on the far right is a long-gone corner clock installed by the West Side Savings Bank. Below each clockface is a panel with unintelligible words, likely the name of the business. With the magnificent tower clock (shown on p. 48) within easy view of this smaller clock, its practical purpose is somewhat limited, yet its presence validates and elevates the status of a company.

The following selection of projecting clocks were created by businesses who cared deeply about the image they chose to share with passing New Yorkers. Fortunately for us, these beauties have survived, even though the original businesses have long gone.

NATHANIEL FISHER
& COMPANY
146 DUANE STREET
LATE 19TH CENTURY

Nathaniel Fisher, a wholesale shoe dealer, founded his company in 1869 after many years in the shoe trade. His sons, Irving and Nathaniel Jr., became partners in the company, which boasted a double-wide storefront on Duane Street, where this lovely clock can still be found. Made of bronze and now beautifully patinated, this nonworking clock tells the story of a bustling and successful business—an enterprise profitable enough to ornament the exterior of their store with a two-faced projecting clock, which also functioned as a form of advertising. The script at the top of the cartouche-style frame, now barely readable, says "Nath'l Fisher & Co." The clockface, a later replacement, advertises a more recent business that seems to have moved on.

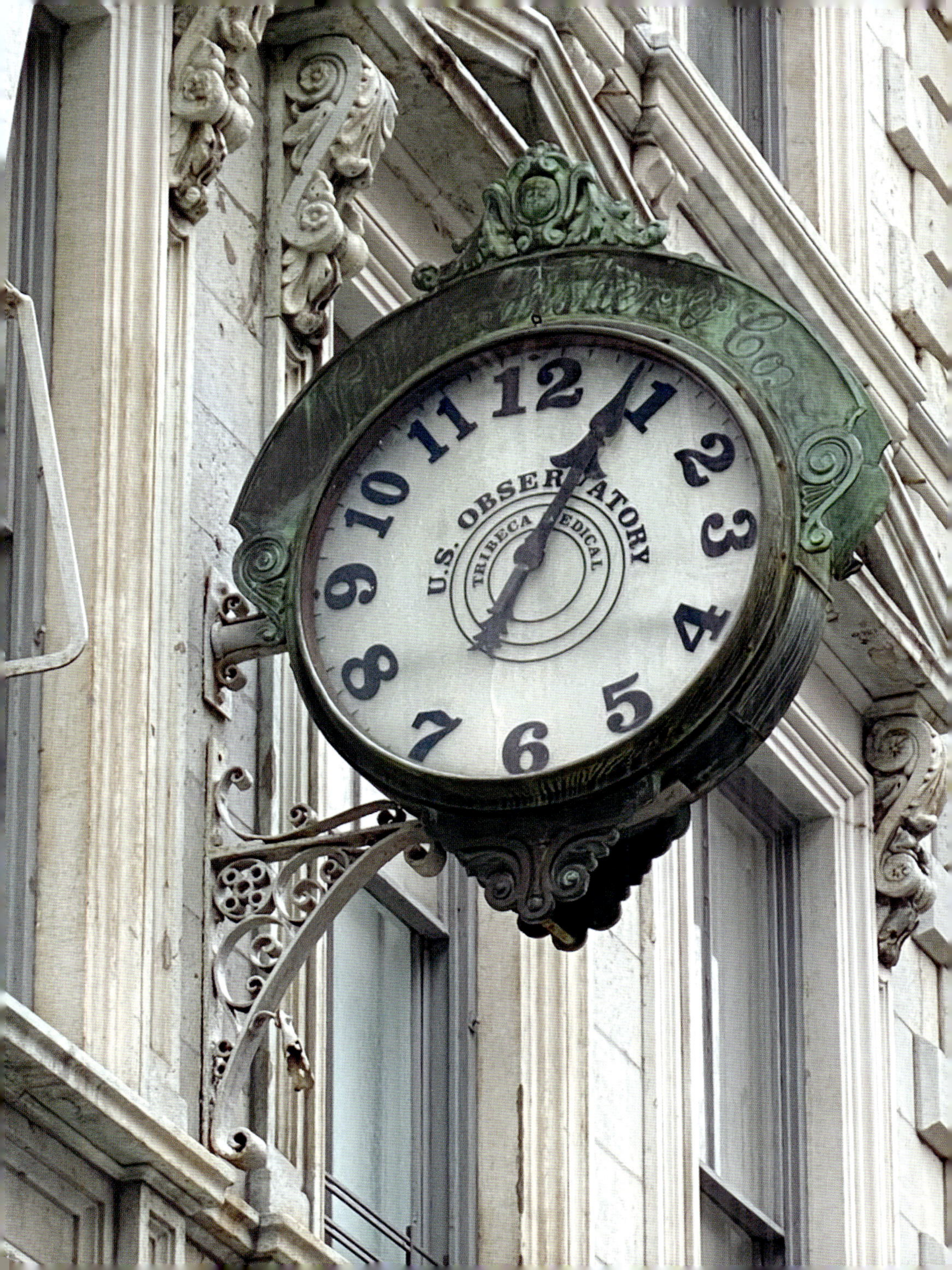
12
11
1
10
2
9
3
8
4
7
5
6
U.S. OBSERVATORY
TRIBECA MEDICAL

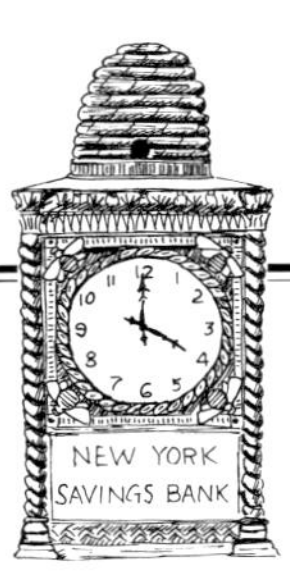

NEW YORK
SAVINGS BANK

81 EIGHTH AVENUE
LATE 19TH CENTURY

On the corner of West 14th Street and Eighth Avenue is an extraordinary bronze clock crowned by a beehive with a honeybee at each corner of its two clockfaces. Bees have long symbolized industry and a strong work ethic, two helpful attributes for a person seeking to put their money into a solid bank. The clock is attached to a white marble building, which was originally known as the New York Savings Bank, an elegant templelike structure crowned by a dome. Designed by architect R. H. Robertson and built in two sections in 1896 and 1897, this beautiful building has had many uses over the years, and was landmarked in 1988. This jewel of a clock brings a sense of whimsy to the otherwise grandly classical building.

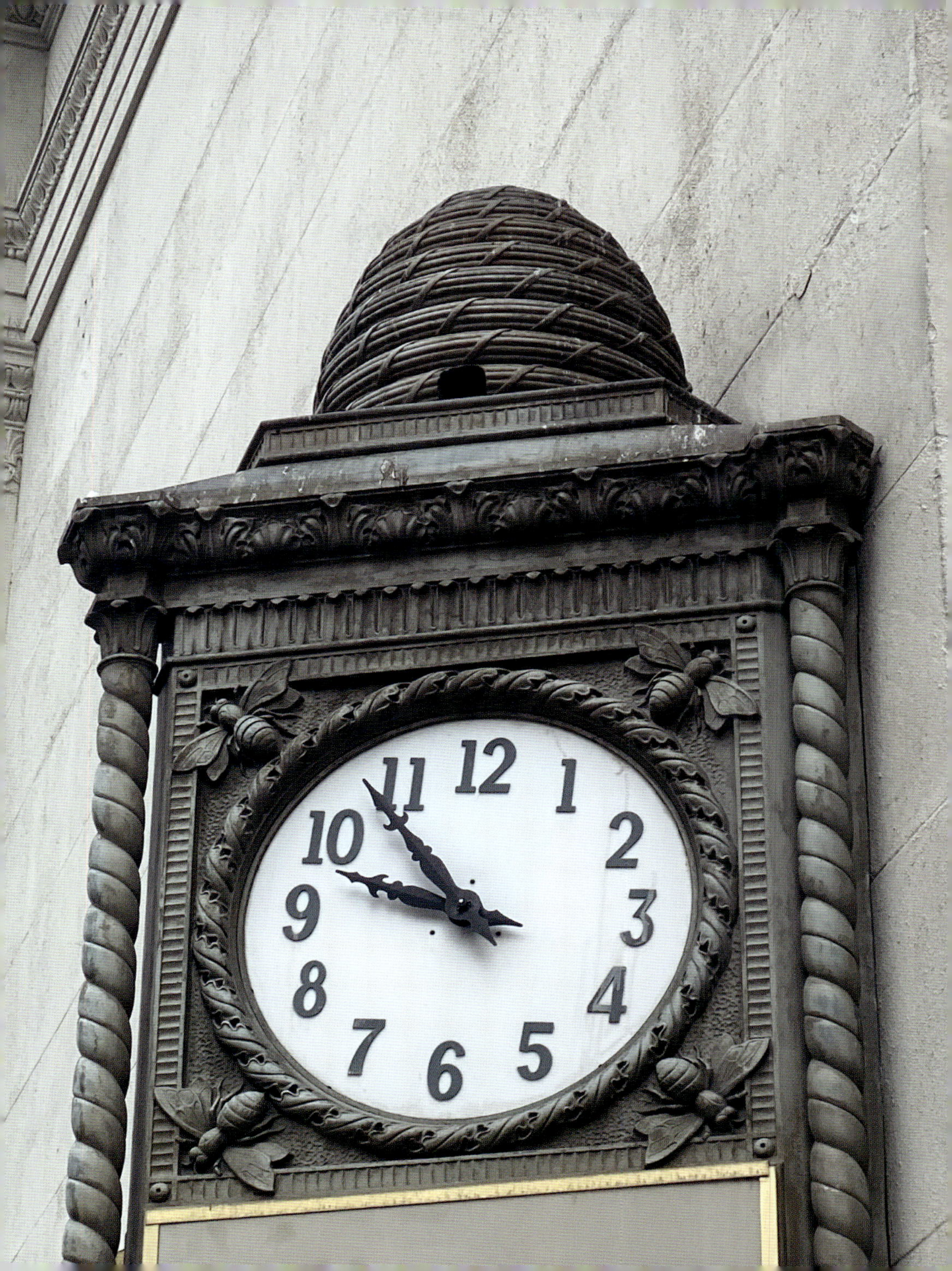

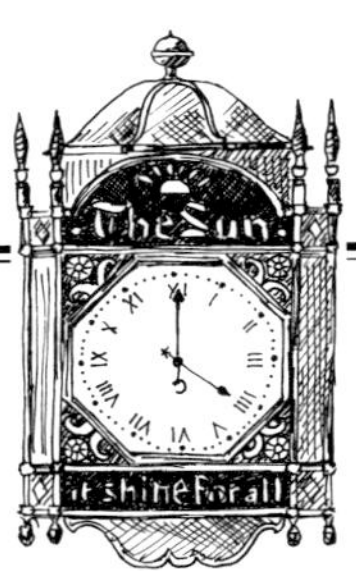

THE *SUN*
NEWSPAPER CLOCK
280 BROADWAY
C. 1919

After the *New York Sun*, a newspaper created for the working class, purchased the department store building at 280 Broadway, this highly detailed bronze four-faced clock appeared on the southern corner. At the top, it reads "The Sun" and below, "It shines for all." A coordinating, double-faced bronze thermometer is mounted at the northern edge of the building (not pictured). These lovely enhancements to this beautiful Italianate building, known as "the marble palace," were intended to send a direct message to the paper's core audience: information is for every New Yorker. A solid sentiment beautifully designed on the clock, while also promoting the business. One wishes that every American company would create something that supports their business while also enhancing the neighborhood, as this clock has done for over a century.

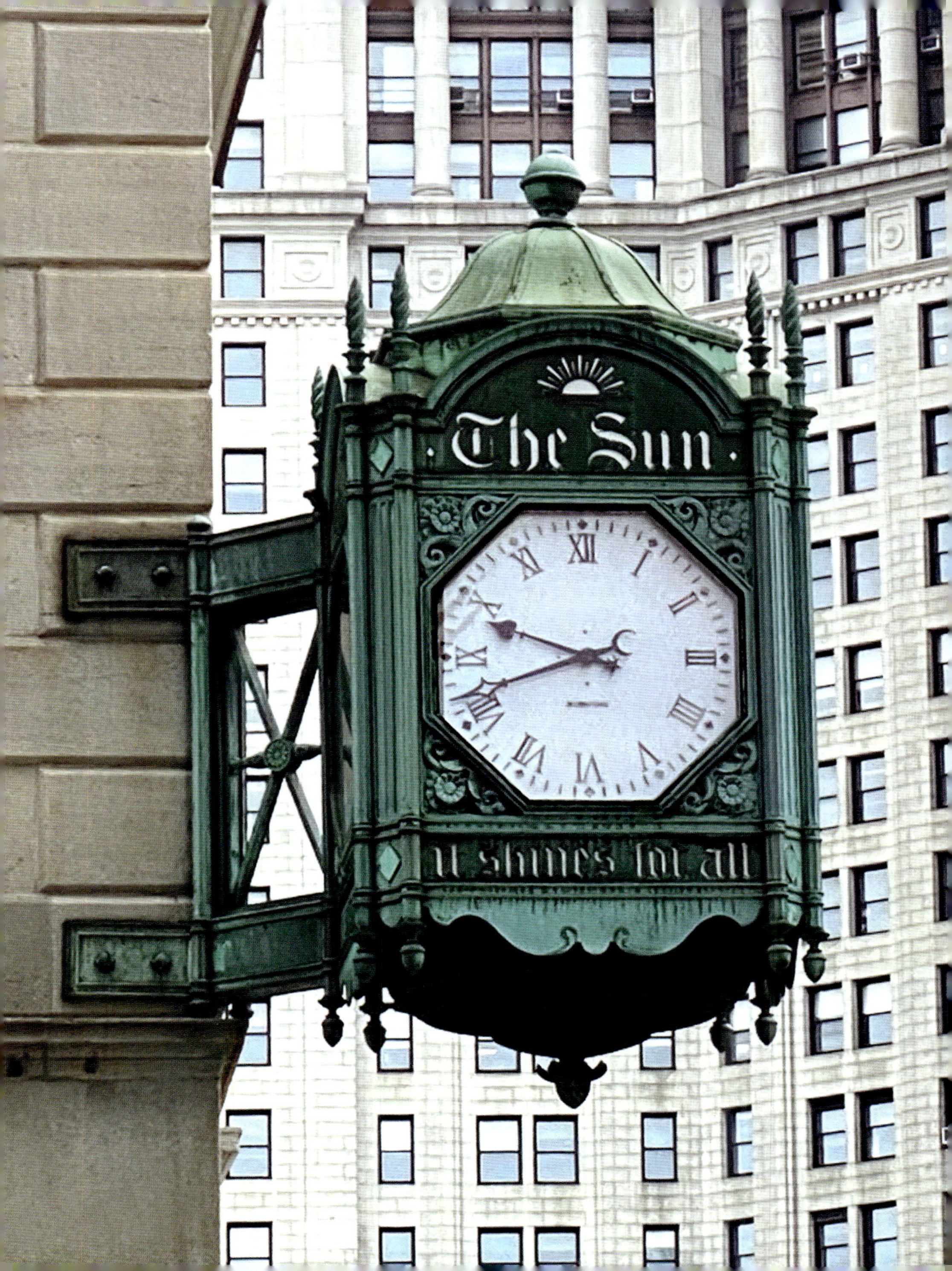

The Sun
U Shines for All

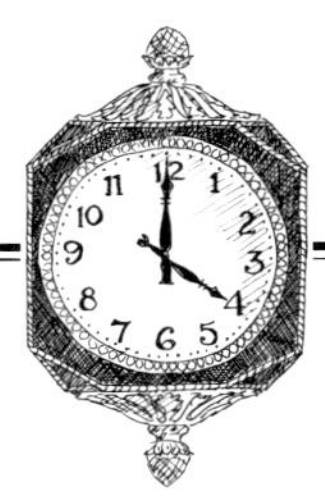

CORNER CLOCK

FIRST AVENUE AND
79TH STREET
1930S

Projecting from the corner of an unassuming brick building at First Avenue and 79th Street on Manhattan's Upper East Side is this refined four-faced clock. The building was a branch of Manufacturers Trust Company, a Brooklyn bank founded in the 1850s, though the clock likely dates from the 1930s. The four round clockfaces are framed by gilded egg and dart molding; at the top and bottom, artichoke-shaped finials are planted into lavish acanthus leaf bases that repeat the octagonal shape of this elegantly restrained neoclassical timepiece. The modest building is thus elevated by a beautiful clock, a lovely marker for this Manhattan neighborhood.

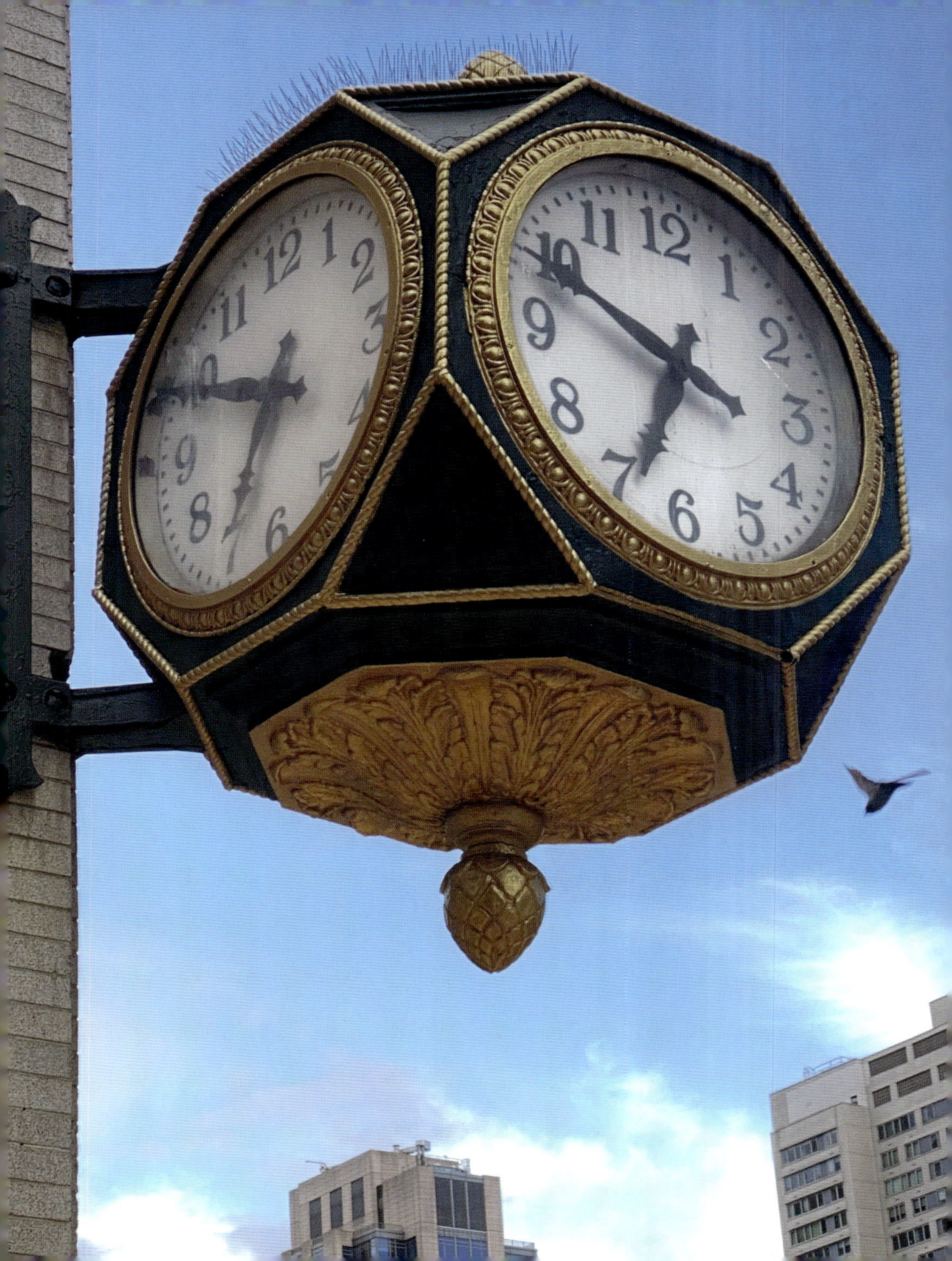

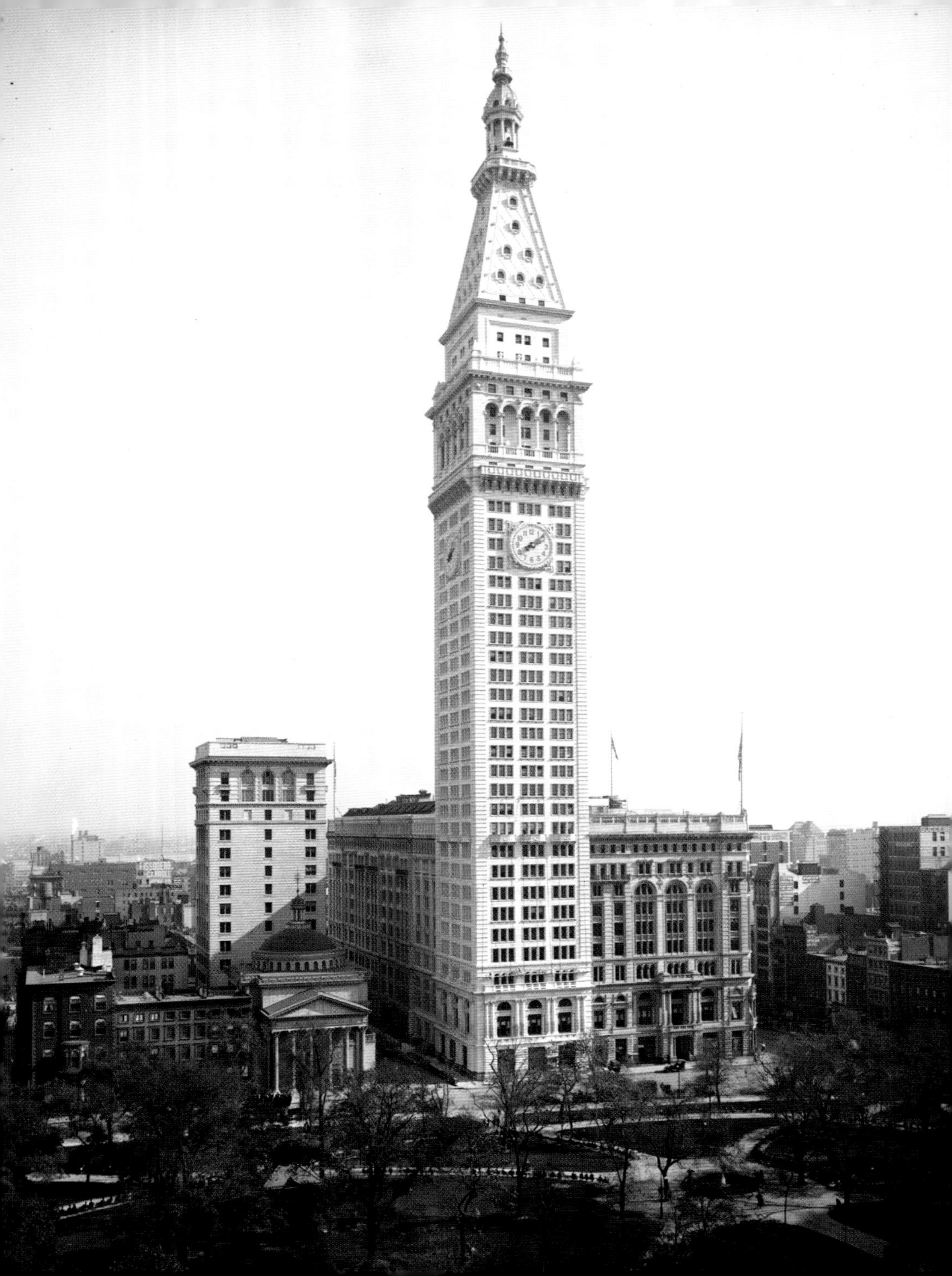

HIGH TIME
SKYSCRAPER CLOCKS

As new technology and building materials advanced in the nineteenth century, making taller buildings possible, the term *skyscraper* was invented. The first hurdle to reaching the sky was surpassed in New York in 1857 with the E. V. Haughwout Building. At only five stories high, it was the first to install a functional passenger elevator, which was more of an attraction than a necessity, but what followed was the inevitable race for taller and taller buildings. As time progressed and high-rise status was achieved, a handful of new skyscrapers added the cherry on top by creating impressive, massive clocks that could be viewed from many miles away.

The long-distance perspective was the purpose of these clocks, since they needed distance to be properly read. As these early skyscrapers popped up, they were not merely tall, but dramatically taller than most of the buildings around them—so the view from afar was largely unobstructed. These buildings and their clocks became the talk of the town, and with early innovative lighting, folks all the way in the boroughs were chattering as they set their watches by them. Even at night, these showstopping timepieces became identifiable icons, giving New Yorkers bragging rights about their ever-expanding, cutting-edge metropolis.

Metropolitan Life Insurance Company Tower, built 1909, 1 Madison Avenue, c. 1909–15

Overlooking Madison Square Park, the MetLife Tower dwarfed every nearby structure, its clock visible for miles.

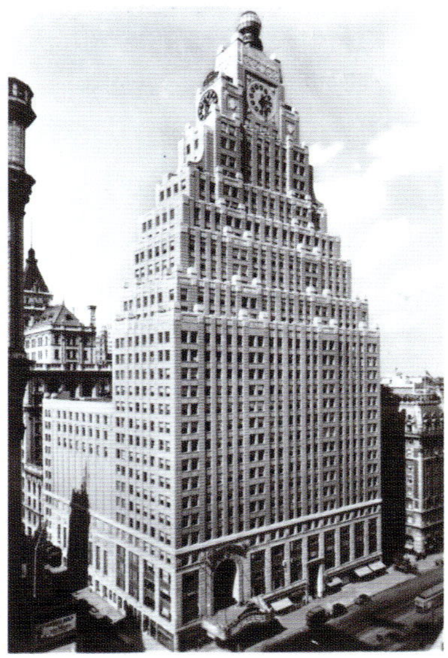

PARAMOUNT BUILDING, built
1927, 1501 Broadway, c. 1927–40

The massive clock, with its
unique use of stars instead of
numerals for the hours, sits atop
this ziggurat-style building in
Times Square and has long in-
vited views from a distance.

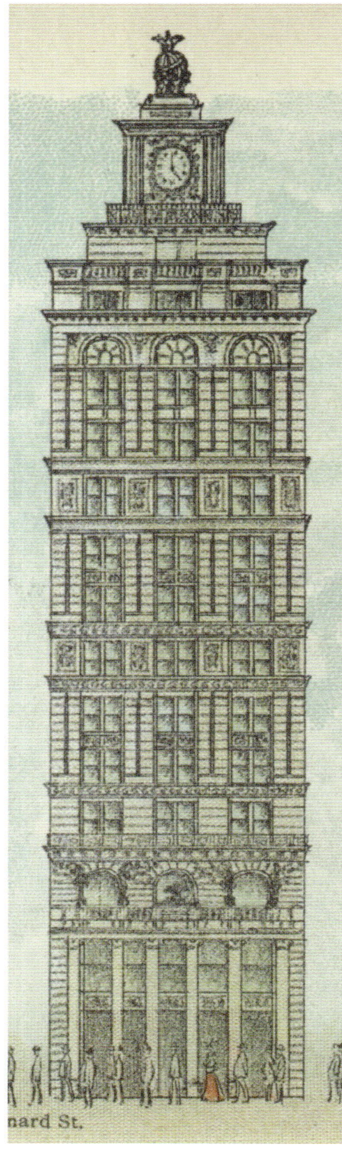

NEW YORK LIFE INSURANCE BUILDING,
built 1898, 346 Broadway, 1899

The sculpture above the four-sided clock of
this early skyscraper disappeared in the 1920s.

In the second half of the twentieth century, high-rises became more monumental and more plentiful, but typically without clocks, making them impressive only because of their size. With New York's skyline always changing, the lavish attention to detail of the earlier skyscrapers began to get lost in the shuffle. The clock-topped skyscrapers of the 1890s and early twentieth century no longer stood head and shoulders above the rest, limiting their impact while muffling the clocks' practical use.

The Metropolitan Life Insurance Company Tower on Madison Square, shown on p. 74 shortly after it was built, gives an idea how the seemingly lofty buildings erected in prior years could not compete with the stratospheric height of what was—for four years—the tallest building in the world. Other notable examples shown opposite include the New York Life Insurance Company Building, which was built roughly a decade before and not only had a beautiful clock but a thirty-plus-foot sculpture crowning it, now lost; and the Paramount Building, whose clock was once enjoyed with an unobstructed view by New Yorkers near and far.

As you walk through the city today, you may be wowed by the recently erected, needlelike glass high-rises. For me, they offer architectural empty calories that rarely tempt a repeated viewing. I deeply admire the United Nations building, but it was built in the 1940s, making today's glass-box structures a rather old idea, even if engineers have devised ways to heighten them. I find the regurgitation of these glass boxes lazy and visually exhausting. Thankfully, tucked here and there among New York's forest of redundant towers stand larger-than-life ticking clocks, masterfully incorporated into highly original buildings. Those century-old buildings and their talk-of-the-town timepieces remind us even today to live in the now. Here are some of the surviving skyscraper clocks that touch the sky and continue to make a statement.

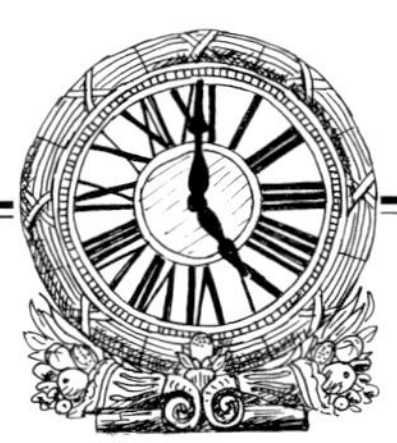

NEW YORK LIFE INSURANCE COMPANY BUILDING
346 BROADWAY
1898

Above this twelve-story building, once the New York Life Insurance Company headquarters, is a sensational four-faced clock housed within a neo-classical tower. Each clockface measures twelve feet in diameter. The marble-clad building was designed by architect Stephen Decatur Hatch, who passed away in 1894 during construction, so the illustrious firm McKim, Mead & White were brought on board to complete the building, including redesigning one of the facades. A thirty-three-foot-tall sculpture created by Philip Martiny, a student of Augustus Saint-Gaudens, once crowned the clock tower. It was a massive armillary-type sphere supported by four crouching Atlas figures, and on top a massive eagle perched with spread wings. The sculpture was removed sometime after 1928, its whereabouts still unknown. This clock is one of the last in the city to be wound by hand rather than run by electricity. The clockworks, created by the E. Howard Clock Company, and the building are both landmarked.

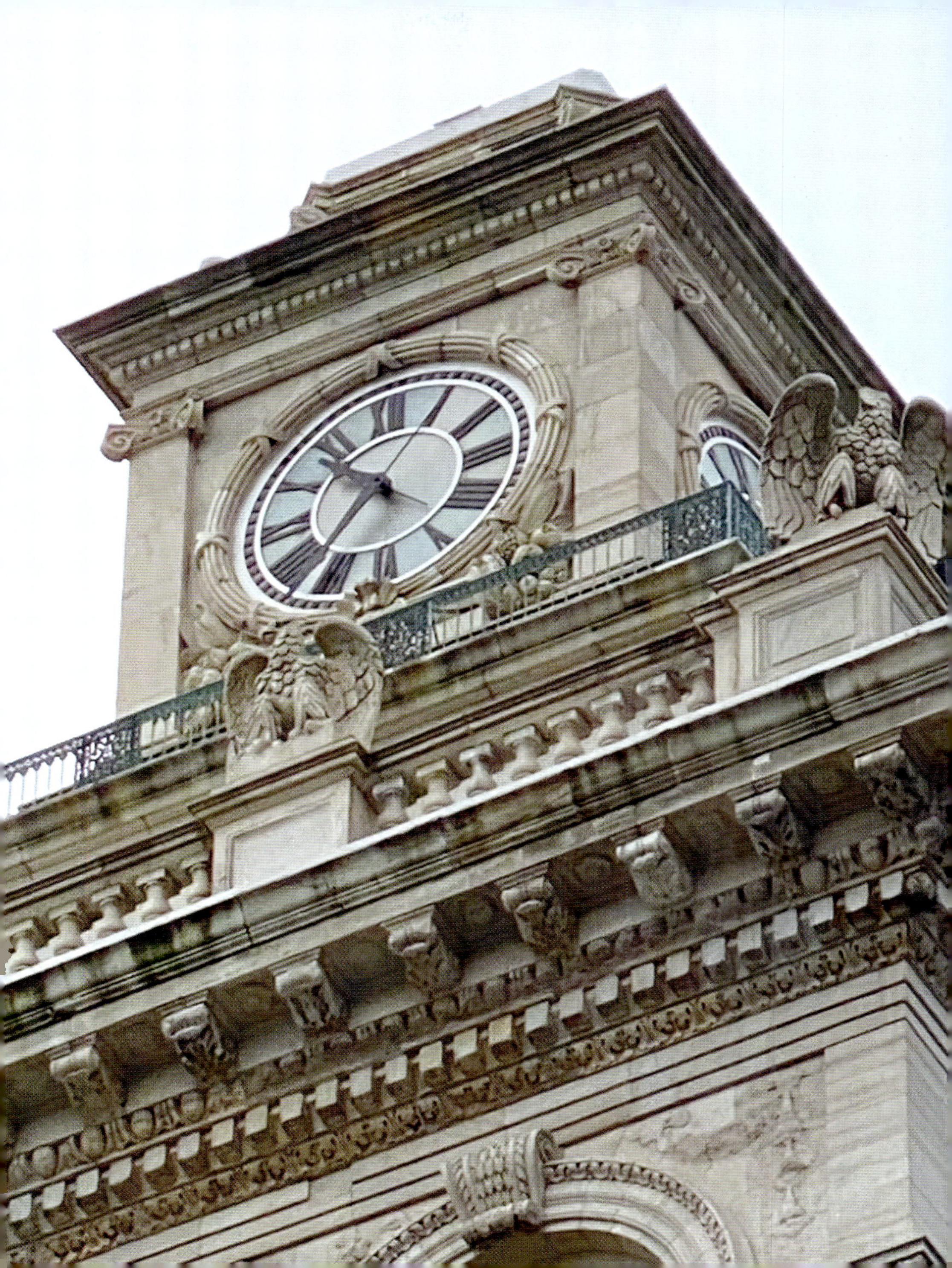

METROPOLITAN LIFE INSURANCE COMPANY TOWER

1 MADISON AVENUE
1909

While this building is officially a skyscraper, it was inspired by a tower—St. Mark's Campanile in Venice. Pierre LeBrun of Napoleon LeBrun & Sons designed the building, the tallest in the world until 1913. Given the building's fifty-story height and the clock's 26.5-foot diameter, the four clockfaces were visible from miles around. These were the largest clockfaces in the world at that time, positioned between the twenty-fifth and twenty-seventh floors. The numerals are four feet tall and the minute hands seventeen feet long, weighing one thousand pounds each. The master clock was electric, unusual for the time. The mechanism controlled all four clockfaces, plus a hundred other clocks within the building. Pierre LeBrun designed the sculptural ornamentation of the four faces, which includes dolphins, shells, and a laurel leaf wreath to frame the faces. This building is, surprisingly, older than the Campanile in Venice; though the original tower was completed in 1514, it collapsed in 1902 and was rebuilt in 1912.

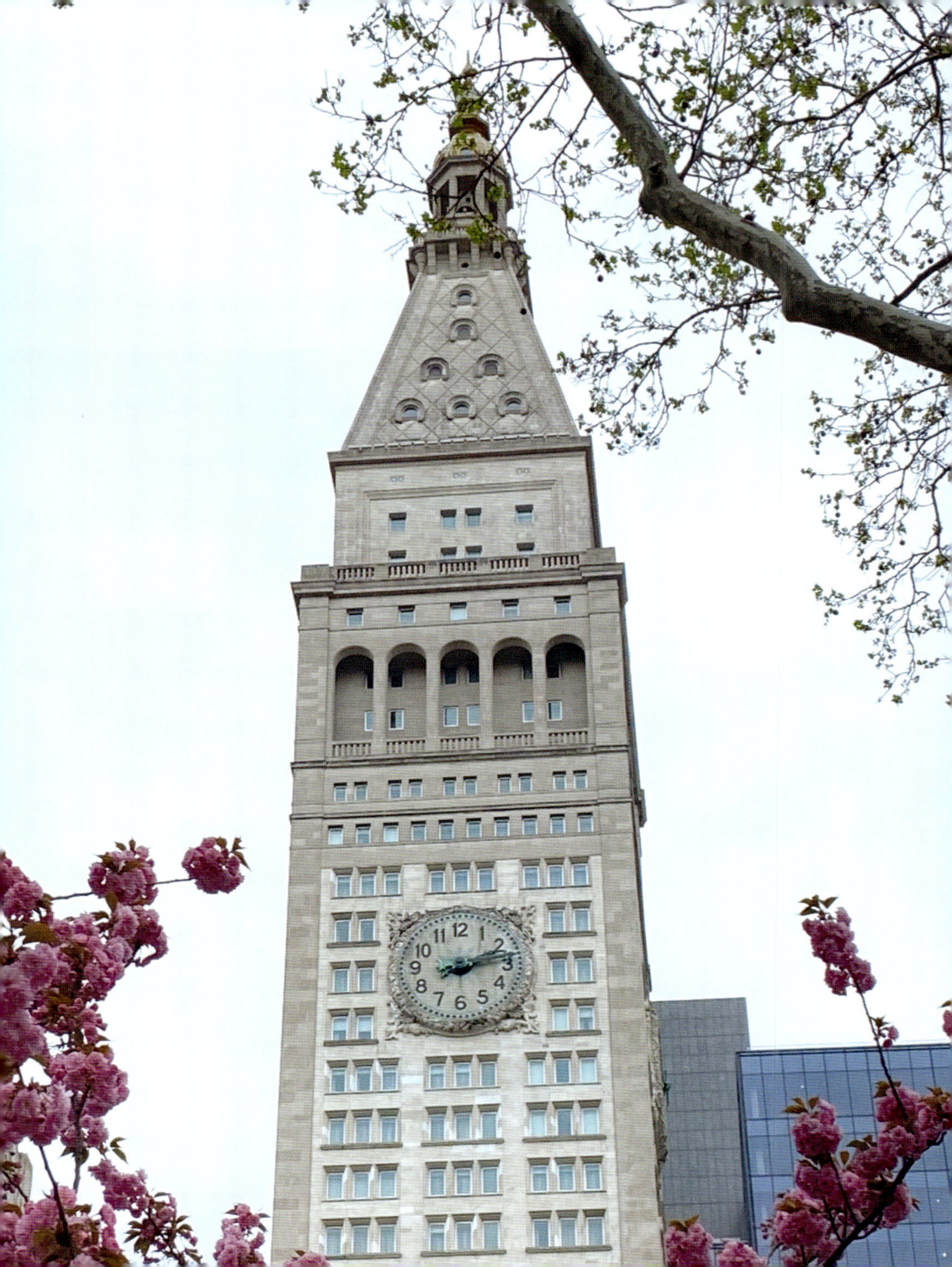

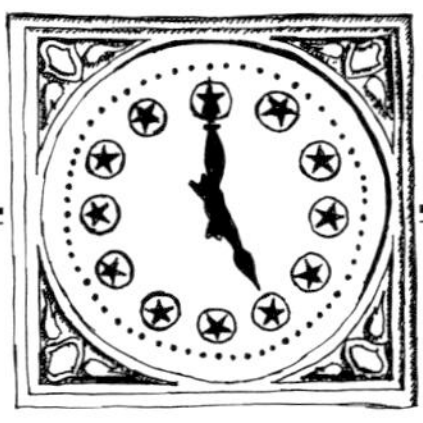

PARAMOUNT BUILDING

1501 BROADWAY
1927

At the center of Times Square and New York's famous theater district stands the thirty-three-story Paramount Building designed by architects Rapp & Rapp. When it was constructed, it was the tallest building in Times Square (known in the nineteenth century as Long Acre Square). The theatrical architectural style is a blend of Beaux Arts and Art Deco, with a massive four-sided clock on the thirtieth floor. Instead of numerals, the hours on these Seth Thomas Clock Company clocks are depicted as simple glass circles lit from behind to allow viewing from a distance at night. Each circle measures four feet in diameter, and within these circles are five-pointed stars, referencing Paramount's famous logo. The east and west clockfaces measure about twenty-five feet across, and the north and south clockfaces measure twenty-two feet in diameter. Topping it all is an illuminated glass globe made of ninety panels that were originally painted with a world map. The building initially held a three-thousand-plus-seat Paramount theater, which featured live performances of some of Hollywood's most illustrious stars.

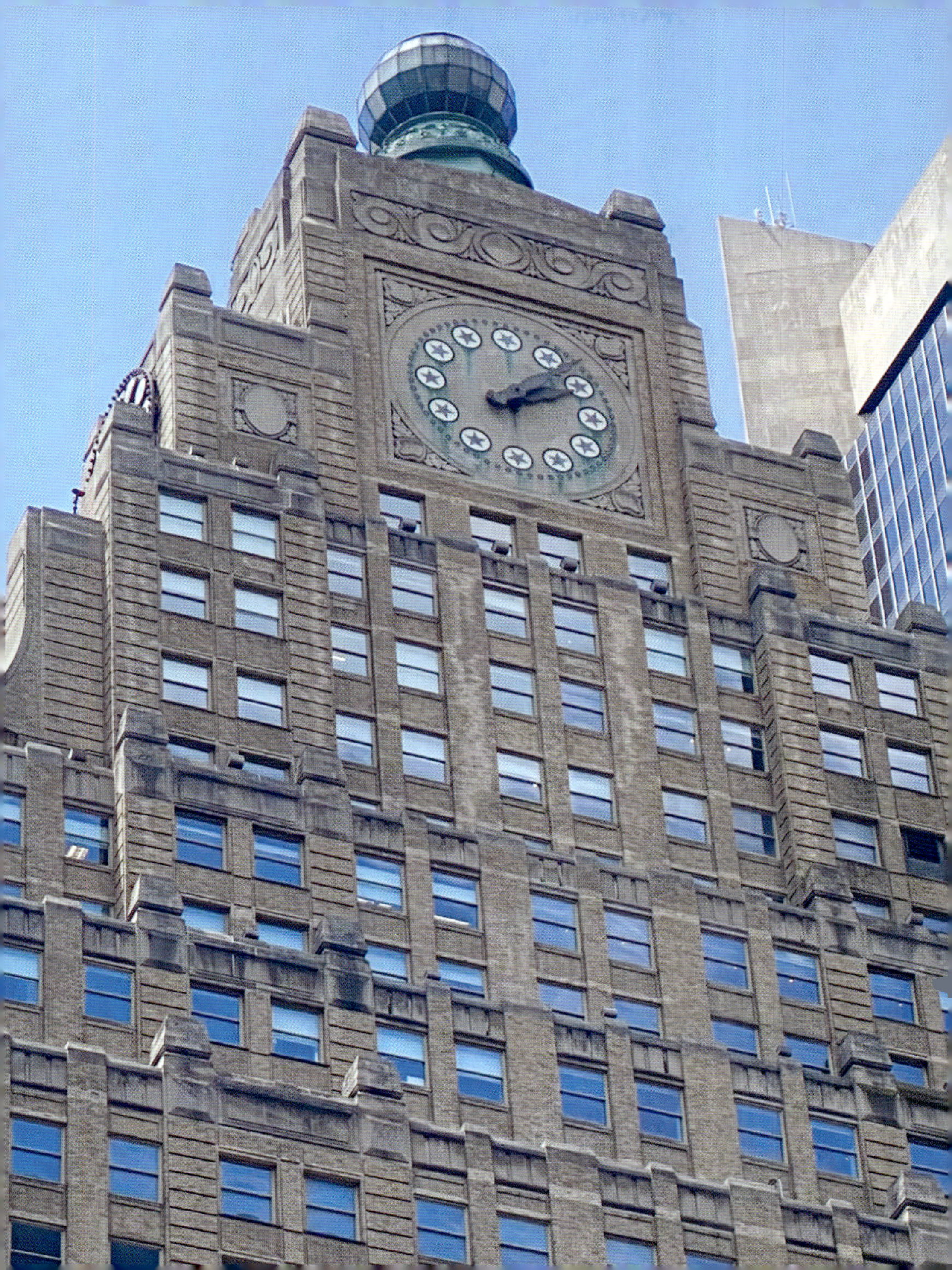

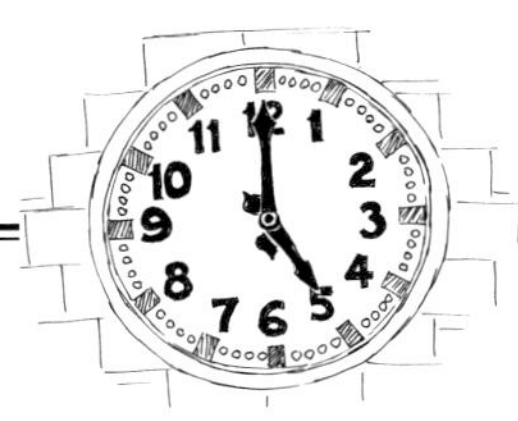

CONSOLIDATED EDISON BUILDING

4 IRVING PLACE
1927

Designed by Warren & Wetmore, the temple-like structure atop the Con Edison Building is crowned with a massive lantern. Four clockfaces are set in the base of the columned temple, which helped to create an instantly iconic addition to the New York skyline when the building was completed in the late 1920s. The nearly twenty-two-foot-diameter clocks were made by the Seth Thomas Clock Company, who described them as the "most elaborate installation ever furnished up to the present time." Four monumental bells, one weighing five thousand pounds, hang within the tower and ring every quarter hour. The building was famous for its elaborate lighting system that created spectacular changing colors, giving the glorious topper of this skyscraper a nickname appropriate for a power company: the Tower of Light. These special effects continue to this day.

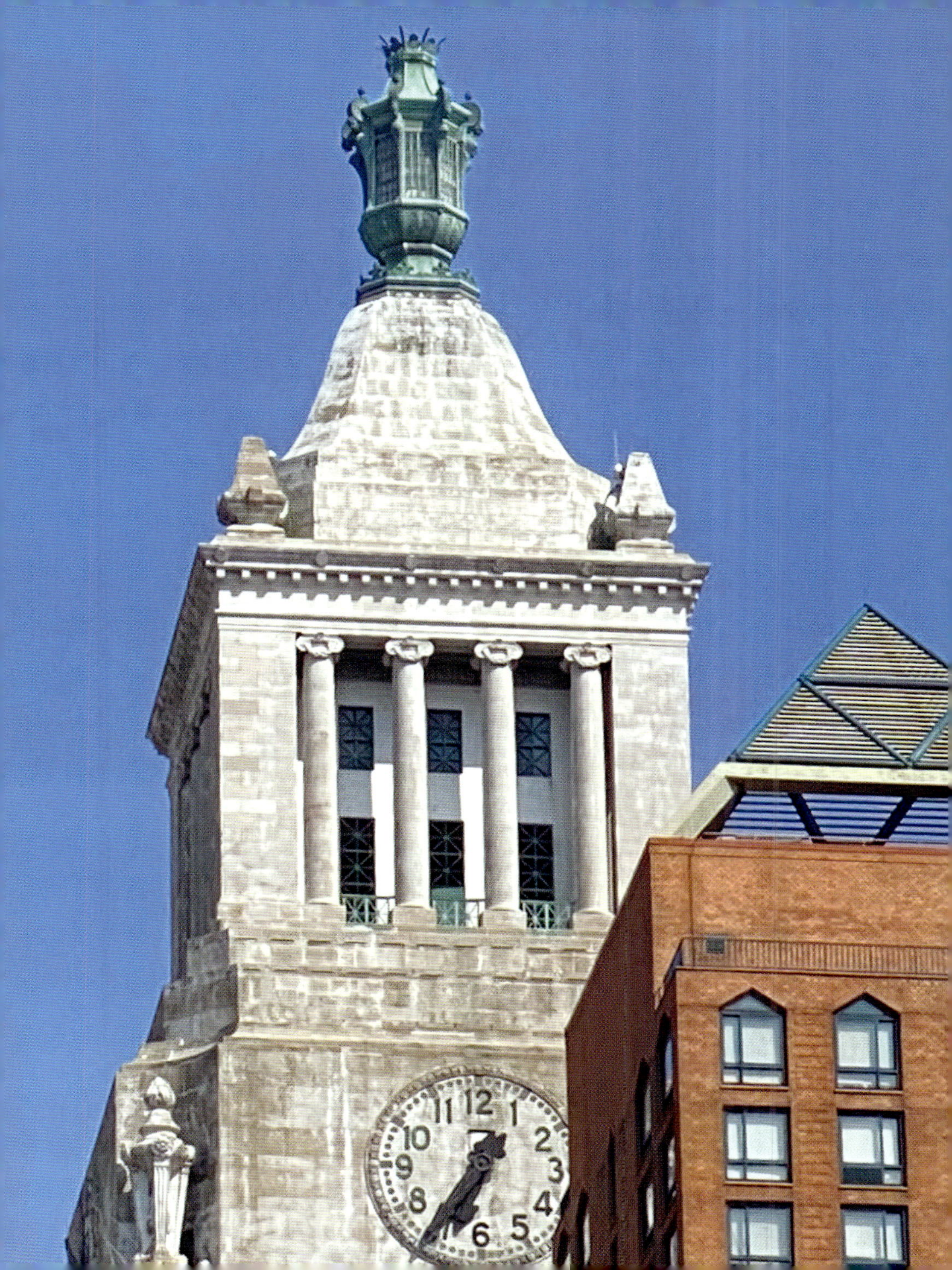

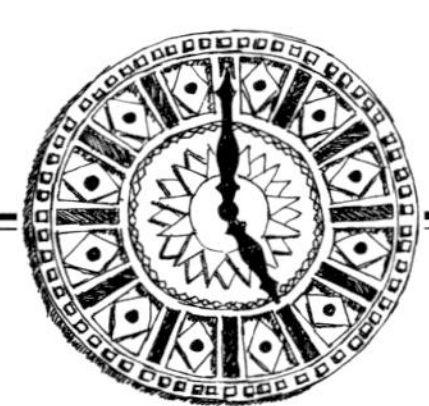

WILLIAMSBURGH SAVINGS BANK TOWER

1 HANSON PLACE, BROOKLYN
1929

In the Fort Greene neighborhood near downtown Brooklyn stands a domed skyscraper designed by Halsey, McCormack & Helmer. It was completed in 1929, and was the tallest building in Brooklyn for eighty years. Its major feature is the massive four-sided clock that resides between the thirty-fourth and thirty-sixth floors. These clocks were the largest in the world at the time, each face measuring twenty-seven feet in diameter with the minute hands being more than fifteen feet long and weighing 523 pounds. The clock was illuminated in 1928, before the building was completed, with lighted dots instead of numerals. According to the *Brooklyn Daily Eagle*, it was visible from thirty miles away. Brooklynites and even folks from neighboring boroughs set their watches to the monumental clock of this much-admired tower.

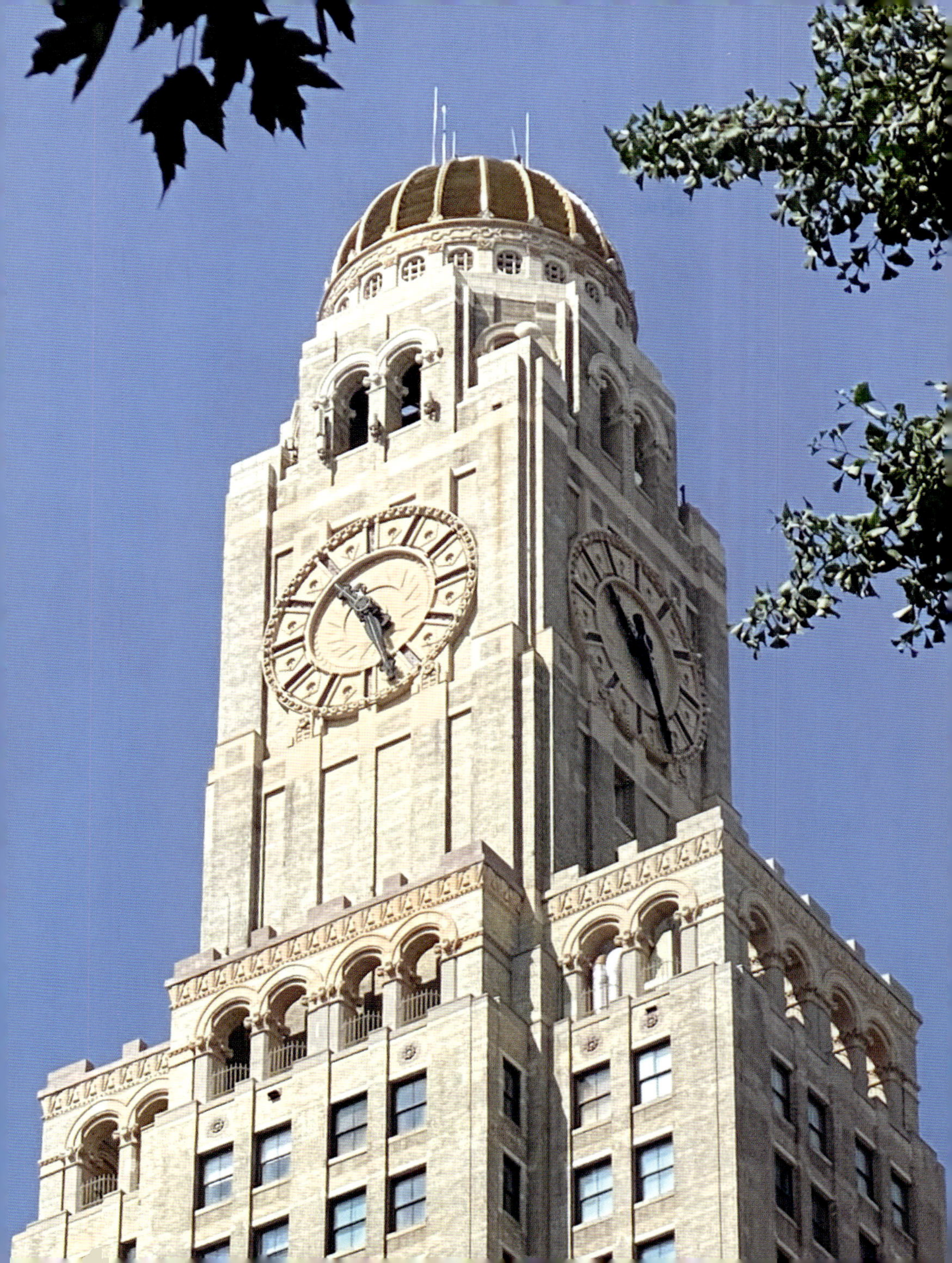

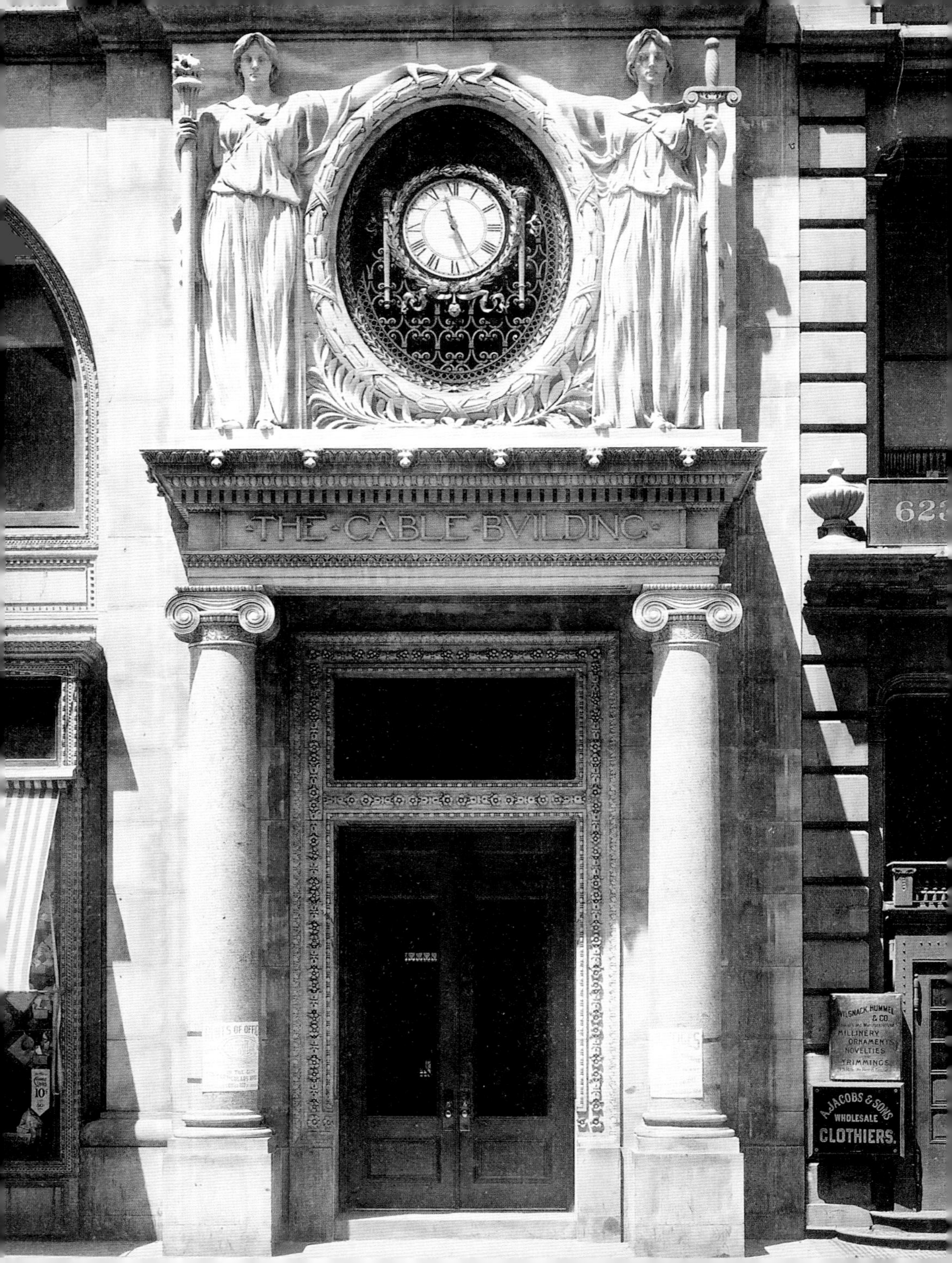
THE · CABLE · BVILDING ·
623
WILSNACK, HUMMEL
& CO.
MILLINERY
ORNAMENTS
NOVELTIES
TRIMMINGS
A. JACOBS & SONS
WHOLESALE
CLOTHIERS.

PRIME TIME
OVERDOOR CLOCKS

Clocks atop skyscrapers are best seen from afar, but when entering those buildings, you cannot check the clock thirty floors above to see if you're late for work. That's what overdoor clocks are for. Jumping out of cabs or rushing upstairs from subterranean trains to madly dash to a meeting is more comforting if you know you can "clock" a clock from the corner of your eye as you push through the door and head toward the elevator. That scenario made sense in a time long before affordable wristwatches became available or smartphones existed. But even with these fairly recent conveniences, overdoor clocks remain a handy and attractive element for a well-appointed building.

An excellent example from the past is the beautiful entrance to the Cable Building in NoHo, designed by Stanford White and completed in 1894. Its striking portal is surmounted not only by a clock inset in an oval window, but by an impressive pair of eleven-foot-tall draped female figures made by Scottish American sculptor J. Massey Rhind. It was called the Cable Building because deep beneath the structure were thirty-two-foot-diameter steel wheels that turned, pulling the cable cars on Broadway—yes, with actual cables. Offices were upstairs. The building and

CABLE BUILDING, built 1894, 611 Broadway, 1894.

The entrance of this building is still intact, but the clock is long gone.

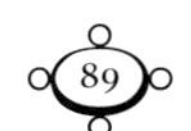

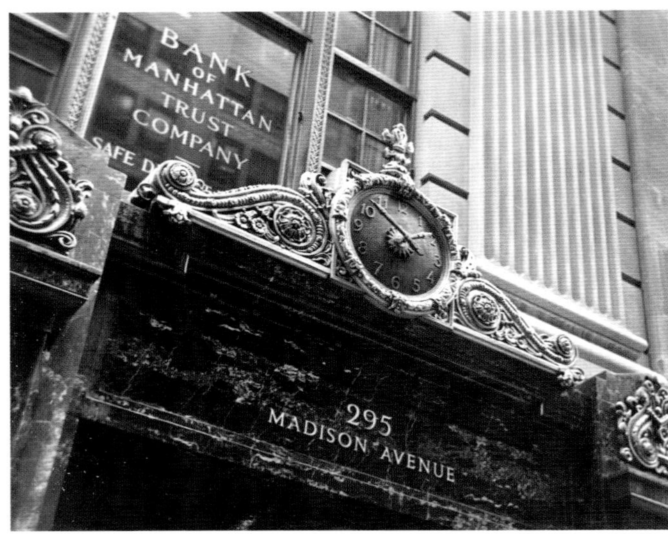

BANK OF MANHATTAN TRUST COMPANY, 1930, 295 Madison Avenue, c. 1930–38

The superb bronze over-door clock that once ornamented this bank entrance is sadly but a memory.

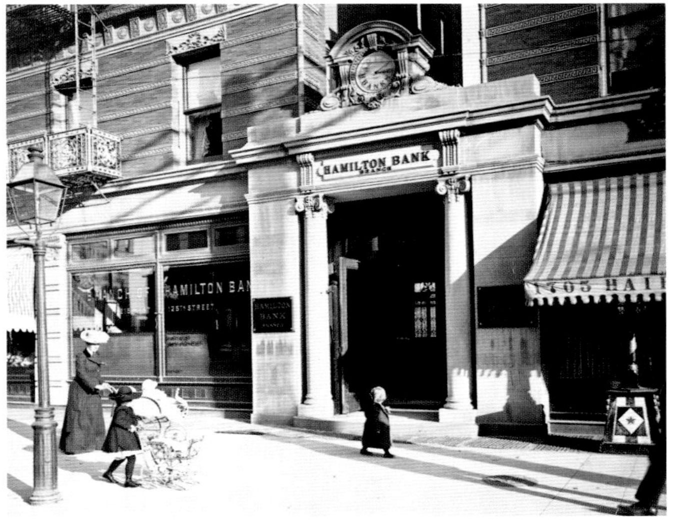

HAMILTON BANK BUILDING, built 1899, 1707 Amsterdam Avenue, c. 1901

In Harlem, this limestone portal on Amsterdam Avenue between 144th and 145th Streets, with its crowning clock casing above it, still stands. The Hamilton Bank and its clockworks, however, are no more.

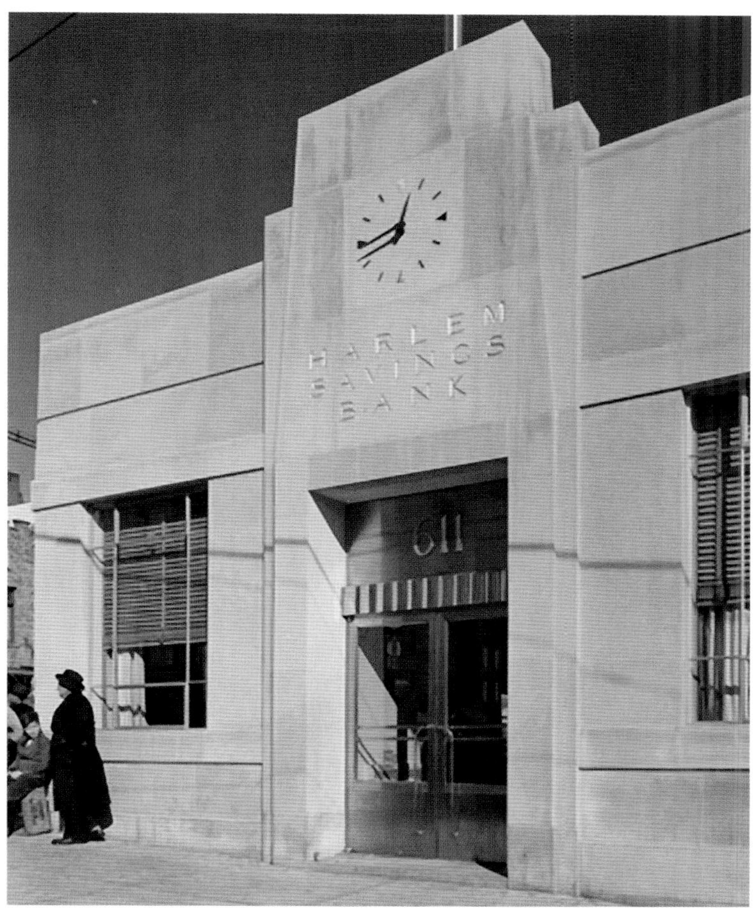

HARLEM SAVINGS BANK, built 1863,
611 West 207th Street, 1940

This image of a Harlem Savings Bank
branch shows how the Art Deco style
was transitioning into something
optimistically fresh and clean.

its beautiful goddess figures survive as an official landmark, but sadly the clock is no more.

I delight in beautiful old structures like the Cable Building, designed by visionaries to house innovative projects. Though this building's original use disappeared long ago, as time marched on creative minds and makers filled the void. Among them was Keith Haring, who created his epochal art here. These are the layers of uniquely New York stories that took place, and still take place, behind the clocks of so many of the city's historic buildings.

In Midtown Manhattan, long considered the business district of the city, there once stood a branch of the Bank of Manhattan Trust Company with a beautiful overdoor clock rendered in an exuberant Empire style (shown on p. 90). Cast in bronze and mounted onto dark marble, it visually references the decorative bronze mounts on very fine Napoleonic furniture. This neoclassical clock was designed to be a representation of the strength and security of the bank within.

Uptown in Harlem, the Hamilton Bank Building resided on Amsterdam Avenue between 144th and 145th Streets. As shown in the 1901 photograph on p. 90, this was the first bank in Harlem above 125th Street offering local service to businesses and residences. The handsome limestone portal of the building sports an overdoor clock in the Renaissance style, but instead of numerals for the hours, the bank cleverly had twelve letters spelled out: H - A - M - I - L - T - O - N - B - A - N - K. The building still stands, but like the Cable Building, its clock is sadly gone. Today the stone clock casing is a relic that feels like an architectural Cyclops missing his eye.

Farther north, on 207th Street, was a branch of the Harlem Savings Bank. Though the bank was founded in 1863, the photo shown on p. 91 was taken in 1940 for what appears to be a sparkling new branch. This building's very spiffy late Art Deco style had an overdoor clock with a breezy, minimal design. It is

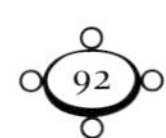

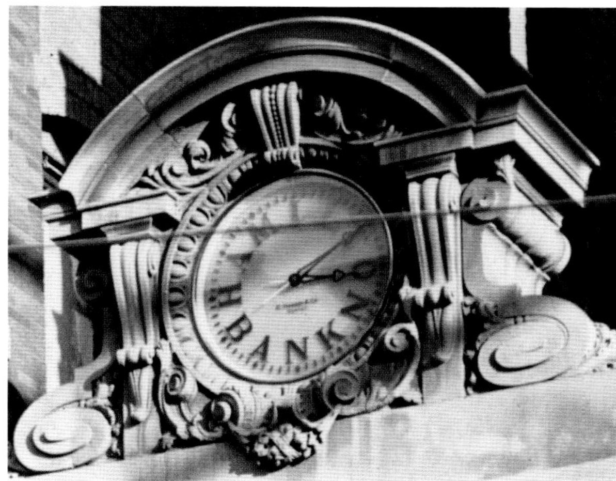

HAMILTON BANK
BUILDING, detail

See p. 90

possible the building survives, but if so, the facade has been dramatically altered, the clock only a memory.

In a vast city with clocks of every size and description, there is something wonderfully intimate about a smaller timepiece over a portal. The four bygone clocks discussed are superb examples of overdoor clocks in an assortment of styles and from a variety of eras, but they are a fraction of those that have been lost. Happily, many still exist, and the following examples are those I find most compelling. They range from neoclassical to super sleek, but what they all share is a sense of great style that still holds up today. Legions of creative minds and daily workers passed beneath these clocks, hopefully on time, as they answered the call to innovate and move our history forward, one tick at a time.

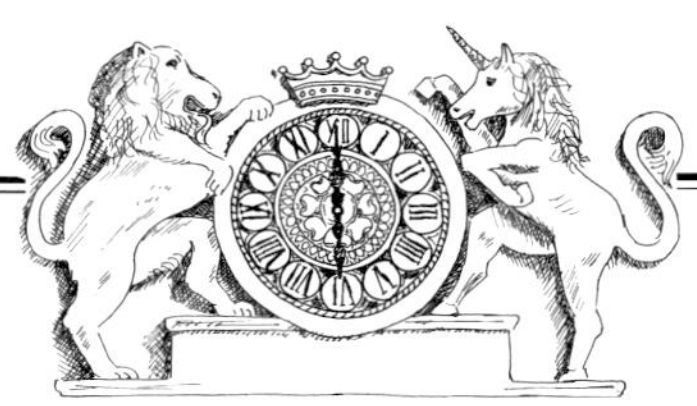

ROYAL LIFE
INSURANCE COMPANY
84 WILLIAM STREET
1907

At the corner of William Street and Maiden Lane in Lower Manhattan is the entrance to a handsome seventeen-floor building created to house the Royal Life Insurance Company in 1907. White marble and brick were combined in a British style by American architects Howells & Stokes. If it wasn't crystal clear what side of the pond this company favored, the over-door clock designed like the British royal coat of arms is there to remind us. Instead of a shield held by the lion and unicorn, we see a marble and bronze clock—perhaps the company's nod to New York City's fast-paced culture? The clockface is eight feet in diameter with marble disks beneath each of the twelve bronze Roman numerals. An elegant crown is perched above.

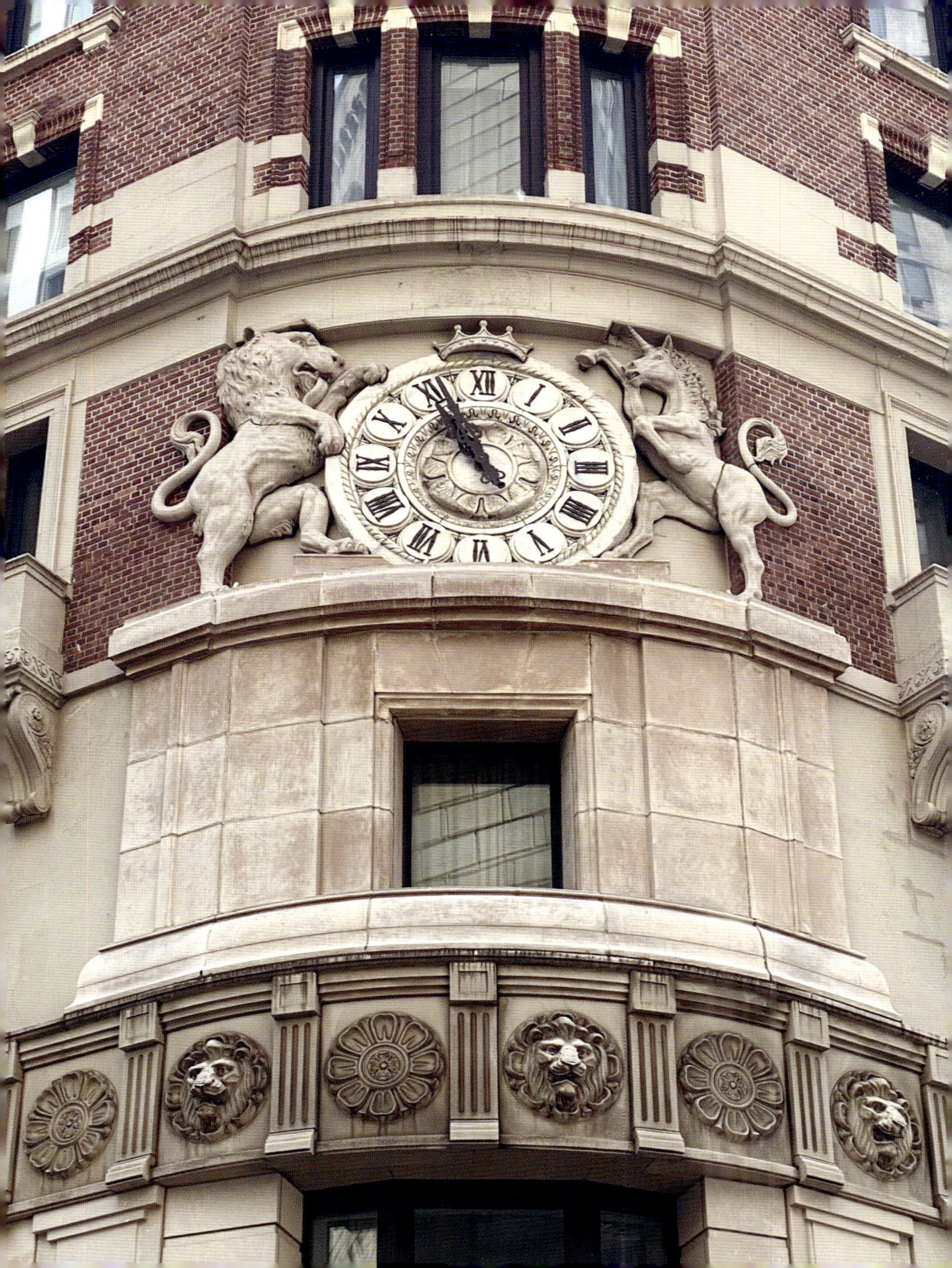

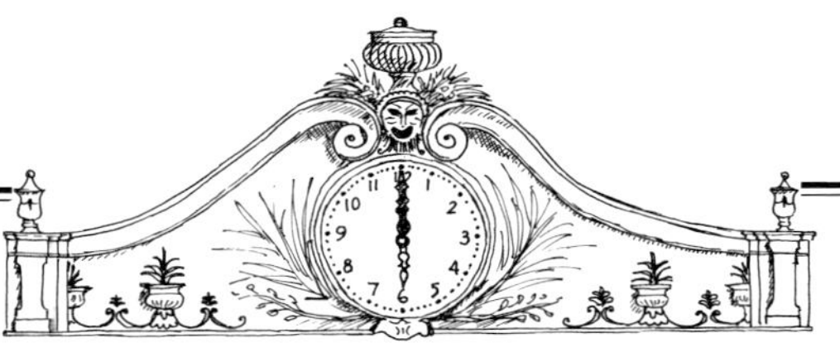

PARAMOUNT BUILDING

1501 BROADWAY
1927

With a comedy mask crowning the overdoor clock, the Broadway entrance to the Paramount Pictures headquarters makes it clear that this is a theatrical enterprise. The decorative metalwork fenestration continues to the elegant transom and doors rendered in polished brass. Built in 1927 in the heart of Times Square, this thirty-three-story skyscraper was designed by the firm Rapp & Rapp (two brothers, George Leslie Rapp and Cornelius Ward Rapp). The architectural design combines both Beaux Arts and Art Deco styles. This clock here nods toward the former, while the massive clock high above on the thirtieth floor leans into the more modern Art Deco (see p. 82).

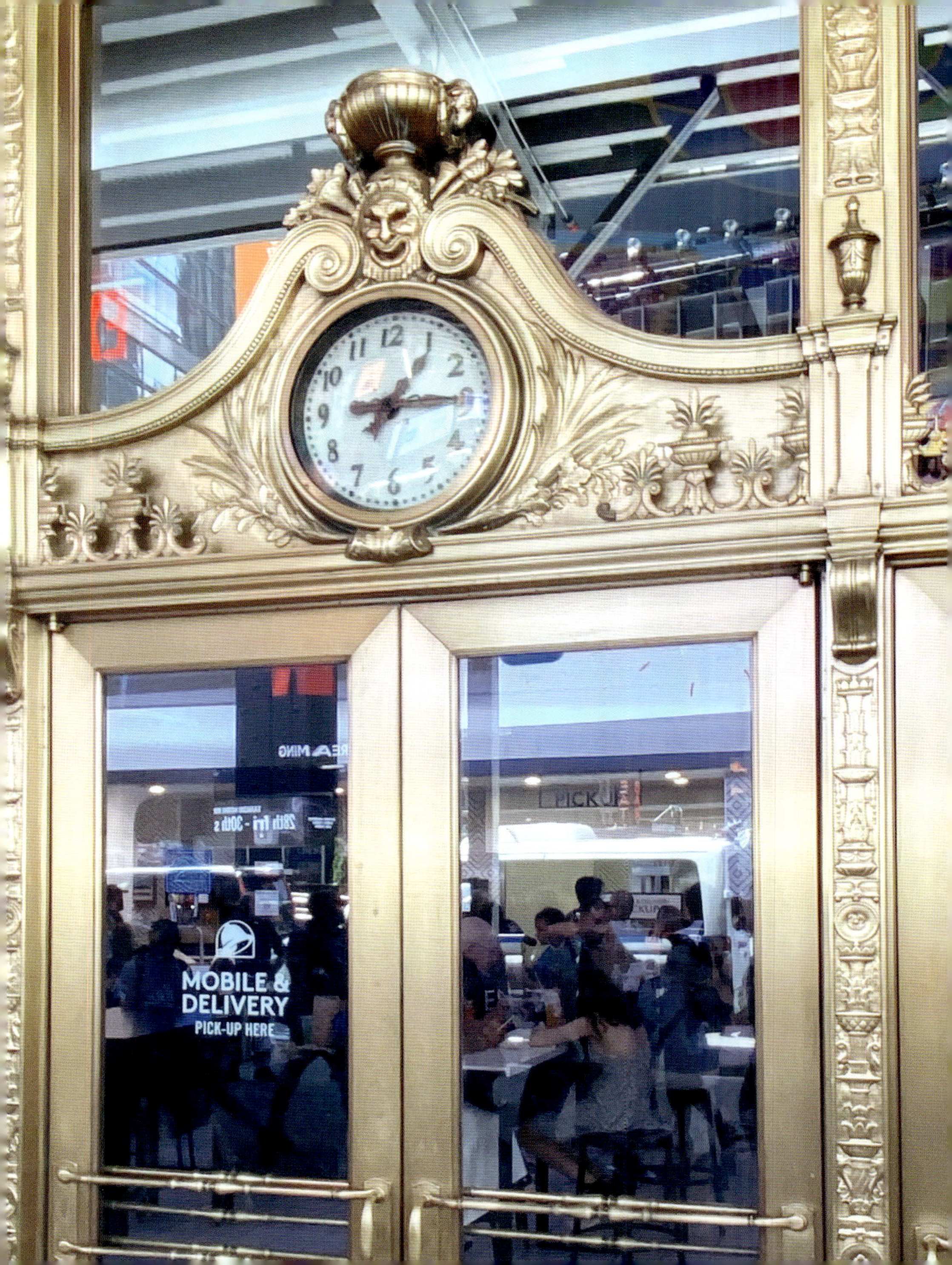
MOBILE &
DELIVERY
PICK-UP HERE
PICKUP

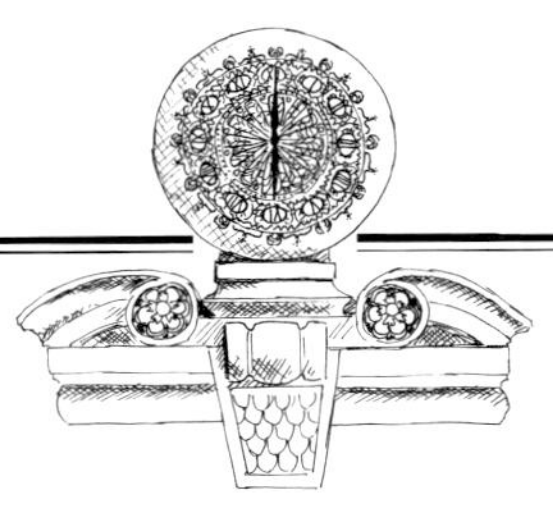

STANDARD OIL
BUILDING

28 BROADWAY
1928

The original Standard Oil Building in Manhattan's Financial District was completed in 1885, with major additions and a dramatic redesign in the 1920s by Thomas Hastings of Carrère & Hastings. This newer and very robust Renaissance Revival–style building was created to impress, even down to the overdoor clock at the 28 Broadway entrance. This timepiece imparts a visually surreal surprise by blending classical elements with an early twentieth-century flair. The limestone globe is perched above a keystone and flanked by bold scrolls. The globe is fitted with a bronze "shield" in elaborate tracery that references classical designs in a way that is both highly decorative and modern.

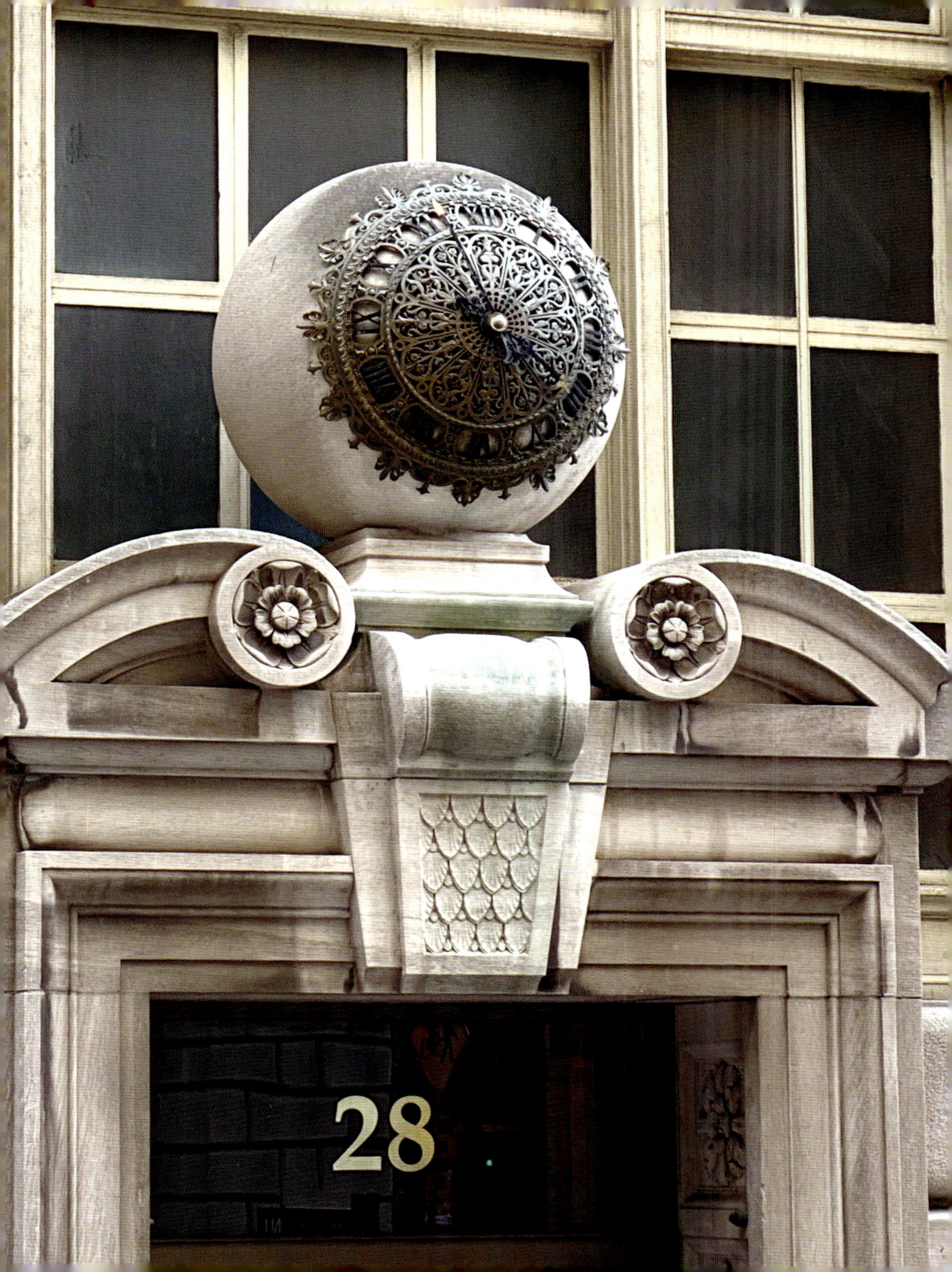

28

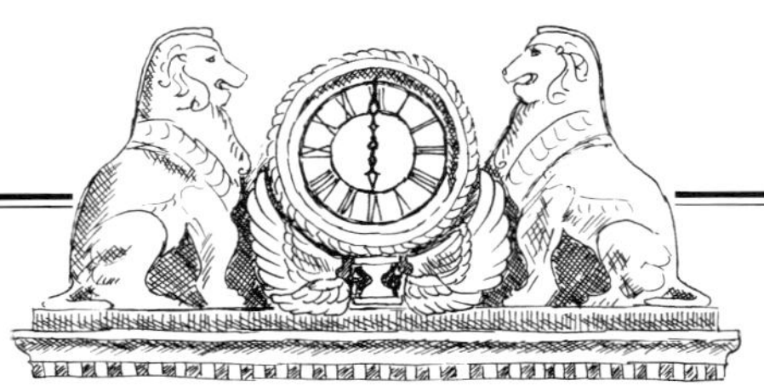

CENTRAL SAVINGS BANK

2100 BROADWAY
1928

During my days as a ballet student living close to Lincoln Center, I regularly walked past what appeared to be an Italian Renaissance palazzo. With its impressively rusticated stone and heavy wrought-iron grills protecting the doors and windows, the noble Central Savings Bank created a sedate and timeless presence in the neighborhood. Above the entrance facing Verdi Square is an overdoor clock flanked by carved stone lions. A small stone hourglass with a pair of wings supports the clockface—this was a discreet reminder to me that, like a ballet dancer's career, time flies. This dignified building, including its stupendous interior, is landmarked. It was designed by architects York & Sawyer and erected in 1928.

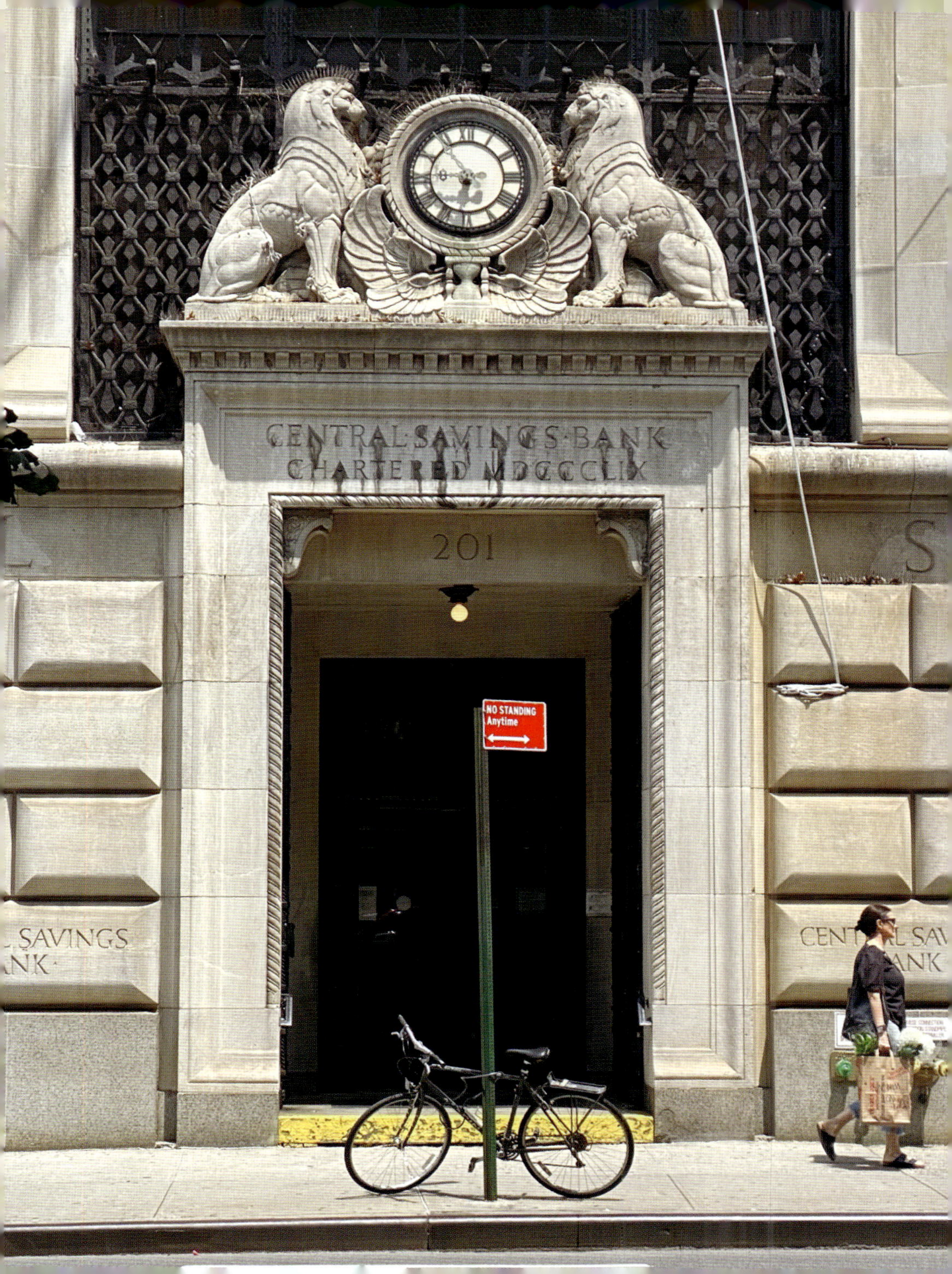

CENTRAL·SAVINGS·BANK
CHARTERED·MDCCCLIX
201
NO STANDING
Anytime
SAVINGS
ANK·
CENTRAL SAV
ANK

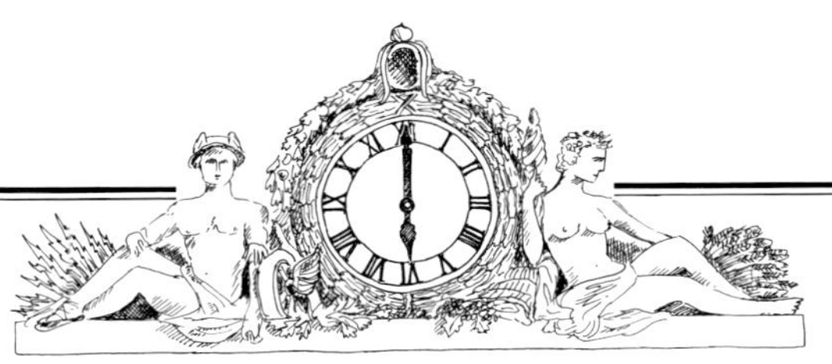

HELMSLEY BUILDING

230 PARK AVENUE
1929

The Helmsley Building clock, looking up Park Avenue from its 46th Street fourth-floor perch, is a beauty designed by sculptor Edward McCartan. The clock is flanked by the limestone semi-reclining draped figures of Mercury and Ceres, representing transportation and agriculture. With their attributes—wings for Mercury and fruits beside Ceres—this neo-classical grouping measures nineteen feet tall and an impressive forty-five feet wide, framing a nine-foot-diameter clock. Built in 1929, the Helmsley skyscraper towers thirty-five stories. Unable to leave well enough alone, developers built the MetLife Building (formerly the Pan Am Building) in the early 1960s, wedging it between Grand Central Terminal and the Helmsley and blocking the once lighter and more pleasing feel of Park Avenue.

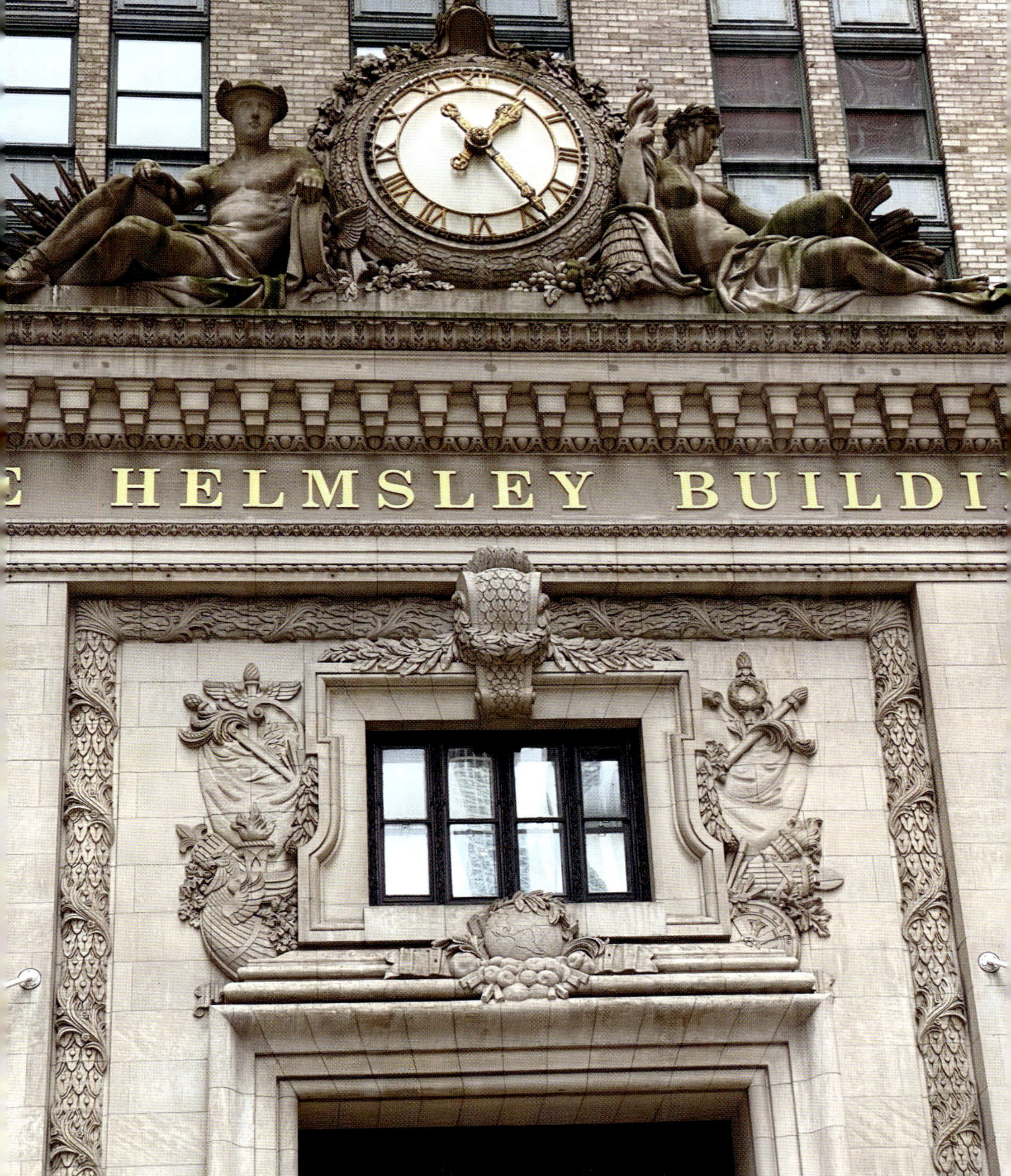
E HELMSLEY BUILDI

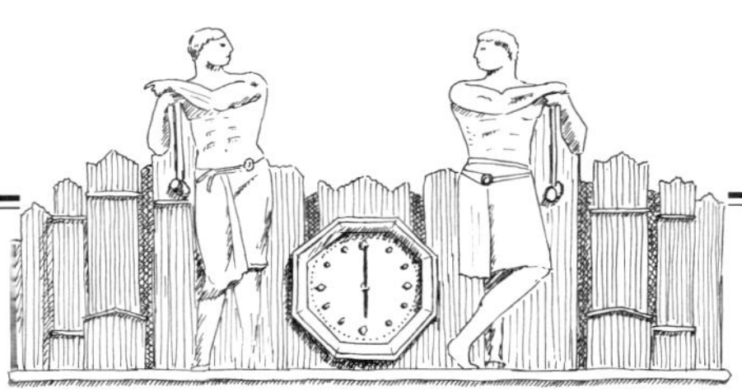

FULLER BUILDING

41 EAST 57TH STREET
1929

The Fuller Building, designed by Walker & Gillette and built between 1928 and 1929, fully embraces the spirit of the machine age. The high contrast of black granite and limestone, combined with glass, bronze, and brass, sleekly encases this stylish midtown skyscraper. The entrance on 57th Street is flanked by pilasters of contrasting stones and crowned on the fourth floor with a limestone sculptural group designed by Elie Nadelman. Here, two godlike construction workers face an octagonal clock, while a stylized city skyline in elegant relief stands behind them. Though it is impossible to check the time while you enter the doors far below, the clock becomes more useful when viewed from across the street, a vantage point to more fully admire this marvelous portal.

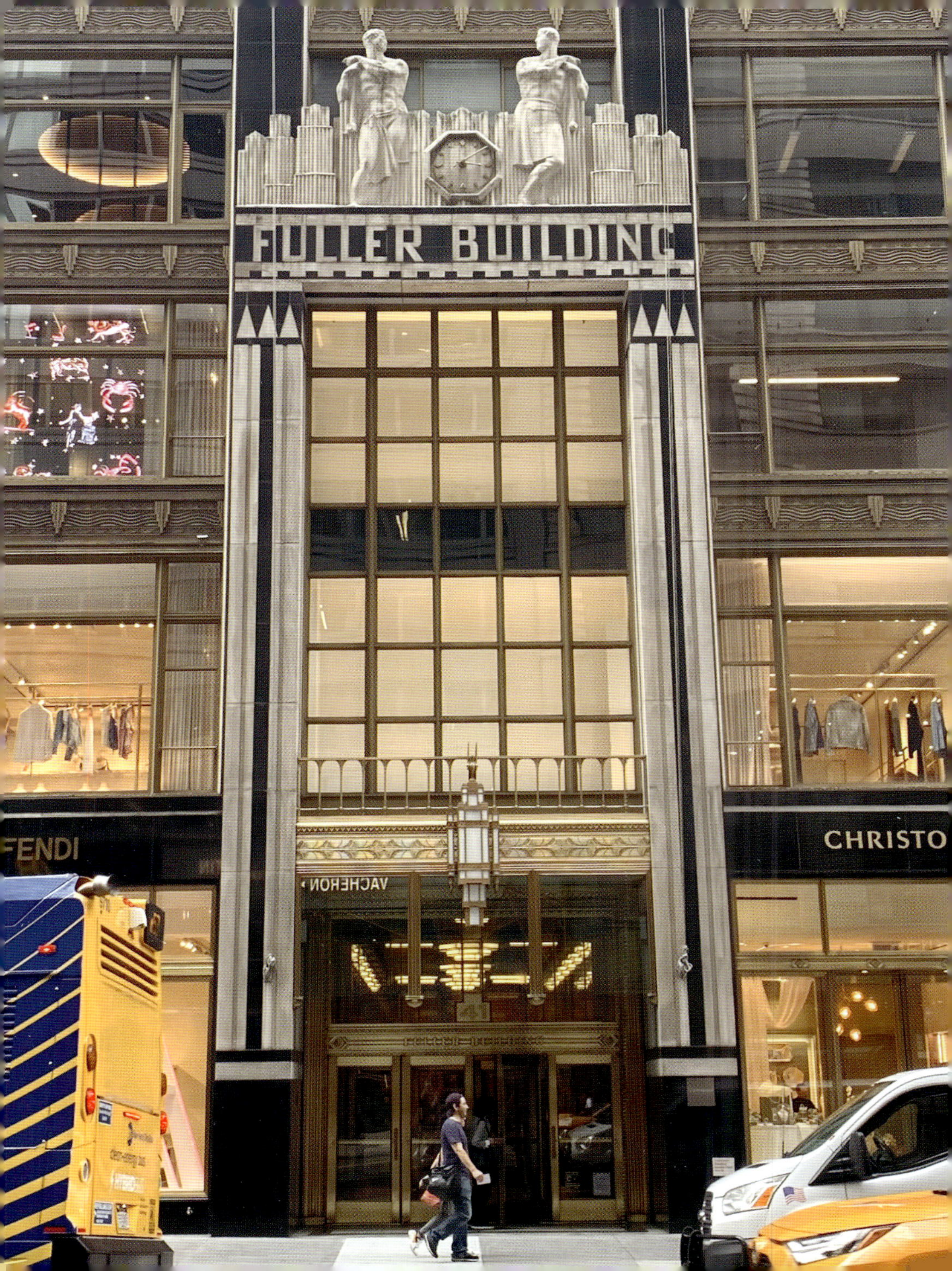

FULLER BUILDING
FENDI
CHRISTO
41

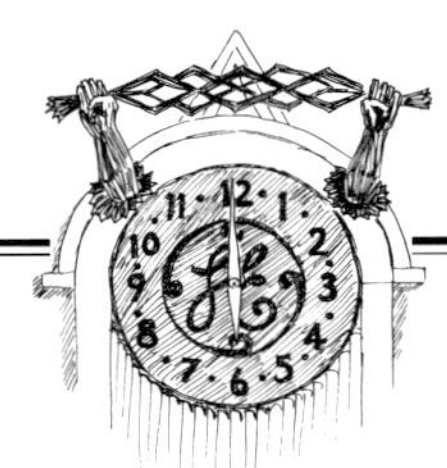

GENERAL ELECTRIC
BUILDING

570 LEXINGTON AVENUE
1931

Positioned on a canted corner flanked by two entrances on Lexington Avenue and 51st Street, an overdoor clock virtually vibrates with electricity. At the top of the clock are two projecting arms with clenched fists taming a stylized thunderbolt. The building housing this clock was designed by Cross & Cross, an architectural firm founded in 1907 by two brothers, John and Eliot, which lasted until 1942. Their diverse and stylish work spans the quickly changing eras of their company's existence, with this building being an example of their more theatrical side. Radiating arches of red marble are accented with nickel silver details, some with lightning-like elements appropriately suggesting the power of electricity.

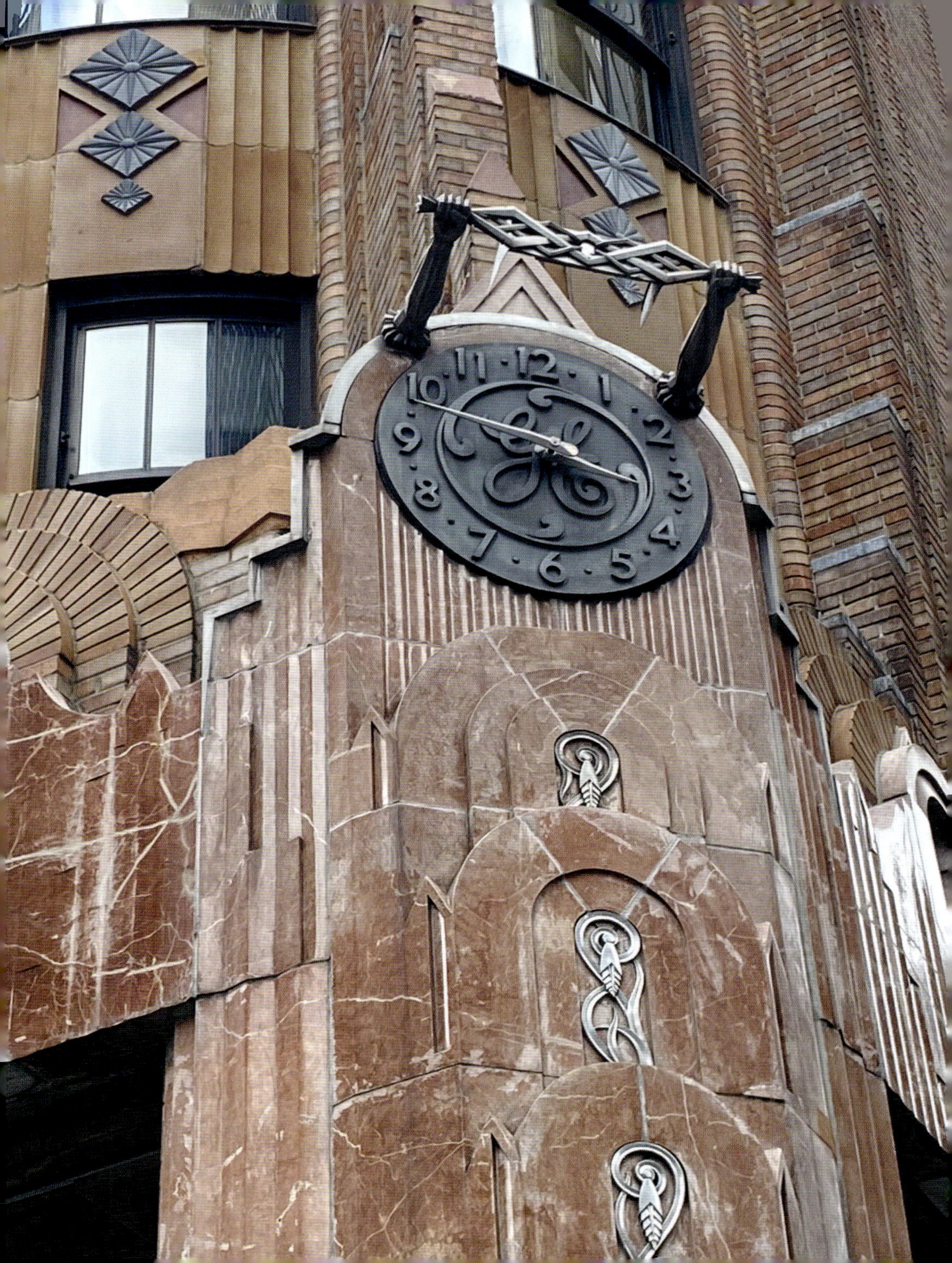

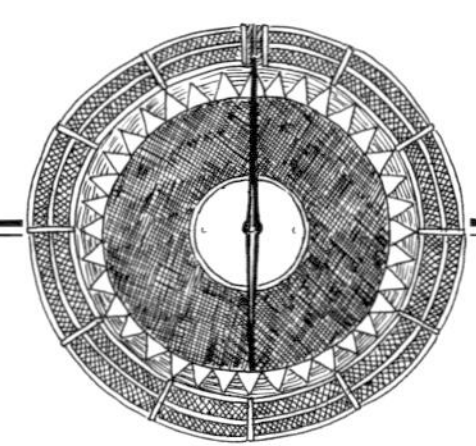

ROCKEFELLER CENTER, FIFTH AVENUE INTERNATIONAL BUILDING

630 FIFTH AVENUE
1935

Rockefeller Center, a stunning expression of American Art Deco, employed not only architects and designers, but artists to create visuals that plainly say *"this* is New York." On the side entrance of the Fifth Avenue International Building is a superb portal with a towering limestone screen incorporated into the facade. It is surmounted by a clock, six feet in diameter. Depicting the story of mankind, this installation was designed by Lee Oscar Lawrie, an American architectural sculptor working with colorist Léon-Victor Solon. The hieroglyph-like panels represent the races, cultures, and progress of man. Centered beneath the clock is the Roman god Mercury, who appears in many clocks around the city, symbolizing travel and commerce—telling all who enter that time is money, so keep moving.

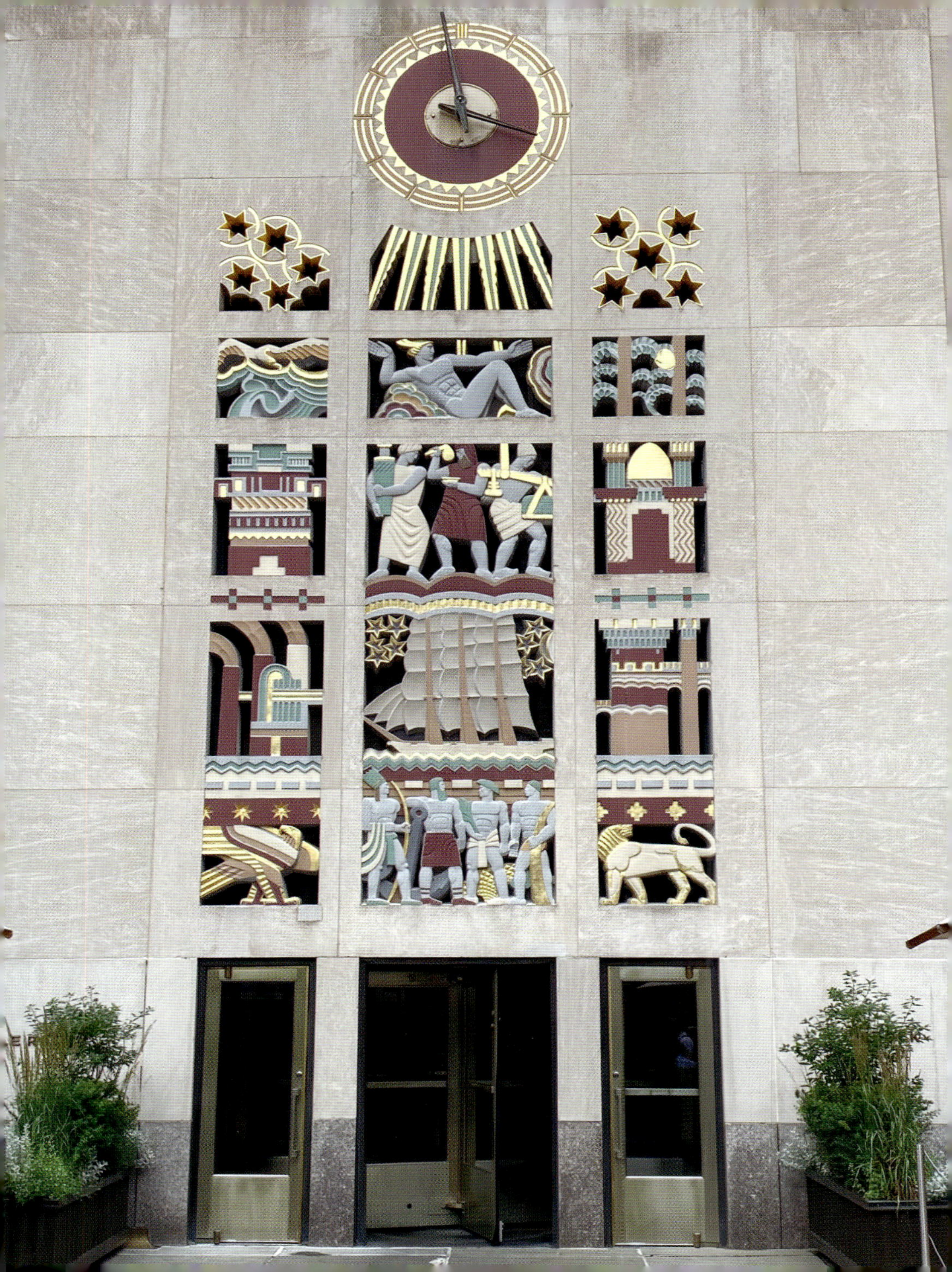

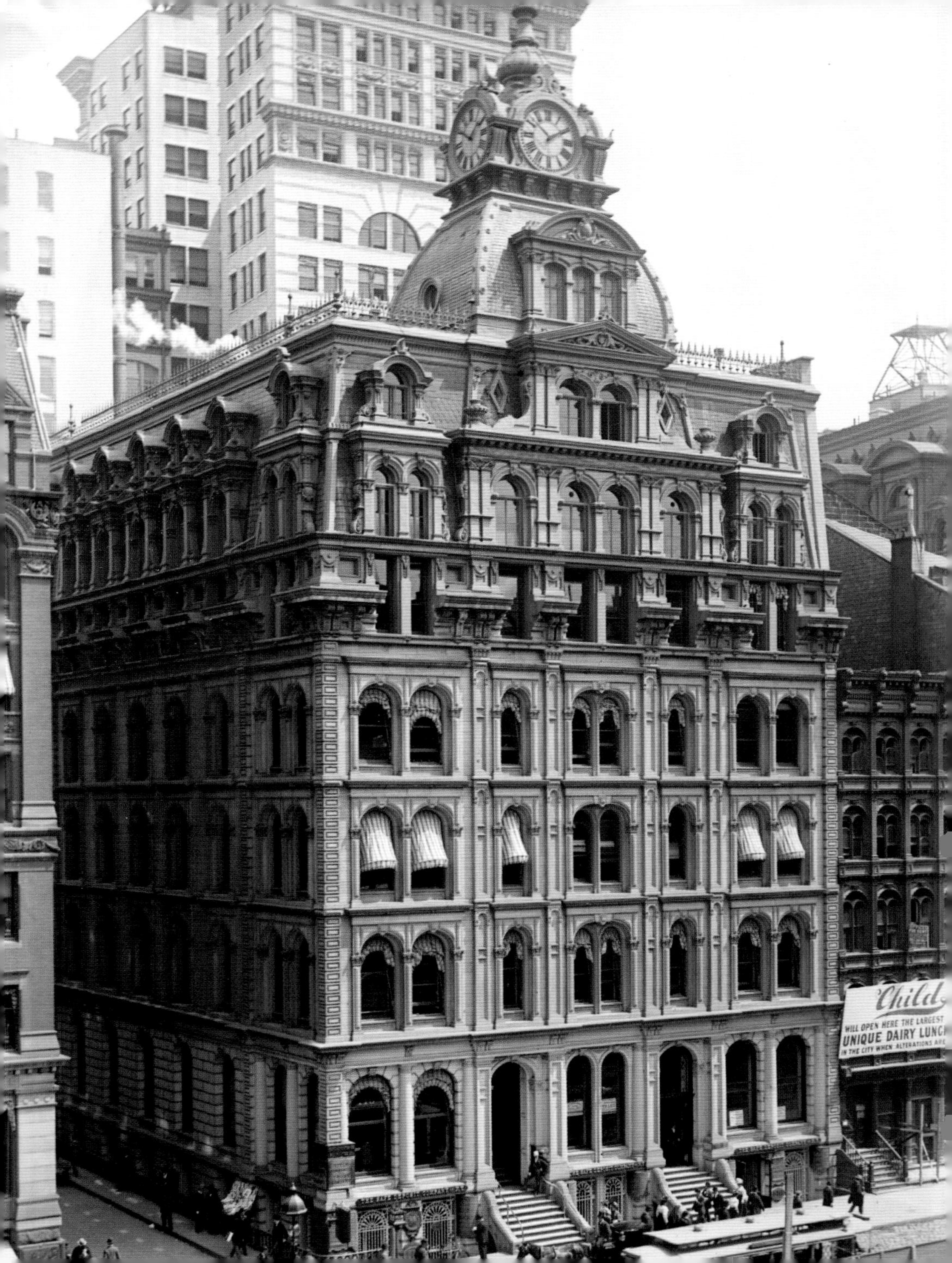
Childs
WILL OPEN HERE THE LARGEST
UNIQUE DAIRY LUNCH
IN THE CITY WHEN ALTERATIONS ARE

THE FULLNESS OF TIME
DOME CLOCKS

I love a dome. Many of my favorite buildings in the world have them, my top two being the Pantheon in Rome, designed and created by Emperor Hadrian c. AD 126, and Basilica Santa Maria della Salute in Venice, constructed between 1631 and 1687. The puffed-up fullness of domes is a delight, like a bubble or an air balloon, and while we know they are made of weighty concrete, masonry, timber, or steel, a proper dome gives the effect of optimistic weightlessness and grandeur. For thousands of years, many cultures have used domes to denote the importance of a building. Small or large, a dome elevates a structure visually and otherwise.

Like steeples, spires, turrets, and towers, domes delight the eye when viewed from a distance but can be pleasurably admired up close to absorb architectural or ornamental details: cornices, columns, finials, sculptures . . . *clocks*. When a dome is embellished with a clock, it gives the pedestrian one more reason to cast their gaze upward. Though domes resemble a bubble just before it pops, they also feel oddly grounded, dependable. Perhaps this is because they've been around for millennia, allowing us to connect with them on an ancestral level.

We already saw the impressive domes of the stations preced-

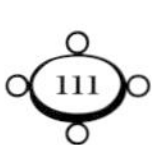

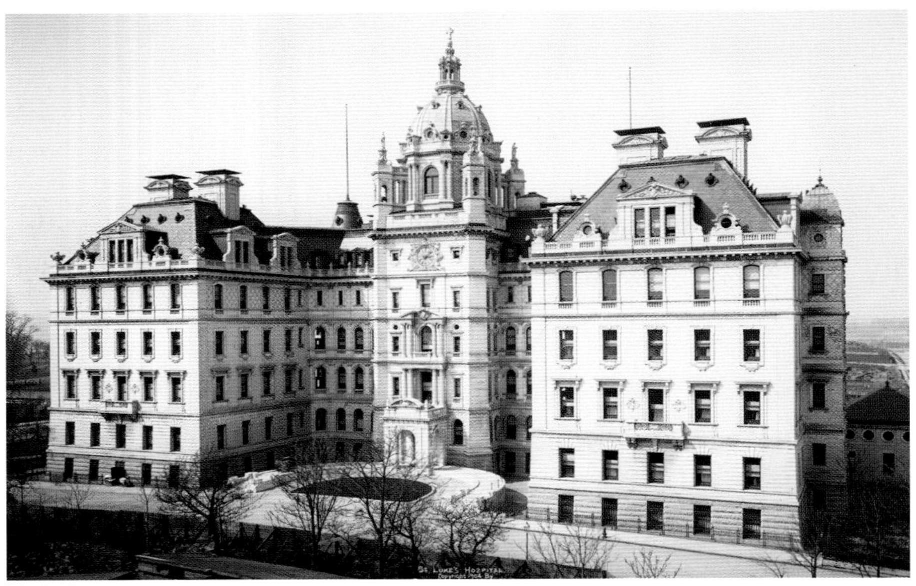

St. Luke's Hospital, built 1896,
1111 Amsterdam Avenue, 1904

This hospital in Harlem shows its beautiful clock beneath one of the city's loveliest
domes (seen at the center of the building).
The building up to the clock surround
survived, but the dome did not.

ing Grand Central Terminal in chapter 1, but the city boasts even
more notable examples. When researching historical images of
clocks, I was pleased to discover an eye-catching dome clock
from the Old Mutual Life Insurance Building at Broadway and
Liberty Street. It was considered an early skyscraper and completed around 1872, only to be demolished less than forty years
later. I call this one "two scoops." I mean, why have one dome

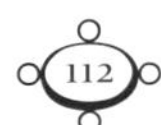

when you can have two, plus a cherry on top? That said, it is quite handsome in that robust Second Empire way of the 1870s.

St. Luke's Hospital, a glorious example of a domed, clock-bedecked building in Harlem, had a long and complicated history. The building shown opposite was designed by Ernest Flagg, a young, relatively unknown architect who some felt received the commission because of his close relationship to Cornelius Vanderbilt II, who was on both the executive and building committees for the hospital. Apparently, some committee members had reservations about the choice and added the established architect Charles W. Clinton to the team. The project began in May 1893 and was not completed until late 1896. Other hospital "pavilions" were added to those shown in the photo, some built well into the 1920s. In 1893, *Harper's Weekly* said that Flagg's design possessed the "appearance of symmetrical perfectness so royal to the French Renaissance, and a harmonious beauty in the rendering of detail." While the clock (seen beneath the dome) and facade remain mostly intact, the crowning dome in all its splendor was demolished in 1966. Even with the beheading of the dome, I've included it in this chapter along with four other buildings that still possess their domes and clocks.

The following buildings are New York landmarks, each one designed to express the structure's status, or at the very least to show they were built to get noticed. I am grateful to the architects, clock makers, stone carvers, and other craftspeople who collaborated in creating these clocks and their crowning domes, and I am equally happy they have survived to give us pleasure today.

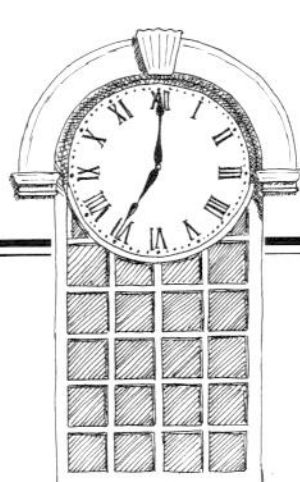

NEW YORK CITY HALL

CITY HALL PARK
1812

New York City Hall is the oldest city hall in the United States to have continuously held the municipal functions for which it was built, and it's considered one of the most beautiful. Originally designed by Mangin & McComb and built from 1803 to 1812, the building has survived two fires and many revisions, restorations, and additions by several architects between 1860 and 1998. The clockworks were replaced multiple times over the years, with the current version made by the E. Howard Clock Company and installed in the early twentieth century, about a century after the original building was constructed. Even with its revisions over the centuries, this important New York City landmark maintains its French-influenced but very American neoclassical aura of restrained elegance.

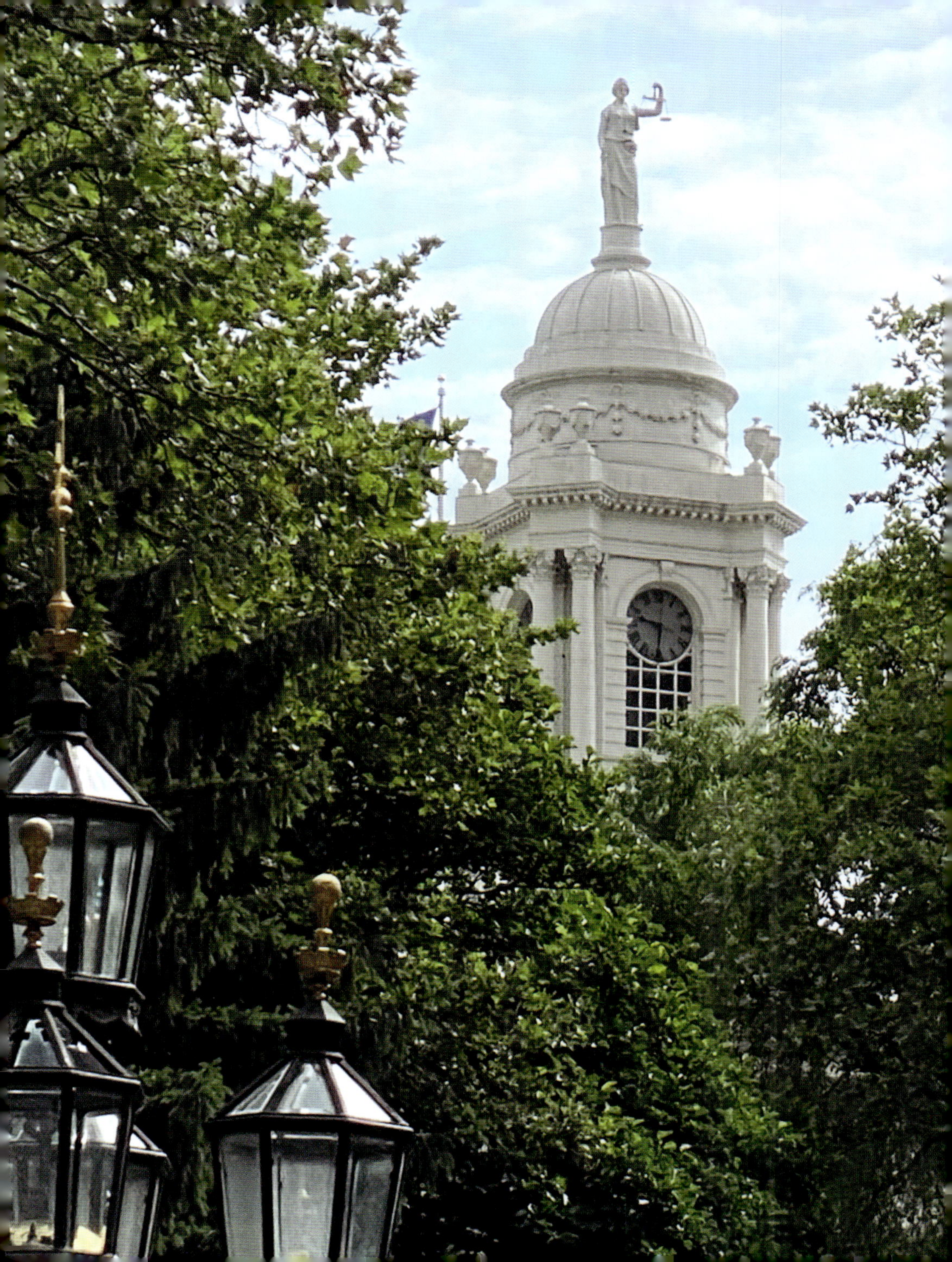

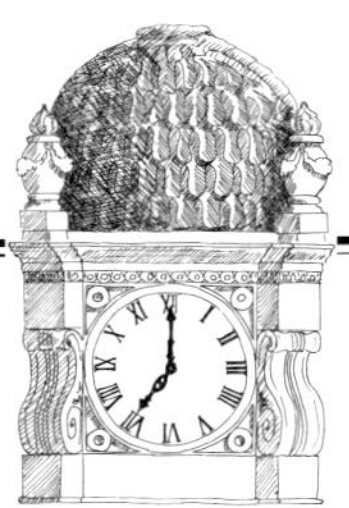

BROOKLYN
BOROUGH HALL

209 JORALEMON STREET
1848

Brooklyn Borough Hall (once called Brooklyn City Hall) was completed in 1848, making it the oldest public building in Brooklyn. Designed in the Greek Revival style by architect Gamaliel King, its Tuckahoe marble temple front sits below an elaborate cast-iron (originally wood) cupola showcasing a clock beneath the patinated copper dome. The original four-sided clock was lost in a fire in 1895 and replaced with a clock by the Self Winding Clock Company in 1898. In the mid-twentieth century, after decades of mechanical problems, the works were replaced by the Verdin Company. The long-awaited gilded sculpture of Lady Justice was planned in 1898, but was installed during a 1989 restoration of the building.

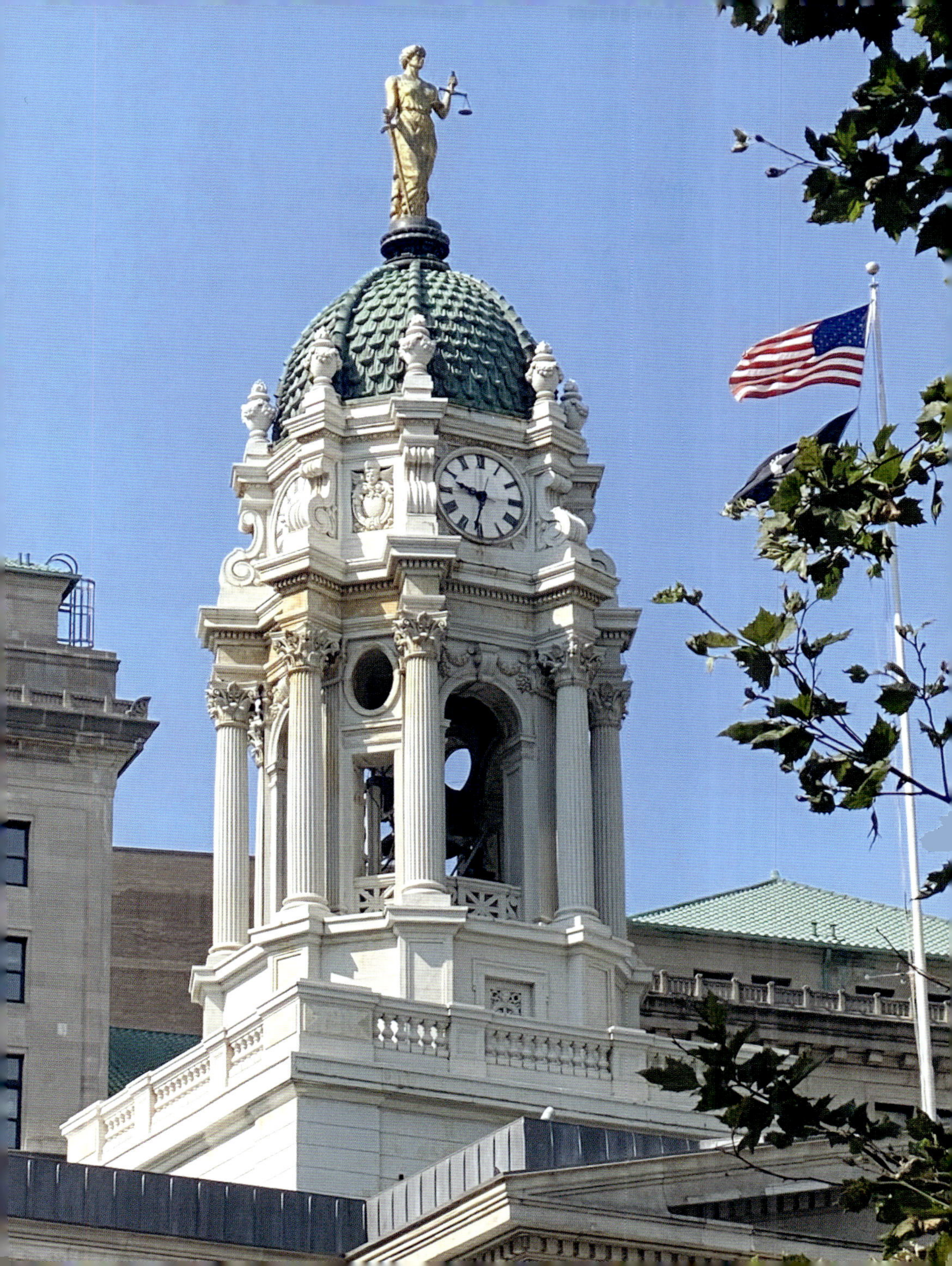

GILSEY HOUSE

1200 BROADWAY
1871

When the Gilsey House opened in 1871 at the corner of Broadway and 29th Street, the hotel cemented its neighborhood as the glittering entertainment district of New York. Architect Stephen Decatur Hatch (of the New York Life Insurance Company building from chapter 5) designed the cast-iron building to be luxurious and cutting edge. It attracted Oscar Wilde and other theatrical luminaries to its well-appointed rooms, elegantly furnished with marble fireplaces, rare woods, tapestries, and bronze chandeliers—and it was the first hotel in New York to offer telephone service to its guests. The highly articulated facade rises to its ultimate embellishment: a fantastic clock with figural ornamentation incorporated onto the three story, dome-like mansard roof. It is this exuberant style that makes Gilsey House among the most elegant cast-iron buildings in the city.

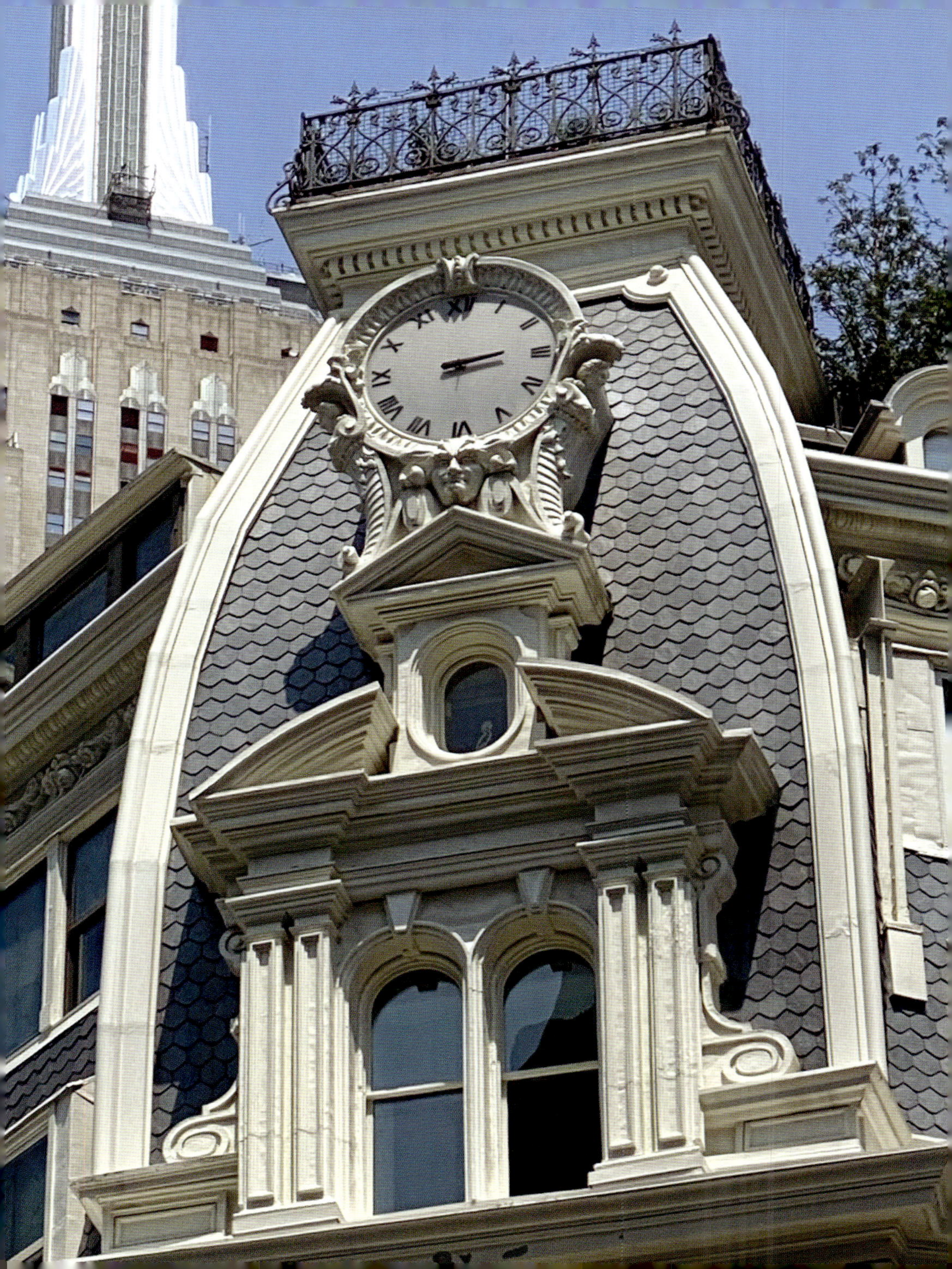

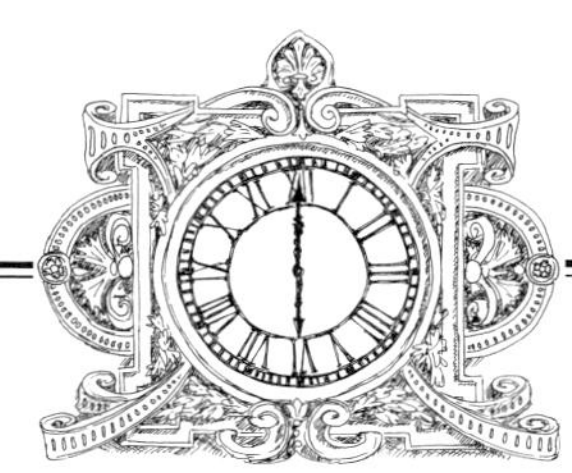

ST. LUKE'S HOSPITAL

421 WEST 113TH STREET
1896

In this West Harlem building, architect Ernest Flagg devised an octagonal dome, shown in its original form on p. 112. Brunelleschi's Florentine Duomo clearly informed the dome shape, and yet Flagg masterfully Frenchified it to create a nearly royal effect, as pleasing as it was grand. Regretfully the dome is no more, but on the fifth floor below where the dome once stood is this sensational clock. Its elaborate Renaissance-style frame, incorporating scrolls, fluted strapwork, and foliate designs all deeply carved in limestone, creates a heraldic architectural moment. While it's lovely to see that the clock housing survives, we are left with a dome-less building and a handless clock. One can only hope a proper restoration of the clock will bring this building's beating heart back to life.

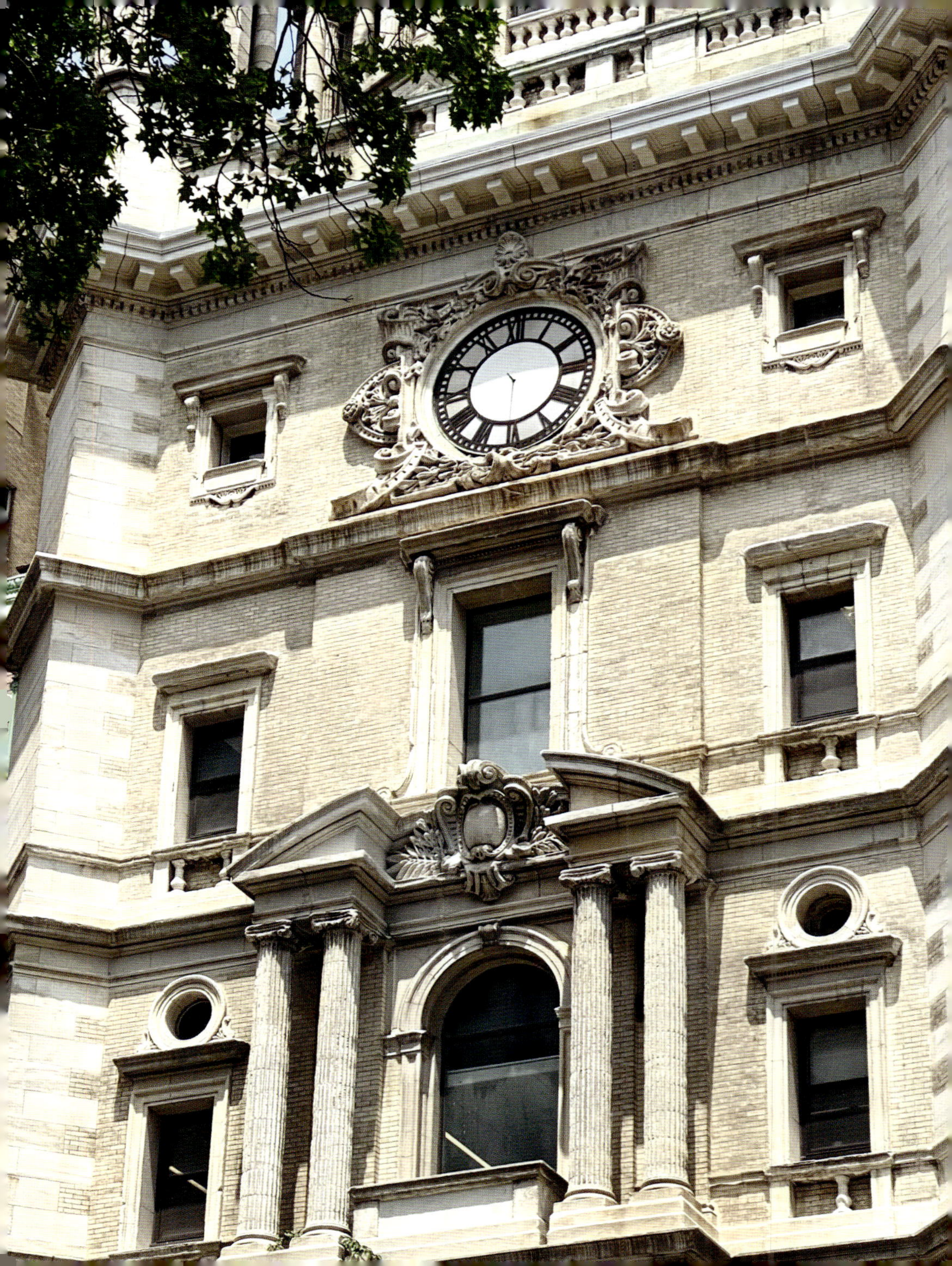

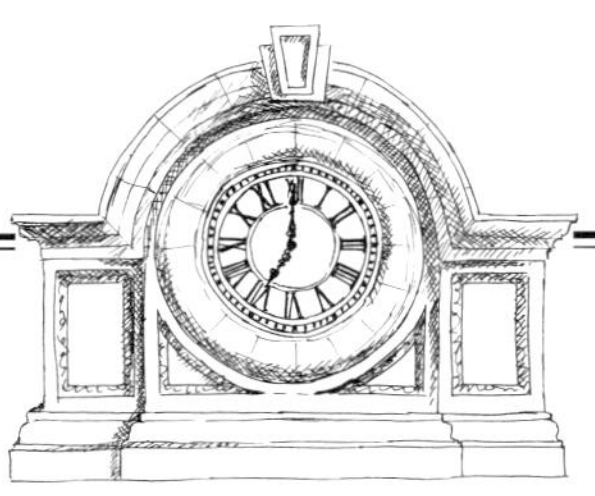

NEW YORK CITY POLICE
HEADQUARTERS

240 CENTRE STREET
1909

Built between 1905 and 1909, the New York City Police Headquarters was designed by Hoppin & Koen and was used by the police force until the 1970s. It remains an extravagant interpretation of Baroque style and a perfect expression of the City Beautiful movement of the late nineteenth and early twentieth centuries, when municipalities, developers, and businesses all shared a sense of civic pride by striving to create edifices that enhanced the experience of being a city dweller. The dome is supported by Corinthian columns and surrounded by four clocks installed by the Seth Thomas Clock Company.

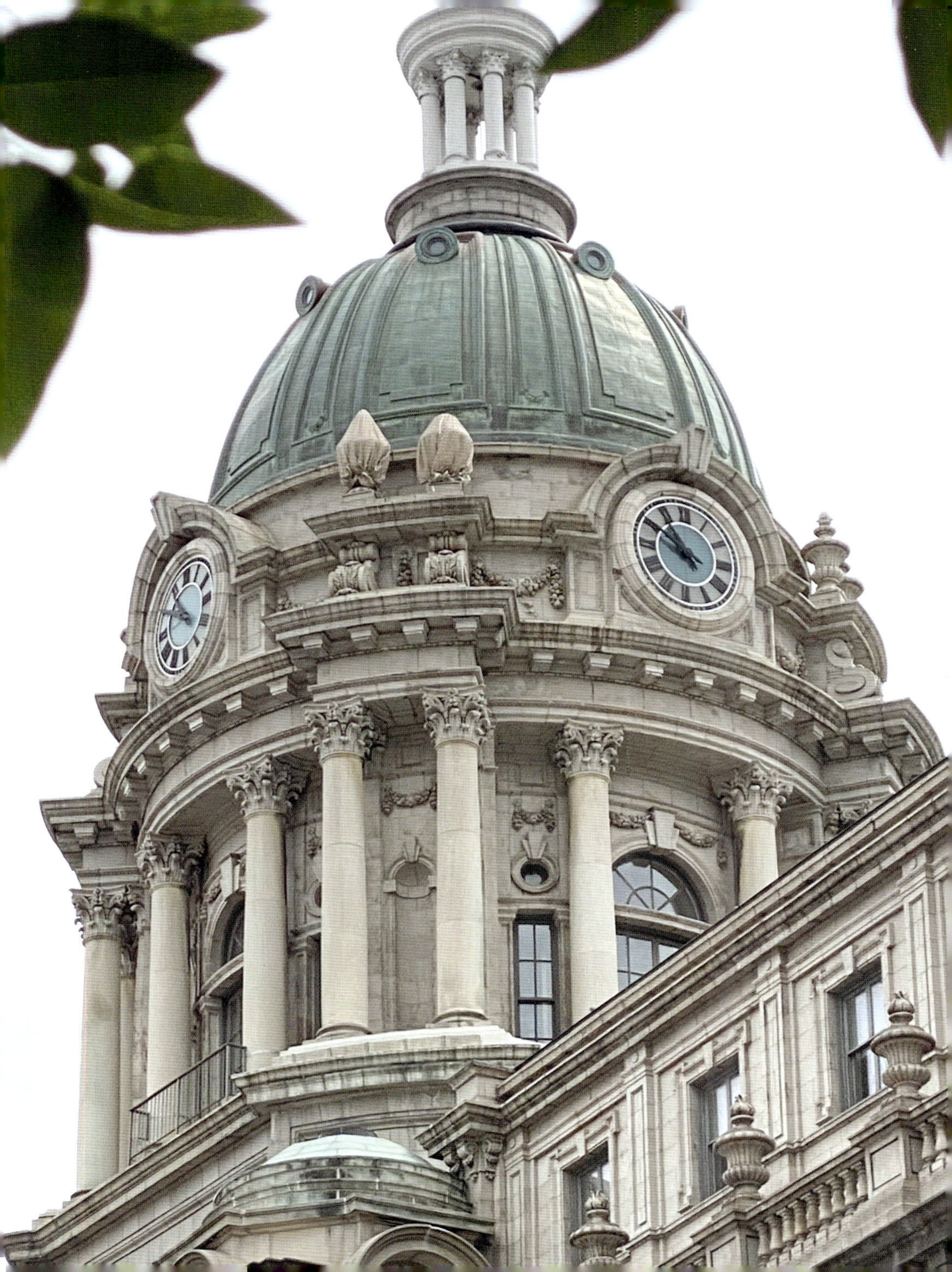

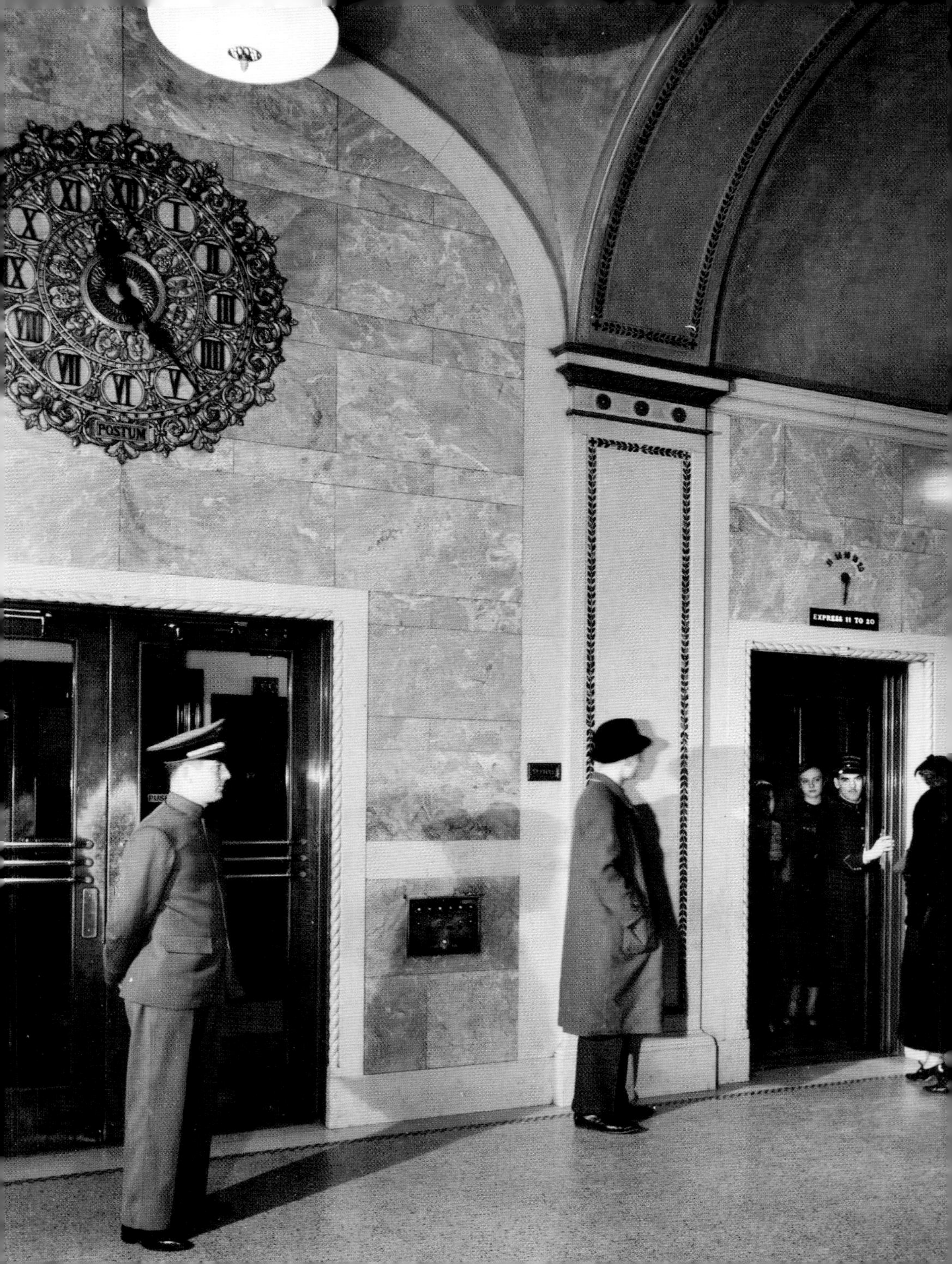

POSTUM
EXPRESS 11 TO 20

RIGHT PLACE— RIGHT TIME

LOBBY AND INTERIOR CLOCKS

After you negotiate trains, cabs, and crowded sidewalks to reach your destination in New York City, it's reassuring to confirm the time by glancing at a lobby clock before boarding the elevator to begin the workday upstairs. Perhaps your inner clock remains fully engaged while immersed in work, but as the day flies by, time may slow down a tad. Let's say a shared drink has been scheduled with a new romance at a hotel bar. The after-work hotel lobby clock provides a pleasing buffer between the urban energy of city sidewalks and that quiet corner table waiting for you. This transition between exterior to interior, rushed to hushed worlds can be enhanced by the solacing presence of a well-placed lobby clock. It is in that moment, when you take a deep breath, that city life slows down and transitions to something wonderfully civilized.

At 250 Park Avenue stands the beautiful old Postum Building, one of only two pre-war office buildings remaining on that avenue. Designed by Cross & Cross and Phelps Barnum, the building was completed in 1924. Like most old New York offices, the original lobby was stripped out and redesigned with the goal of seeming "current" to attract new tenants. The image opposite shows the original lobby with its spectacular tracery clock

Postum Building, built 1924, 250 Park Avenue, 1936

This lobby shows off its huge, lacy bronze clock.

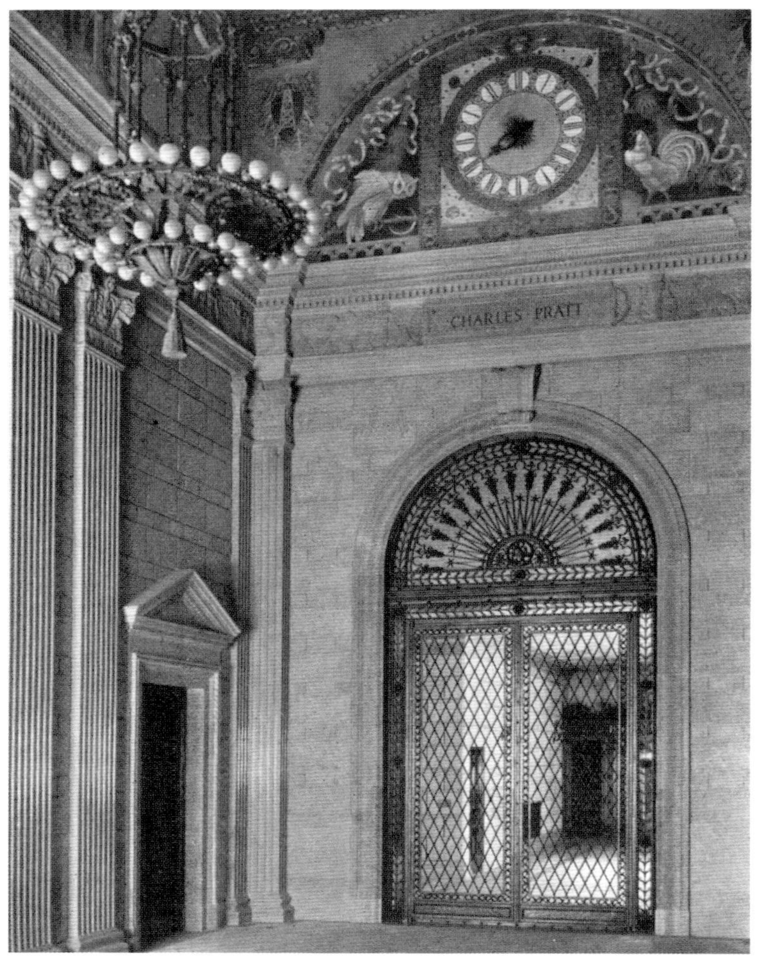

Standard Oil Building, built 1885, 26 Broadway, 1923

Few building lobbies survive the heavy hand of progress, but this one downtown did, mostly. The Roman numerals on the clock are set within medallion-like roundels, and the clock is framed with painted and partially gilded figures of the zodiac. The delightful ceiling and wall painting surrounding the clock, however, was painted over, including the owl and rooster symbolizing night and day.

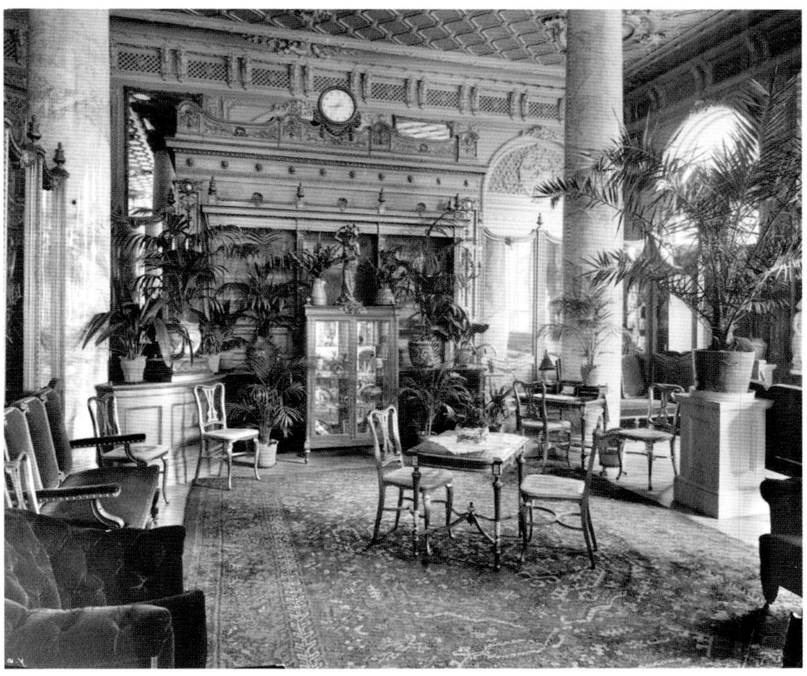

Even the more intimate public
rooms at the old Hotel Astor had
well-placed timepieces, such as this
elegant example crowning a tall
cabinet (center background).

rendered in bronze; a uniformed lobby attendant looks on as office workers board an elevator.

The Standard Oil Company building (whose overdoor clock we encountered on p. 98) also has a lobby clock of note. This barrel-vaulted lobby still exists, as does its beautiful painted and

gilded clock. Sadly, the delightful painting of an owl and crowing rooster flanking the clock, and the decorative ceiling above, appears to have been removed or painted over. The historic photograph on p. 126 shows the original design with the birds representing night and day and the passing of time. Would it not be lovely to see these artful designs restored, completing the intention of the designers of this beautiful space while bringing joy to those who pass beneath it?

Contrast the two images on pp. 124 and 126 with the elegant public room of the old Hotel Astor, pictured on p. 127, which was built in 1905 on Long Acre Square. The massive hotel had one thousand rooms, banquet halls, multiple ballrooms, and an enormous roof garden. This modestly sized room feels like a place for an intimate lady's tea, with a discreetly situated clock reminding the elegant guests when it was time to head home to change for the opera followed by supper. New York City has always made time for serious work and serious leisure.

The contrast between the exterior cacophony and interior spaces of New York is perhaps more extreme than in most American cities, where public transportation is less frequently used. Here one can go from a sprint to something approaching calm in a very short time, like changing gears from a speeding highway to a stroll, without the stress of driving one's own car. A New Yorker can also find solitude, even with people around, on public transportation and busy sidewalks. There are places where the tick of a clock is a given, but it can feel suddenly changed, even contemplative.

One of my favorite spaces in New York City for removing the high-octane aspect of urban life is the Rose Main Reading Room at the New York Public Library. Before ascending the grand staircases inside, you might see the inscription that reads "The City of New York has erected this Building to be maintained forever as a

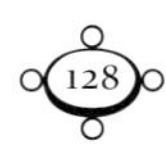

free Library for the use of the People." Every corner of this building is a gift, but upon entering the reading room, one finds sweet solitude even when every desk in this massive space is occupied. It's the people that bring down the pressure here, at least for me. The room is hushed, as most libraries are, but the humans representing every walk of New York life create a sort of camaraderie, a coming together of quietude. That feeling, thanks to the free entrance to all who enter, is a beautiful and uniquely New York experience. Faces of endless variety, eyes reading, hands writing, minds thinking. Everyone feels somehow in sync. And because this is New York, there is, of course, a clock. In the pages that follow you'll see the Rose Main Reading Room clock, among others. Some are meant for time-telling while facing high-pressure pursuits; others hover above more relaxed urban activities. All tell an interior story of one of the world's great cities.

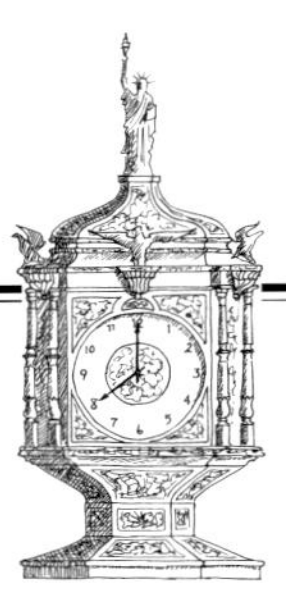

WALDORF ASTORIA
FOYER CLOCK
301 PARK AVENUE
1893

One of New York's most storied timepieces is the Waldorf Astoria foyer clock. Weighing in at four thousand pounds, this free-standing, four-faced gilded bronze confection was created for the Chicago World's Fair of 1893 by the Goldsmiths' Company of London. The clock is topped with a small model of the Statue of Liberty, a gift to Mrs. Astor from the French government. This figural finial was not part of the original design but was added in 1902. The Waldorf-Astoria, two hotel buildings joined together, was razed in 1929 to make way for the Empire State Building. The clock was the only fixture moved to the newly built Art Deco Waldorf Astoria that still stands on Park Avenue. The new hotel was completed in 1931, and the famous clock was given a central location in the lobby. At the writing of this book, the clock has been magnificently restored and is on display at the New York Historical. It awaits reinstallation once the work to refurbish the iconic hotel is complete.

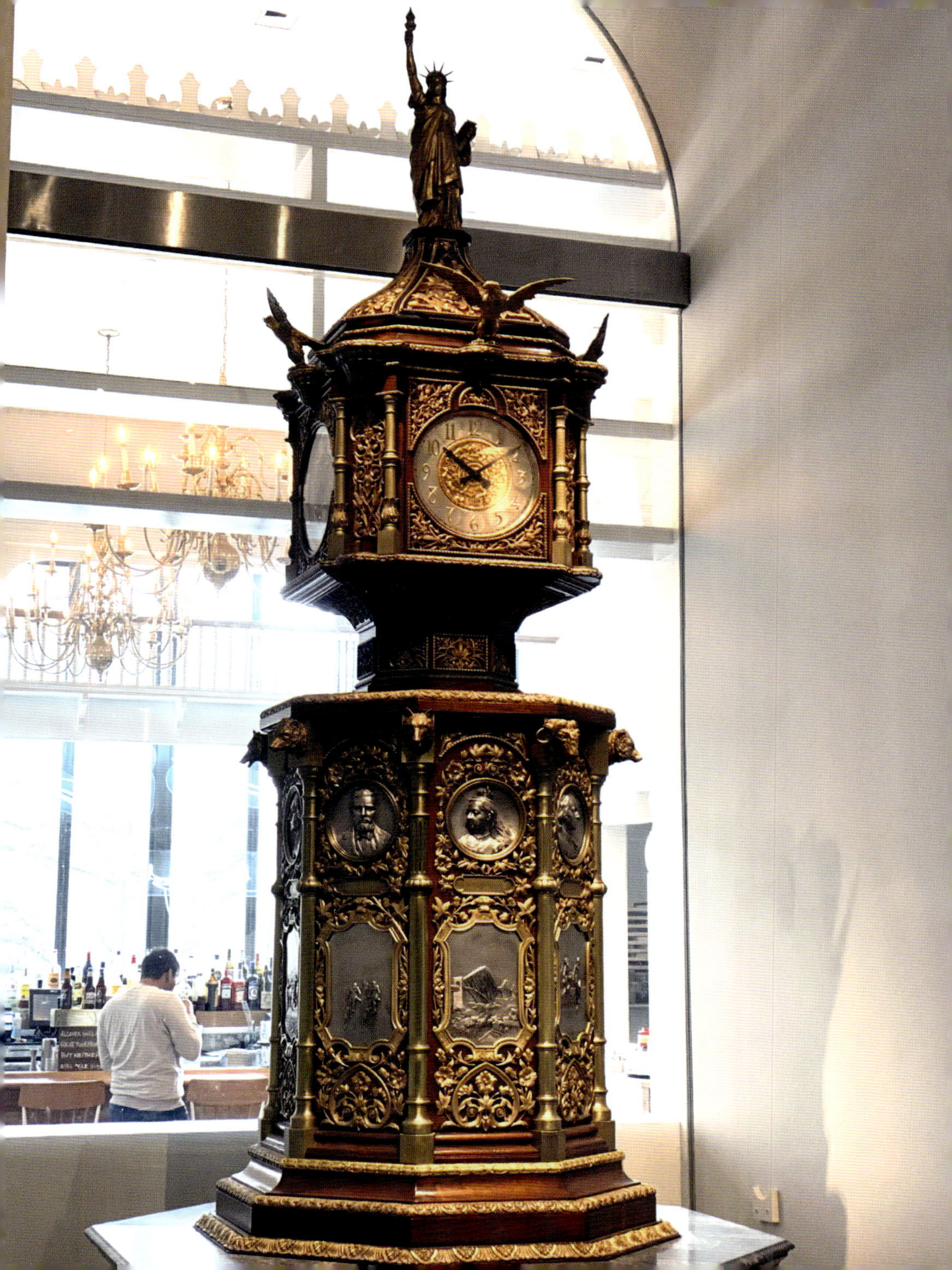

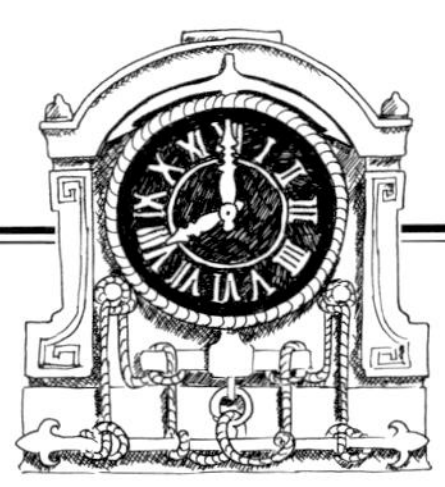

ALEXANDER HAMILTON
U.S. CUSTOM HOUSE
1 BOWLING GREEN
1907

At Manhattan's southern tip stands an impos-ing Beaux Arts government building known as the Alexander Hamilton U.S. Custom House, built be-tween 1900 and 1907 to a design by architect Cass Gil-bert, who was also responsible for the United States Supreme Court Building and several American capitol buildings. The City Beautiful principals suggested that great public buildings also have an interior program suited for site-specific art. As such, in 1900, Gilbert wrote about his plan to create a seamless marriage of engineering, architecture, and fine arts. The oval ro-tunda, an excellent example of this, creates a sort of interior courtyard that rises three full stories. Within the arches above column-flanked portals at each end of the rotunda stands a pair of double-faced clocks with nautical decorative motifs, allowing anyone to see the time upon entering or exiting this magnificent room. Today the building holds government offices and a branch of the National Museum of the Ameri-can Indian.

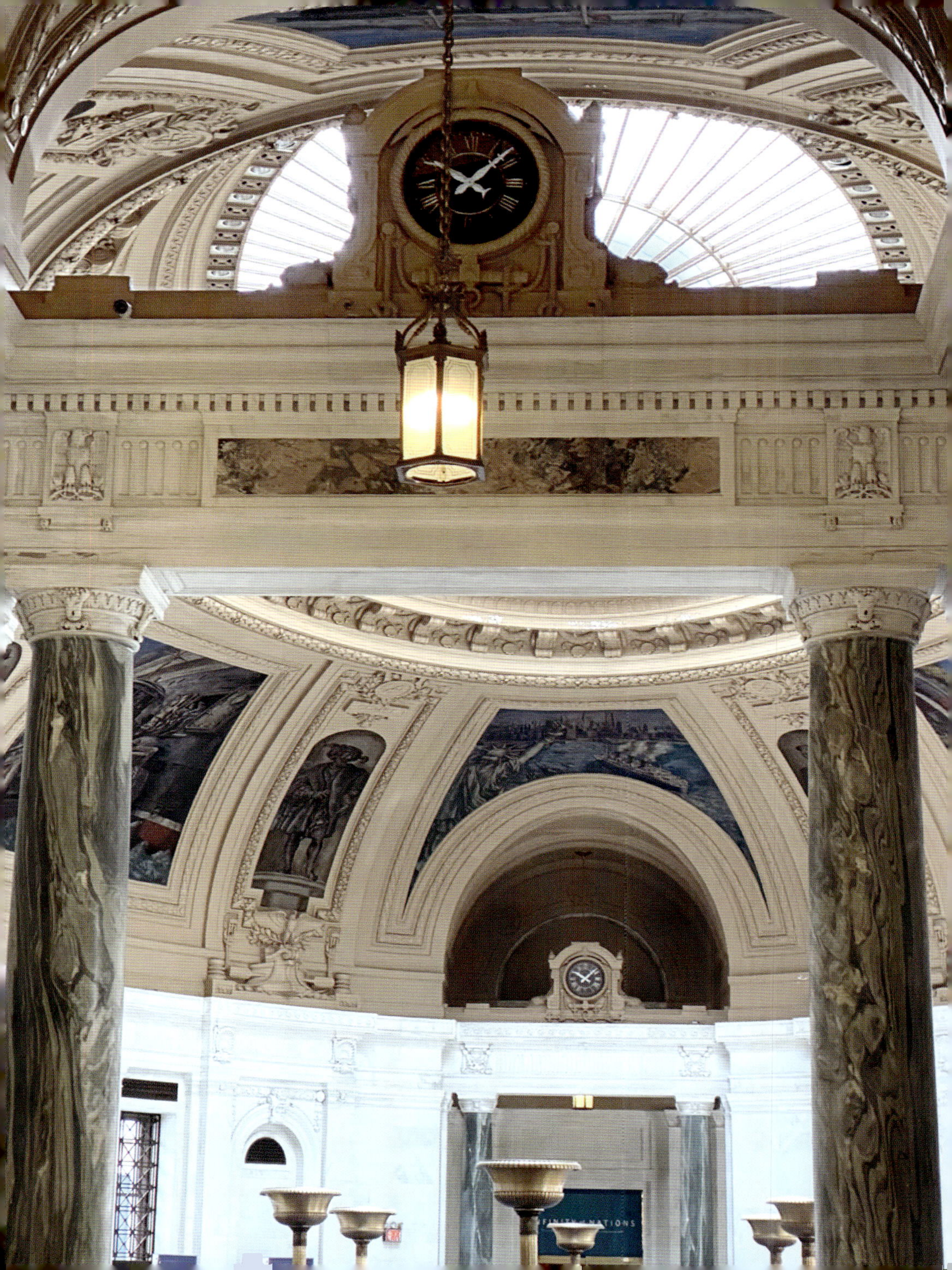

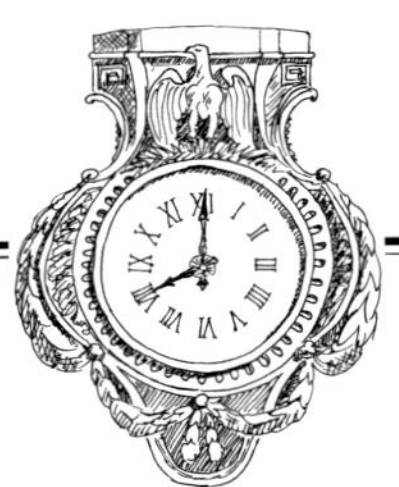

SURROGATE'S COURTHOUSE

31 CHAMBERS STREET
1907

Designed by John Rochester Thomas and completed in 1907, this Beaux Arts structure has gone through very few alterations over the past hundred-plus years. The lobby is largely lined in yellow Siena marble with double staircases inspired by Palais Garnier, the splendid opera house in Paris; the golden tones of this impressive three-story space complement the dark bronze of the lighting and barrel-arched armature of the skylight overhead. In the lobby, a beautiful cast-iron double-faced clock suspends from a rusticated stone arch. At the top is an eagle perched in handsome relief as classical garlands drape the clock's serpentine form.

Originally called the Hall of Records, the building was renamed Surrogate's Courthouse in 1962 when most of the space was used for the court and court-related offices. There were plans to demolish this building along with others nearby to create larger government buildings, but the project was fortunately scrapped with the financial downturn of 1975 and ensuing fiscal crises of New York.

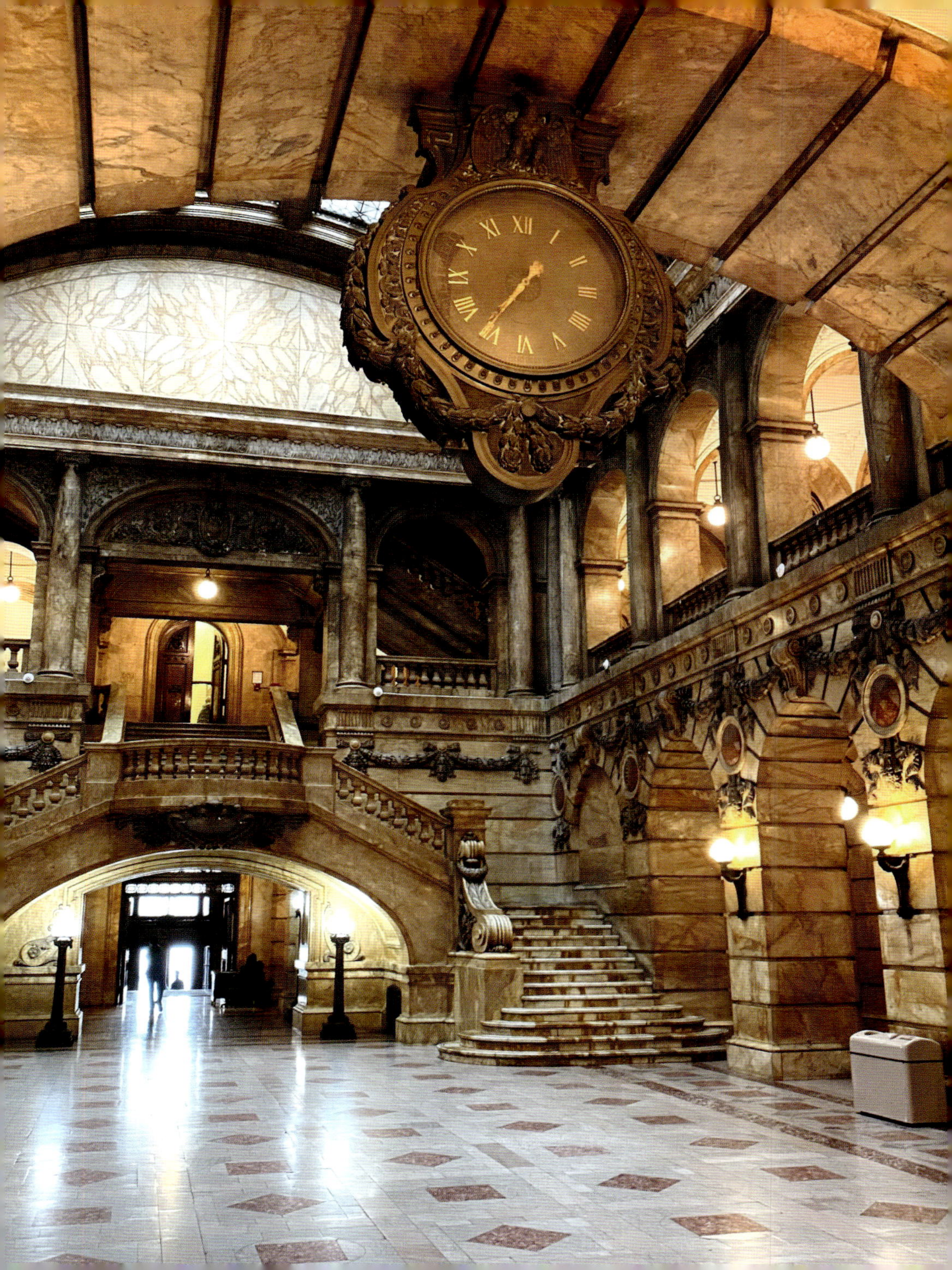

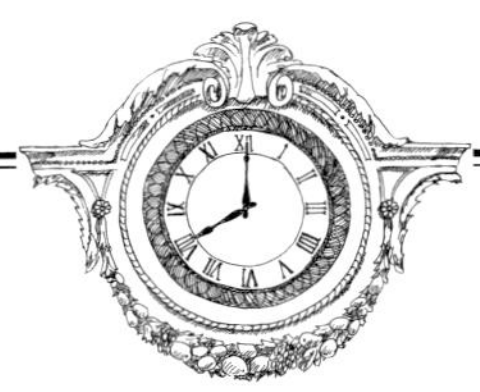

NEW YORK PUBLIC LIBRARY
ROSE MAIN READING
ROOM CLOCK
476 FIFTH AVENUE
1911

Built in 1911 and designed by the architectural firm Carrère & Hastings, the New York Public Library on Fifth Avenue was once the largest marble building in the United States. It remains freely open to the public, and those wishing to read or research are permitted access to the jaw-dropping Rose Main Reading Room. This room measures nearly three hundred feet long with a soaring ceiling that has nary a column to hold it up, and is painted with sky and clouds that seem touched by a rising sun. The ceiling framework is carved wood and plasterwork that is partly gilded. The room is divided in two by a columned wood partition, which holds within it busy librarians in small offices. On each side of this partition of small rooms—which doesn't come anywhere close to the celestial ceiling above—a clock festooned in carved oak flourishes comfortably resides, letting researchers, writers, and students know how long they have toiled within this inspiring space.

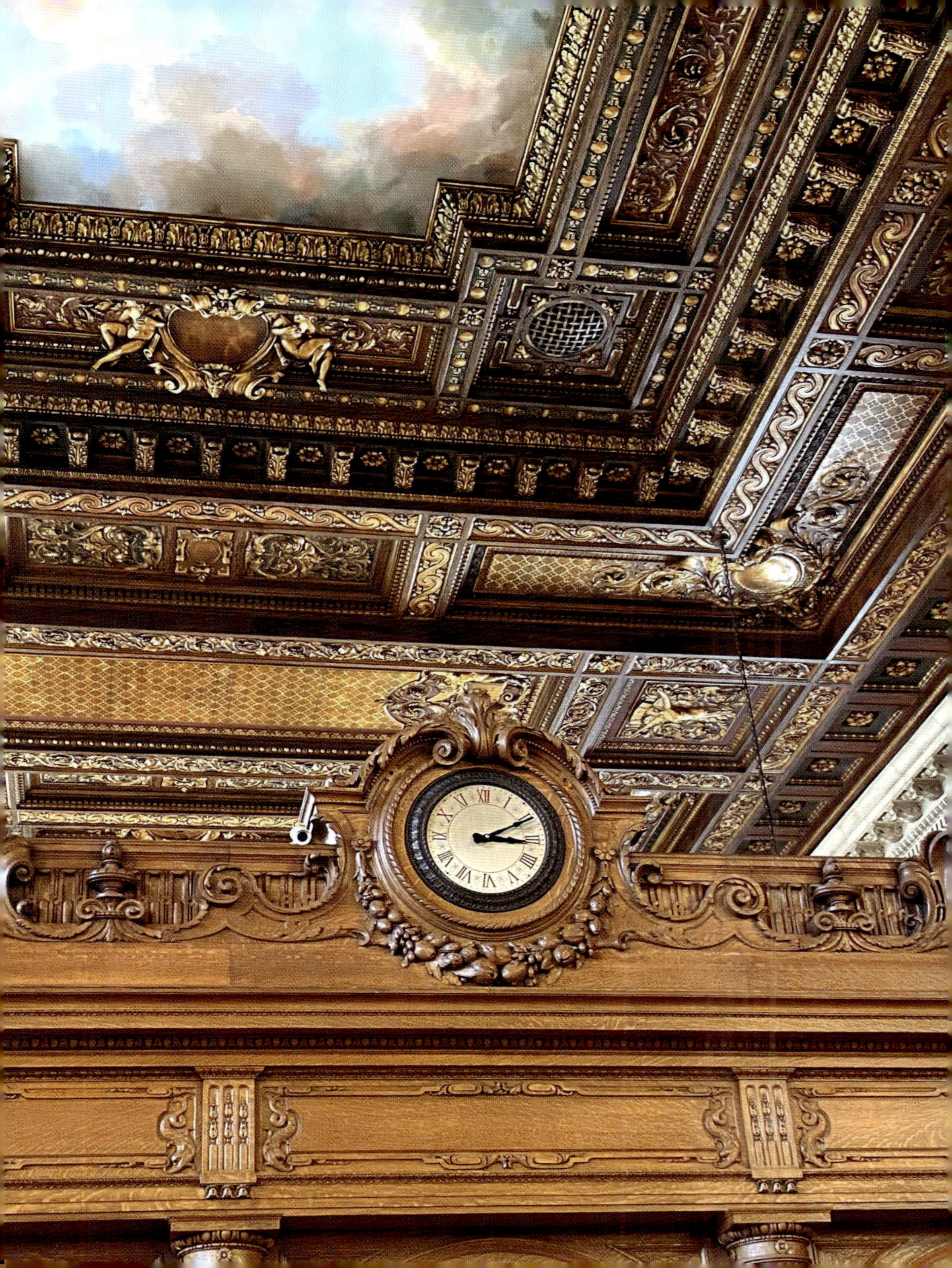

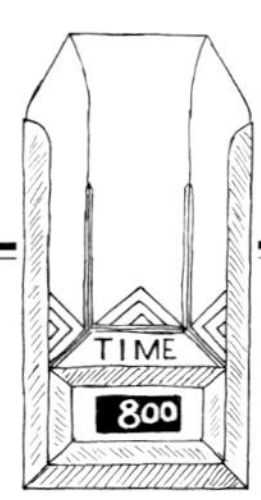

CHRYSLER BUILDING
LOBBY CLOCK
405 LEXINGTON AVENUE
1930

To enter the lobby of the Chrysler Building is to enter a time capsule of cutting-edge twentieth-century design. The space feels more like a futuristic movie set than an office building lobby. Lavish use of red Moroccan marble—accented by other marbles, onyx, aluminum, and steel—creates an interior of exceptionally striking Art Deco style. It is wonderfully strange, even otherworldly. In the vast, soaring three-story lobby, the clock is quite unassuming. No dial or traditional clock here; this one is digital, rare for a public clock of this era. When entering this high-style space I can't help but picture fashionable New Yorkers of the 1920s catching the clock from the corner of their eyes as they beeline to the elevators, knowing they were going to fly up the center of a building that was, oh, so briefly, the tallest in the world. I sense that this space actually ushered in the real twentieth century, leaving the nineteenth in the dust with its new, unfussy, minimal machine-age style.

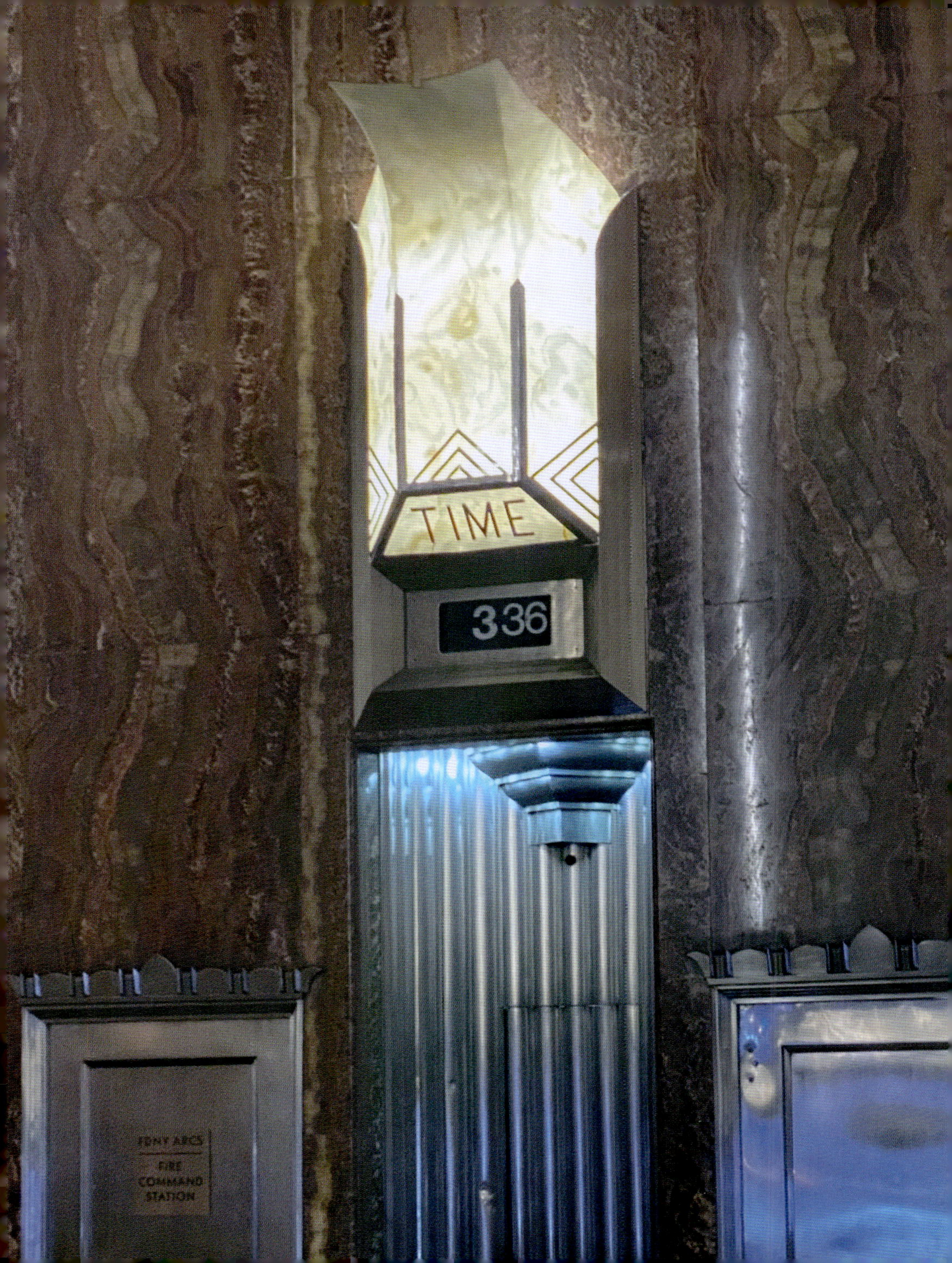
TIME
3 36
FDNY ARCS
FIRE
COMMAND
STATION

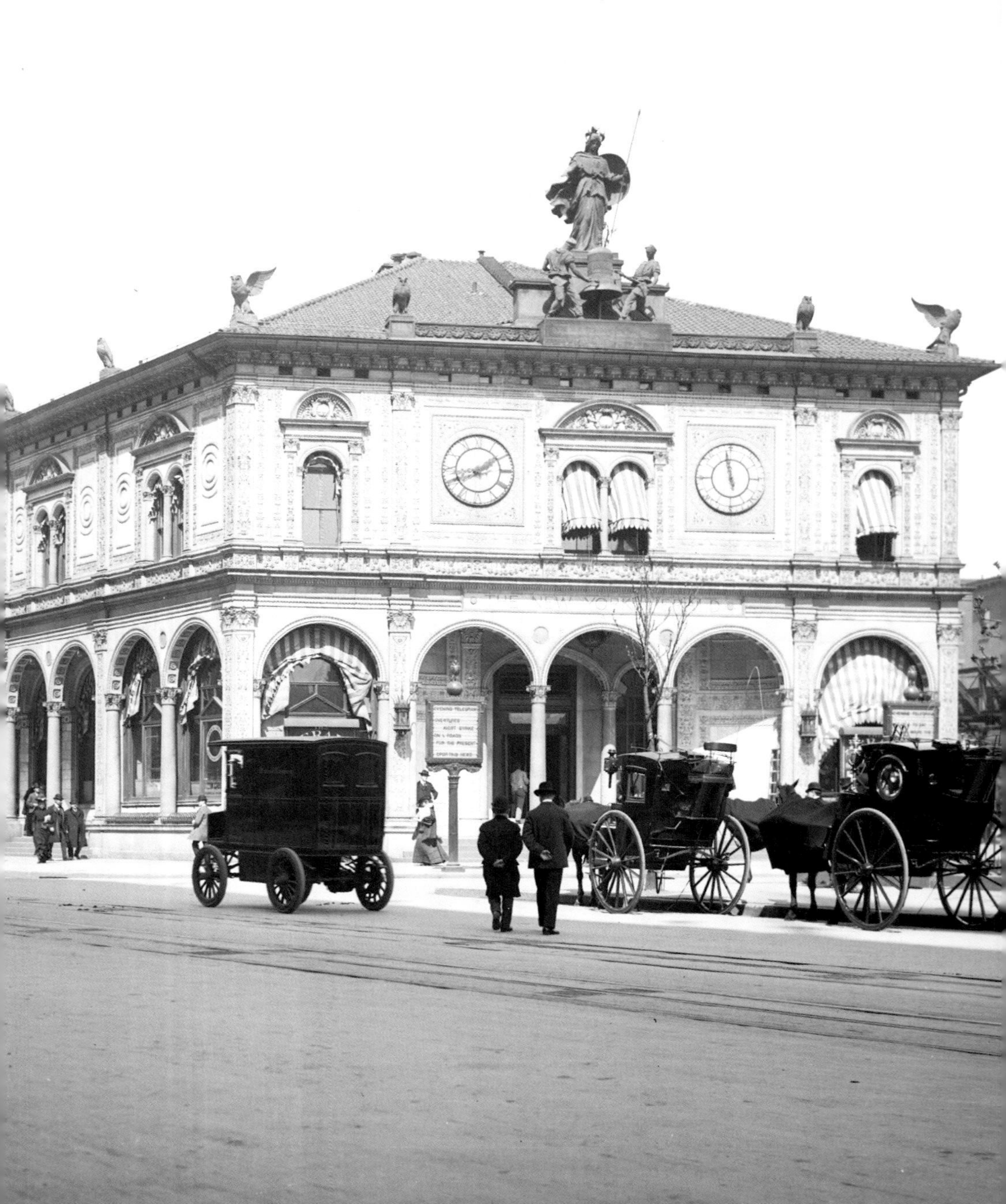

WHEN THE CLOCK STRIKES
AUTOMATON CLOCKS

"Charm" is not the first word used to describe New York City, but if you look for charm you will find it. The timepieces in this book are as diverse in design as the city itself, ranging from simple and workaday to grand on an epic scale. Some are sleekly urbane, and yes, some even have charm. New York's handful of automaton clocks, with figures that move with the ringing bells, reminds us that the city is far more than Gilded Age opulence or canyons of machine-age steel, but a town that holds imagination and magic. Often called glockenspiel clocks, they recall clocks in German town squares. The word *glockenspiel* translates roughly to mean "bell play." Unlike clocks on busy sidewalks or conveniently positioned in Grand Central as you run to catch your train, automaton clocks slow the city rush and beckon us to pause and take in the show. Maybe even while enjoying an ice cream.

My favorite European mechanical clock is not in Germany but in Venice, Italy. On top of the clock tower of Piazza San Marco stands a pair of massive bronze figures who pivot at the waist to strike a bell cast in Venice in 1497. This automaton clock has stopped locals and tourists in their tracks since the early Renaissance. On high religious holidays, three delightfully carved

New York Herald Building, built 1895, Broadway and Sixth Avenue, c. 1900–10

141

This much-admired structure was demolished, but the bronze figures were retained and reused in what is now Herald Square.

wooden kings led by an angel with a trumpet are set upon a track. As the clock strikes, they enter our view through a door on the left in a little procession as they "walk" around the Virgin and Child, bowing as they pass, and then exit a door on the right side.

As New York joined other great world capitals as a powerful metropolis, its business leaders and urban planners often looked to European cities for inspiration. New York government and business owners took on the challenge, securing excellent architects and artists and, in some cases, makers of automaton clocks. These types of clocks were born partly to express civic pride, just like the glockenspiels in nineteenth-century Germany or the San Marco clock in fifteenth-century Venice. Every automaton clock was a delightful gift to New Yorkers and tourists alike.

The grandest example of a New York automaton clock was made possible by James Gordon Bennett Jr., the eccentric publisher and son of the founder and editor of the city's most successful newspaper, the *New York Herald*. Stanford White of McKim, Mead & White was engaged to design the new building, and he turned to Italy for his inspiration, specifically an early Renaissance palazzo in Verona called Palazzo del Consiglio. White's highly praised two-story building was completed in 1895. Besides the indisputable elegance and, one could say, charm of the building, it was the ornament and splendid clock that put it over the top. Bennett Jr., who was obsessed with owls, had White line the edge of his roofline with a series of bronze owls that stood in silence as if surveying the streets below. Centered high above the front entrance was Minerva, goddess of wisdom, who is often seen accompanied by an owl—connecting the *Herald* with this noble attribute of wisdom was no mistake. At Minerva's feet, a bronze bell was centered between two bronze men wielding large mallets. It is these figures, attired as newspaper typesetters, that make the clock an automaton. They appear to strike the bell

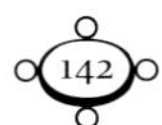

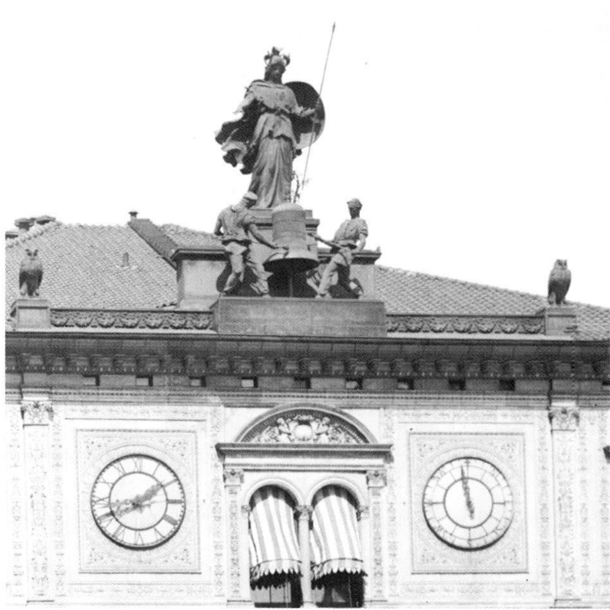

New York's most extravagant automaton clock was on this building, exquisitely designed by Stanford White.

on the hour, rotating at the waist. (The bell is actually struck by a hidden mallet.) The sculptural group was created by Antonin Carlés for the handsome sum of $200,000. On the main facade of the building, below the bronze figures, is a clock on the left, balanced by a dial on the right that shows velocity of the wind.

Sadly, this stunning building was demolished in 1921 when the *Herald* moved uptown. It stood in the triangular plot immediately north of what is now Herald Square. Fortunately, the clock, figures, bell, and some of the owl sculptures were retained and eventually reinstalled in the James Gordon Bennett Memorial, which is shown in the following pages, along with two other singular automaton clocks. And yes, they are charming.

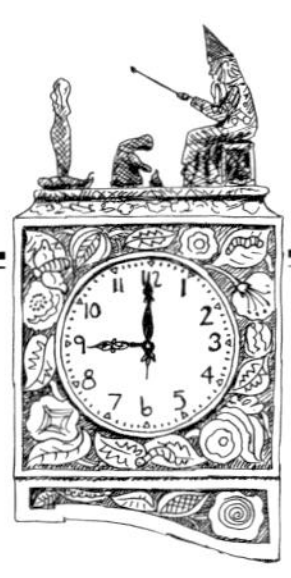

SCHWARZENBACH
BUILDING "SILK CLOCK"
462 PARK AVENUE SOUTH
1926

One of the city's most unusual and delightful clocks was created for the original owners of the Schwarzenbach Building at Park Avenue and 32nd Street. Schwarzenbach Looms was a company in the silk trade, and commissioned the Seth Thomas Clock Company to create this automated clock in 1926. At the top is a wizard with a wand, a blacksmith, and a cocoon. On the hour the wizard waves his wand, and the blacksmith begins forging a sword with a hammer while a lady rises from the cocoon and twirls. On the surface of the double-faced clock is a foliate relief depicting mulberry leaves—the food of silkworms. The artists responsible for the sculpted elements were William Zorach, who sculpted the figures, and his wife, Marguerite, who created the floral relief. In addition to its design, this clock is unusual in that it has never been electrified, a rarity for old clocks in New York City.

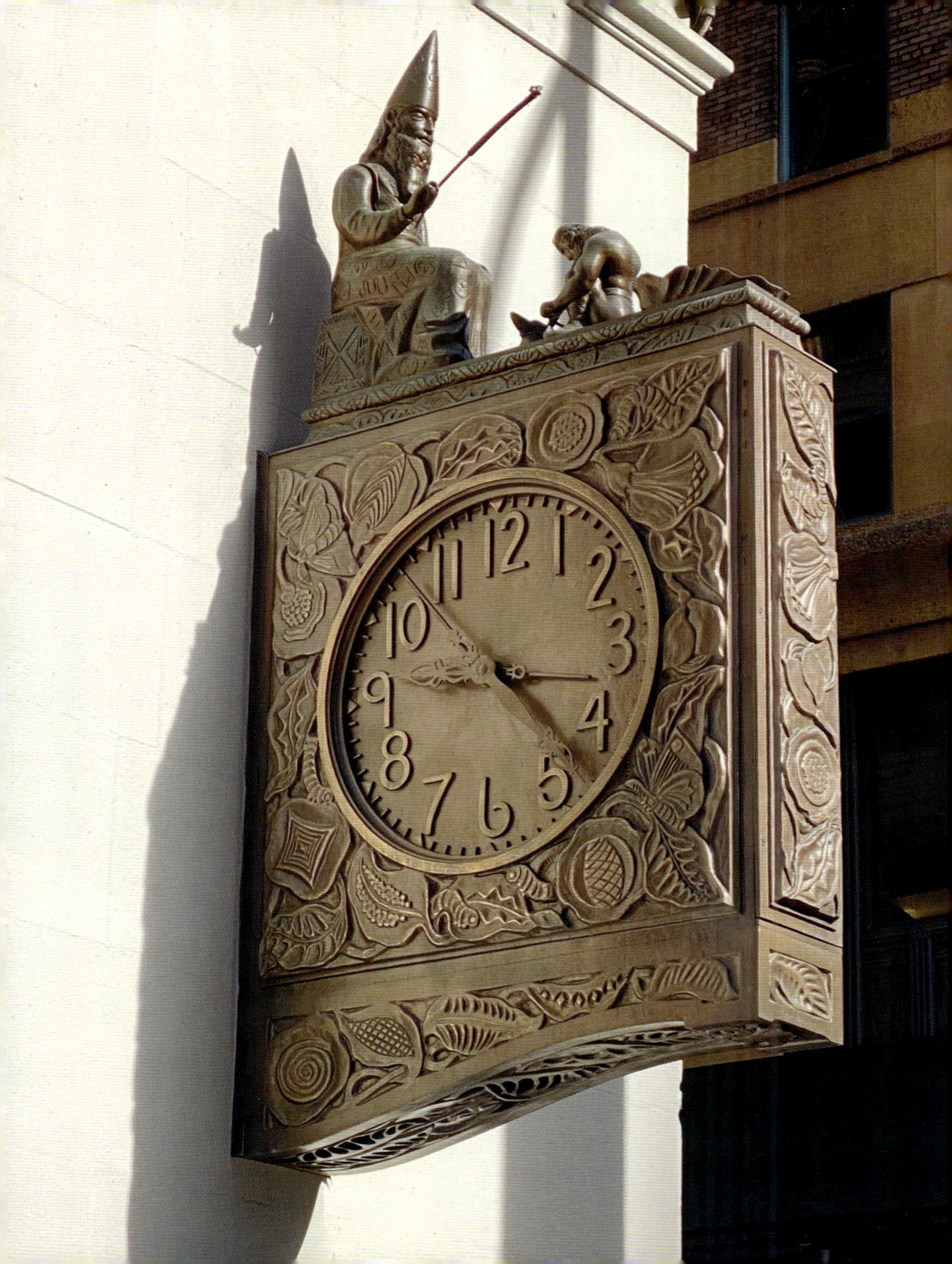

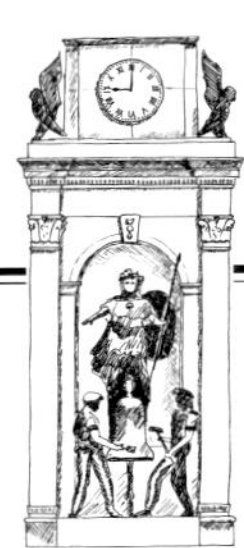

JAMES GORDON BENNETT
MEMORIAL CLOCK
1 HERALD SQUARE
1940

Known as the James Gordon Bennett Memorial, the impressive pink granite pedestal in Herald Square was installed in 1940. The bronze sculptures by Antonin Carlés integrated into the pedestal were originally created for the New York Herald Building that once stood across 35th Street to the north; James Gordon Bennett Sr. was the founder, editor, and publisher of the *New York Herald*. Minerva is the central figure of the grouping, perhaps because of her various attributes, but more likely because her sacred creature is the owl, an animal that Bennett Jr. was obsessed with. In fact, the roof of the old building was lined with multiple owl sculptures. Two of the surviving owls top the monument with eyes that light up at night. Minerva, surmounted by the clockface, gazes down on the automaton figures, two seven-foot press laborers nicknamed Guff and Stuff, who appear to strike the bell. (The bell is actually struck by a hidden mallet from behind.)

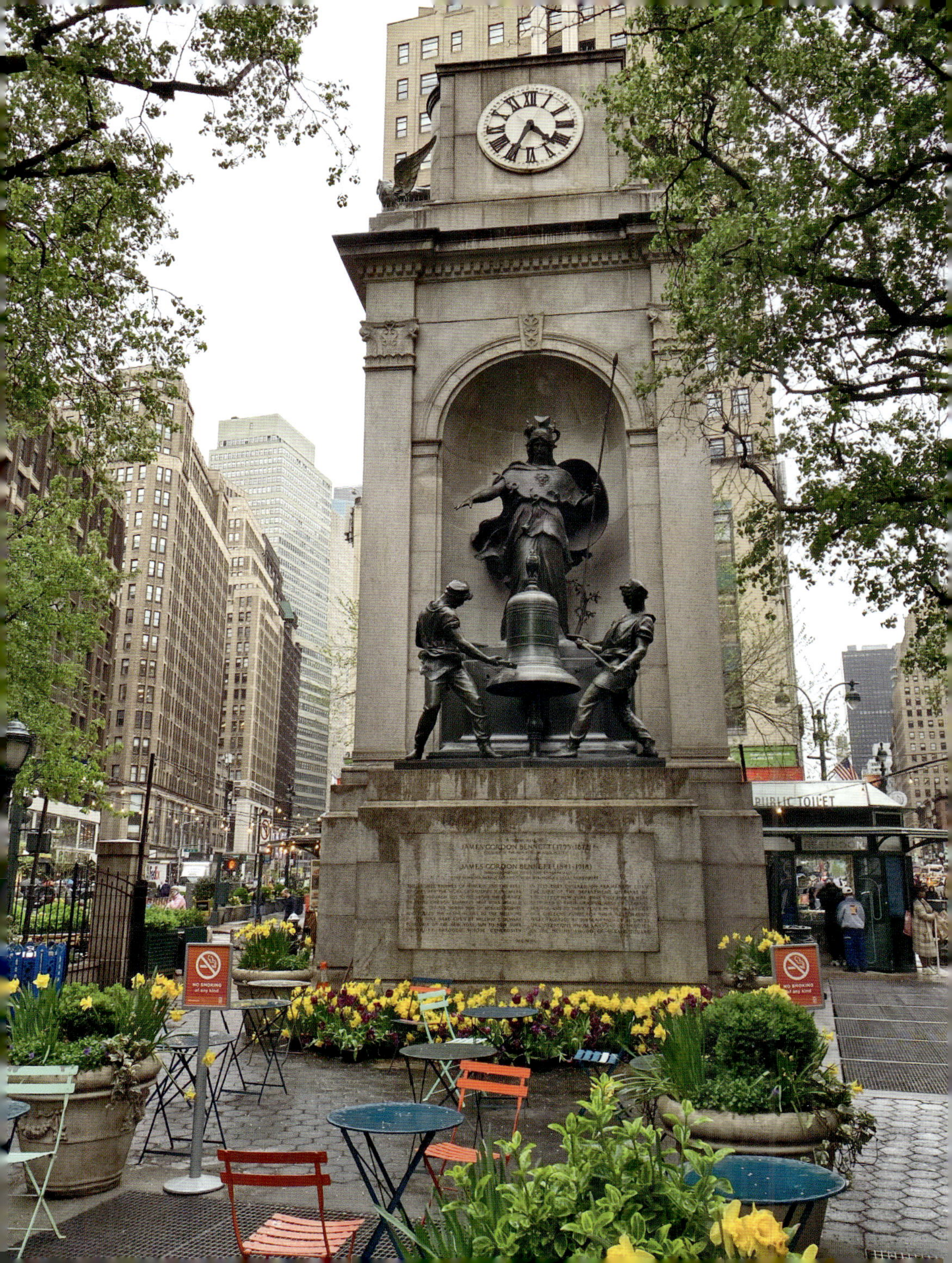

PUBLIC TOILET
RESTROOM
NO SMOKING of any kind
NO SMOKING of any kind

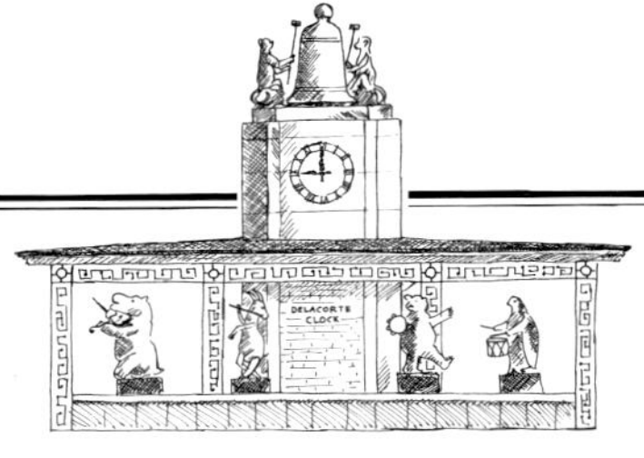

THE DELACORTE
ZOO CLOCK

CENTRAL PARK
1965

The George Delacorte Musical Clock, located between the Children's Zoo and the Wildlife Center in Central Park, was dedicated in 1965. Every half hour a menagerie of animal figures circles the clock base, twirling as they hold musical instruments. Surmounting the clock, a pair of monkeys with mallets flank a bronze bell. As they appear to strike the clock, various nursery rhymes chime. Delacorte, a publisher and philanthropist, was inspired to give this gift to the city after seeing glockenspiel clocks while traveling in Europe. Spanish designer Fernando Texidor collaborated with architect Edward Coe Embury to create a supportive arcade for the clock that complemented nearby zoo buildings. The animals were created by Italian artist Andrea Spadini. Besides the monkeys on top, the dancing animals include a bear, elephant, goat, hippo, penguin, and kangaroo. If ever there was an NYC timepiece that charmed, it is this one.

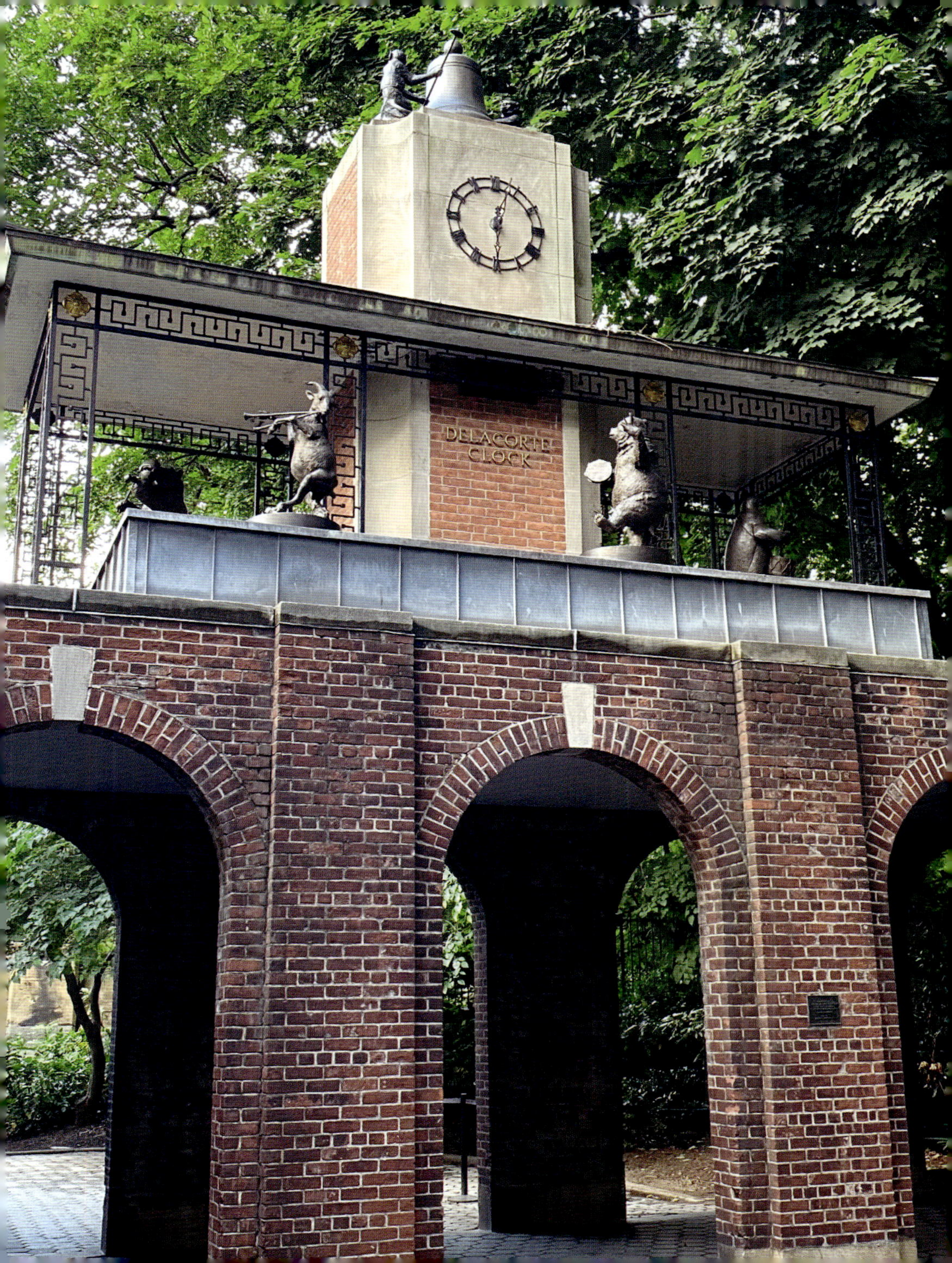

DELACORTE
CLOCK

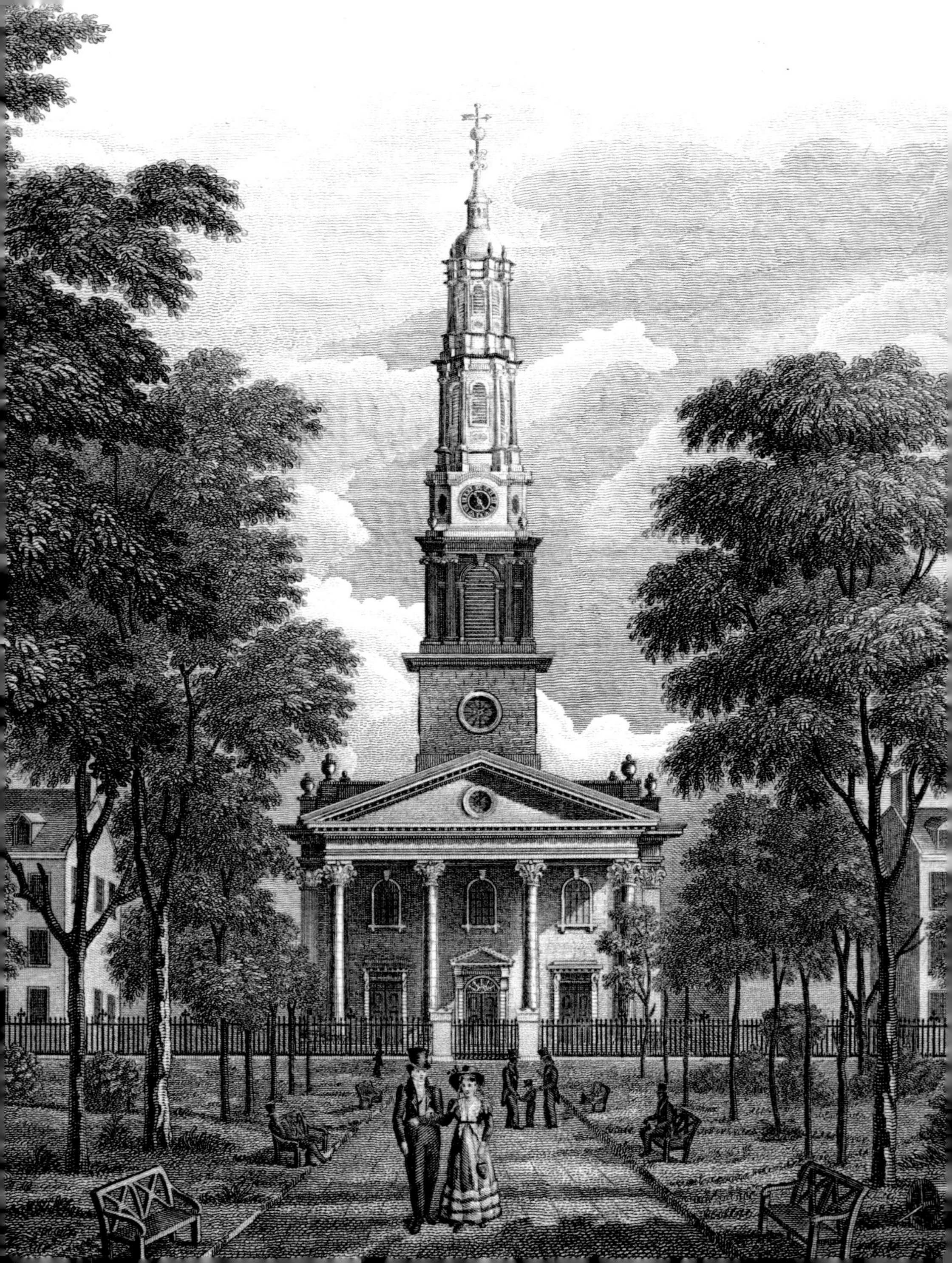

GET ME TO THE CHURCH ON TIME
CHURCH CLOCKS

The oldest still-running clock in the world is in southern England at Salisbury Cathedral, believed to date from around 1386. Given this early example, it makes sense that New York City's oldest and only surviving colonial-era church would also have a clock. That clock continues to tick at St. Paul's Chapel, which is unsurprising given the astonishing staying power of this deeply loved landmark. It makes sense as well that clocks grace the bell towers of many urban churches since they were often the tallest and most centrally located structures in their neighborhoods back in the day. Like clocks on important office or government buildings, it was desirable for churches to show their power, authority, and community spirit by installing public clocks. Plus, it might have been a subtle (or not) reminder to straggling parishioners that they should get to church. On time.

An early New York church that didn't have St. Paul's staying power was St. John's Chapel. St. John's was among the most mourned New York City buildings, lost to—you guessed it—redevelopment. Completed in 1807 in what is now Tribeca, with its classical portico and 214-foot-tall clock and bell tower, this lovely church was considered an architectural masterpiece even

St. John's Chapel, built 1807, Varick Street, 1829

This engraving shows the simple but austere clock situated high in the chapel's tower.

in its day. Its beauty inspired a park surrounded by Federal-era mansions creating the most fashionable and, by all accounts, most beautiful residential neighborhood in the city at that time. Architect John McComb Jr., who had previously designed New York's much admired City Hall in 1803, was responsible for the chapel. St. John's survived only a century. The *New York Times* shared the city's great loss in print on October 6, 1918: "In the demolition of St. John's Chapel New York has lost not only a revered landmark but one of the choicest specimens of Georgian church architecture in the United States. . . . Architects have agreed that St. John's had few if any superiors of its kind . . . and it has been said that neither the justly admired St. Michael's Church in Charleston, Christ Church in Philadelphia, nor King's Chapel in Boston surpassed it in simplicity of proportion or exquisite refinement of architectural detail."

The push of commerce and its inevitable development steamrolled ever north in Manhattan with old downtown residential buildings, and others, being repurposed or, more frequently, pushed aside to make way for bigger and, on rare occasions, better things. In 1914, just a few years before St. John's Chapel was pulled down to make room for a growing commercial district, the new Fort Washington Presbyterian Church was completed on 21 Wadsworth Avenue in Washington Heights. Thomas Hastings designed the church and seemed to be inspired by the same eighteenth-century English principles that John McComb Jr. admired when designing St. John's. Or perhaps Hastings was paying homage to McComb by creating his version of a Georgian-style church. The 1924 photo opposite may make it seem like Hastings's church was in danger of falling to the wrecking crew, but these excavators were instead digging a new extension of the subway system. Thankfully this church with its elegantly articulated clock and bell tower still stands and now

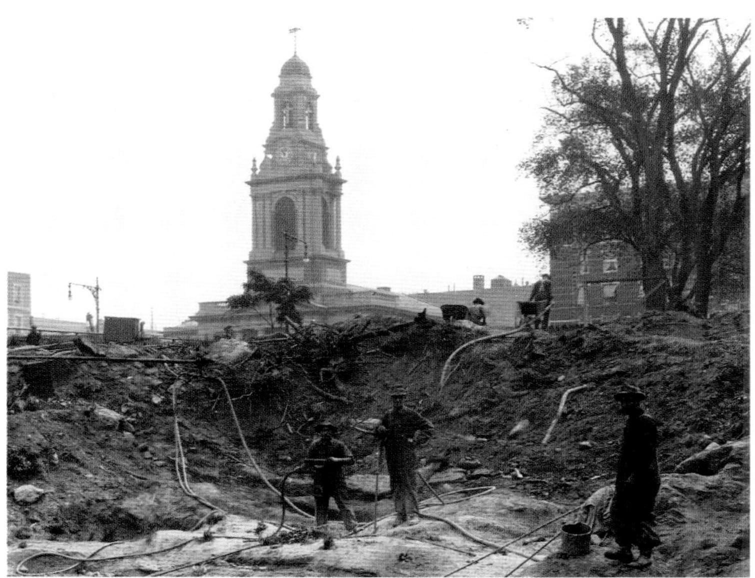

serves the Primera Iglesia Española de Washington Heights, an important part of the Puerto Rican community in New York.

If there is one thing that New Yorkers can count on, it is change, even if glorious historic buildings get in the way. Thankfully the Fort Washington Presbyterian Church can be counted among the survivors despite the above photograph suggesting otherwise. Additional survivors follow with St. Paul's Chapel leading the pack. This church has witnessed an only-in-New-York story with over 250 years of red-letter moments. It joins other examples of ecclesiastical architecture with clocks that have ticked throughout our urban history, and will hopefully continue to do so well into the future.

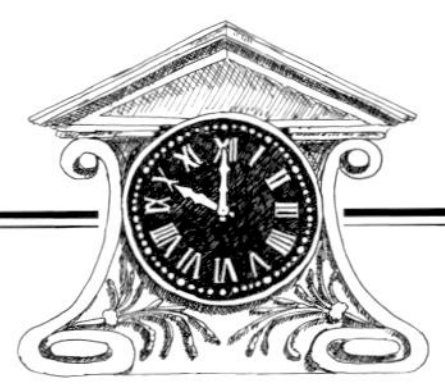

ST. PAUL'S CHAPEL

209 BROADWAY
1766

Designed by Thomas McBean and built in 1766, St. Paul's Chapel is the oldest church building in Manhattan. It survived the great New York fire of 1776, and witnessed the transition from colonialism to a new country as George Washington worshiped here on his inauguration day on April 30, 1789. This historically and architecturally important church miraculously survived the September 11 attack on the World Trade Center, only increasing New Yorkers' love for this beautiful example of late Georgian architecture. The elaborate spire by architect James Crommelin Lawrence with its four-faced clock was added in 1794. St. Paul's still holds the oldest public clockworks in the city, though restorations have replaced or added new parts of the mechanism over the centuries.

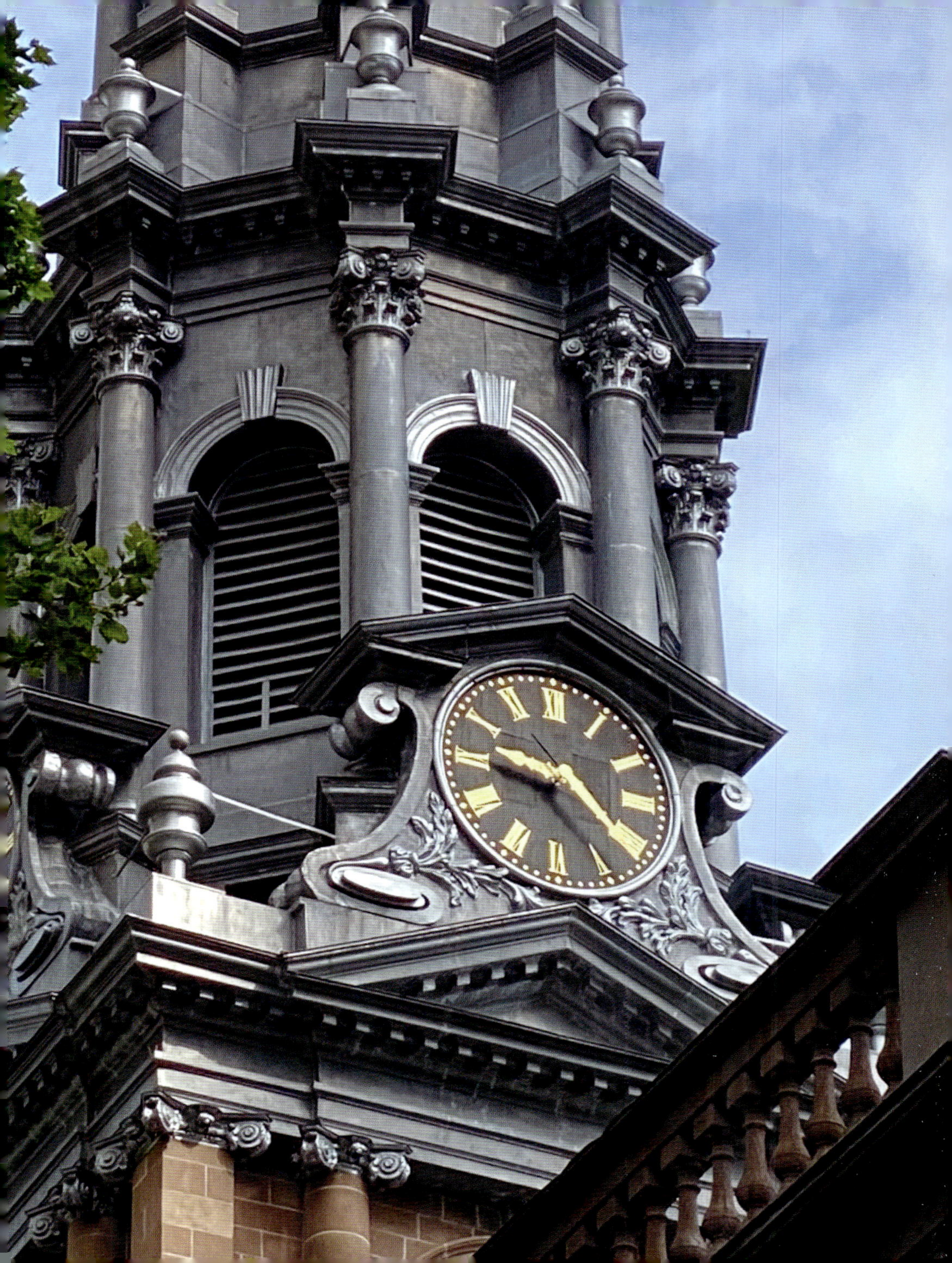

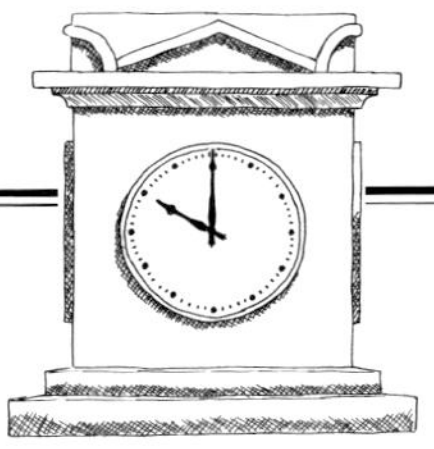

ST. MARK'S CHURCH IN-THE-BOWERY

131 EAST 10TH STREET
1799

St. Mark's Church at Stuyvesant Street and Second Avenue is the second-oldest church in Manhattan. The site, however, has been a continuous place of worship for more than three and a half centuries, since Peter Stuyvesant erected a private chapel on his farm around 1660. The church we see today was designed by John McComb Jr., one of the architects of City Hall. St. Mark's was built in 1799 and made of simple fieldstone in a restrained and elegant Federal style. The neoclassical steeple, designed by Martin Euclid Thompson and Ithiel Town, was added in 1828. The clock came later, in 1836, and was made by John Stokell. In 1881, the Stokell clock was replaced by the E. Howard Clock Company. The unornamented clock face reflects the rather sober yet refined style of this early American structure.

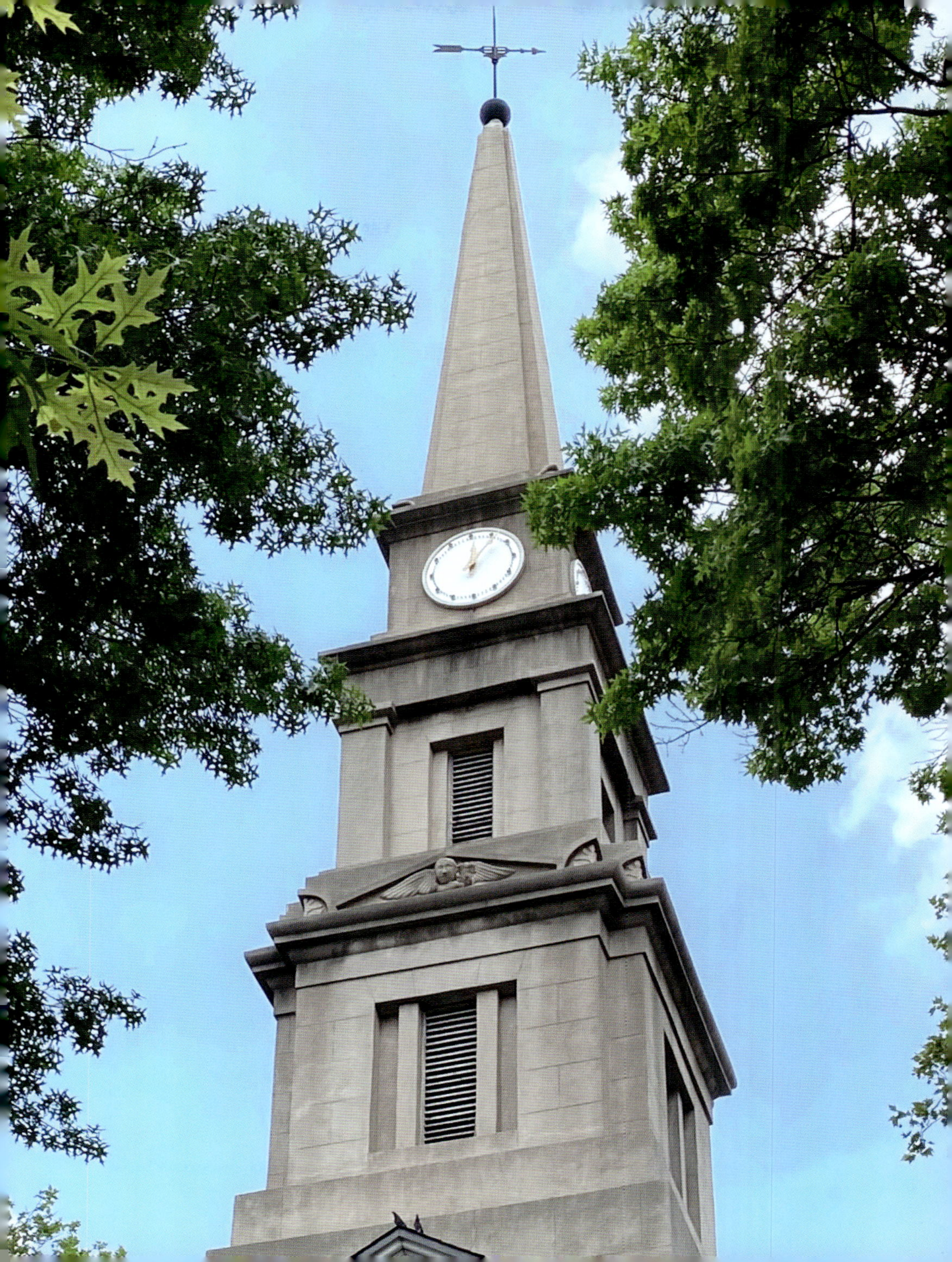

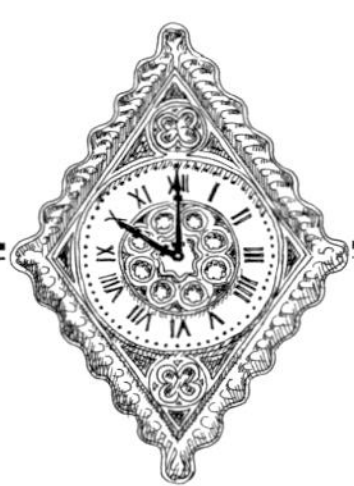

TRINITY CHURCH
89 BROADWAY
1846

Trinity Church was designed by Richard Upjohn (an architect famous for bringing the Gothic Revival to the United States), completed in 1846, and was the tallest building in New York City until 1890. On February 27, 1947, the *New York Times* wrote: "Uncertainty settled over the city's financial district yesterday. . . . The Trinity Church clock, guardian of Wall Street punctuality, had stopped. Most of the tens of thousands of 'Street' employees who several times a day turn their eyes to the gilded hands of the clock's three nine-foot dials, found life normal as they hurried out of buses and ferries to report for work. Those privileged to report to their offices after 9:30 A.M. were the ones first thrown off stride. At that hour workmen inside the brownstone ashlar tower put some monkey wrenches in the works and pointed the hands to 12. They will remain there for several days. The huge clock's entire mechanism is being overhauled and Wall Street will have to struggle along on less convenient timepieces." Trinity Church was 101 years old when the *New York Times* shared the obvious news that public clocks were more than decorative.

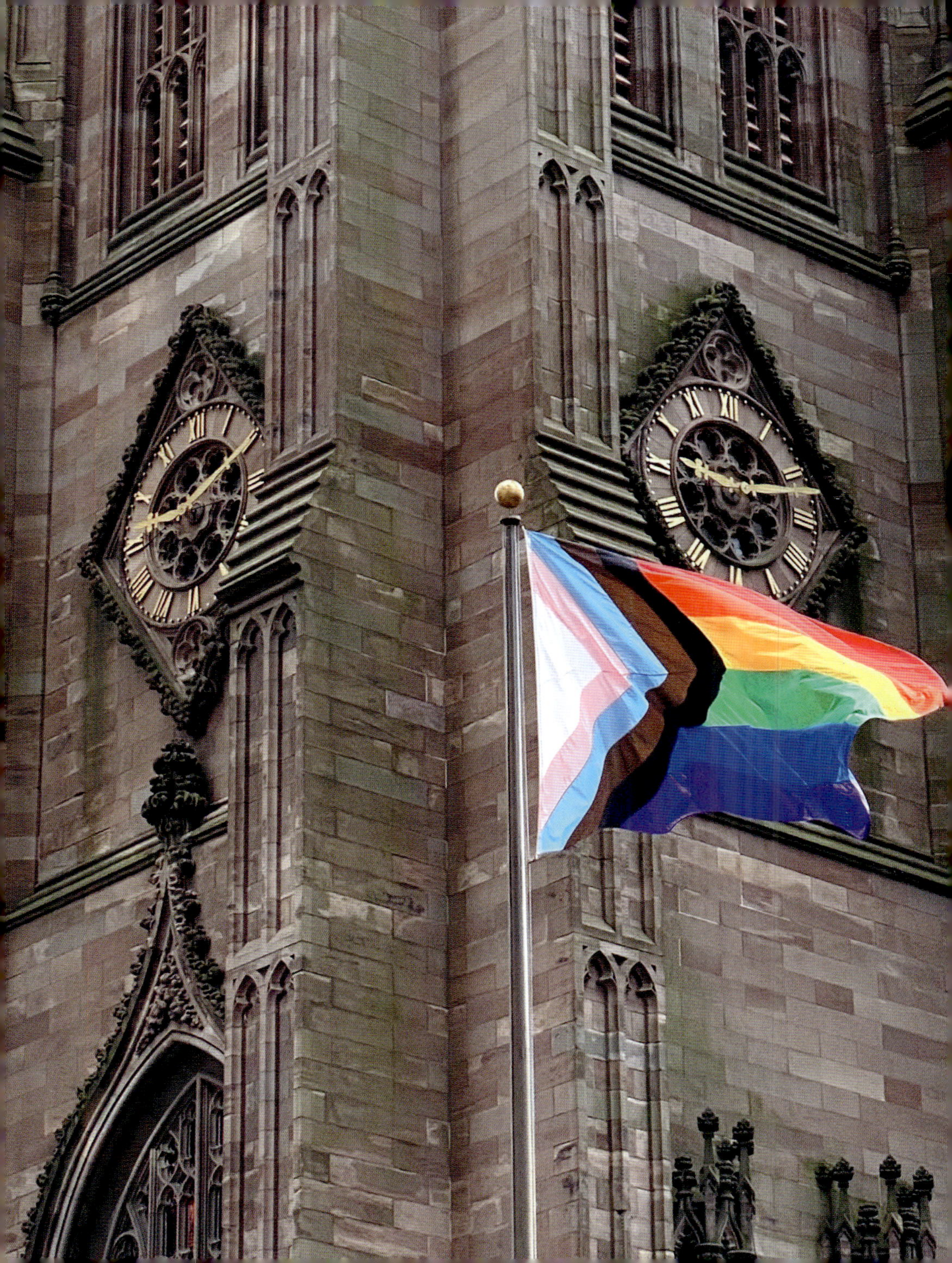

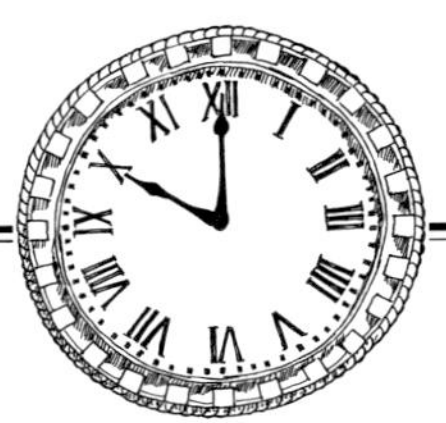

CHURCH OF THE MOST
HOLY REDEEMER

173 EAST 3RD STREET
1852

When this Roman Catholic church on East 3rd Street was built, the neighborhood was called *Kleindeutschland*, or "Little Germany." The German Catholic community was second only to the Irish in America at this time, and other than Berlin and Vienna, New York City had the third-largest German-speaking population of any city in the world. Originally built in a somewhat German Baroque style, it was designed by an architect known as Walsh. The original design had a much taller spire and more elaborate facade but as the affluent moved increasingly uptown, including many German Americans, the church was left with decreased support. In 1913, the spire was dramatically shortened and the facade simplified by Paul Schultz, and it seems the clock survived the renovation.

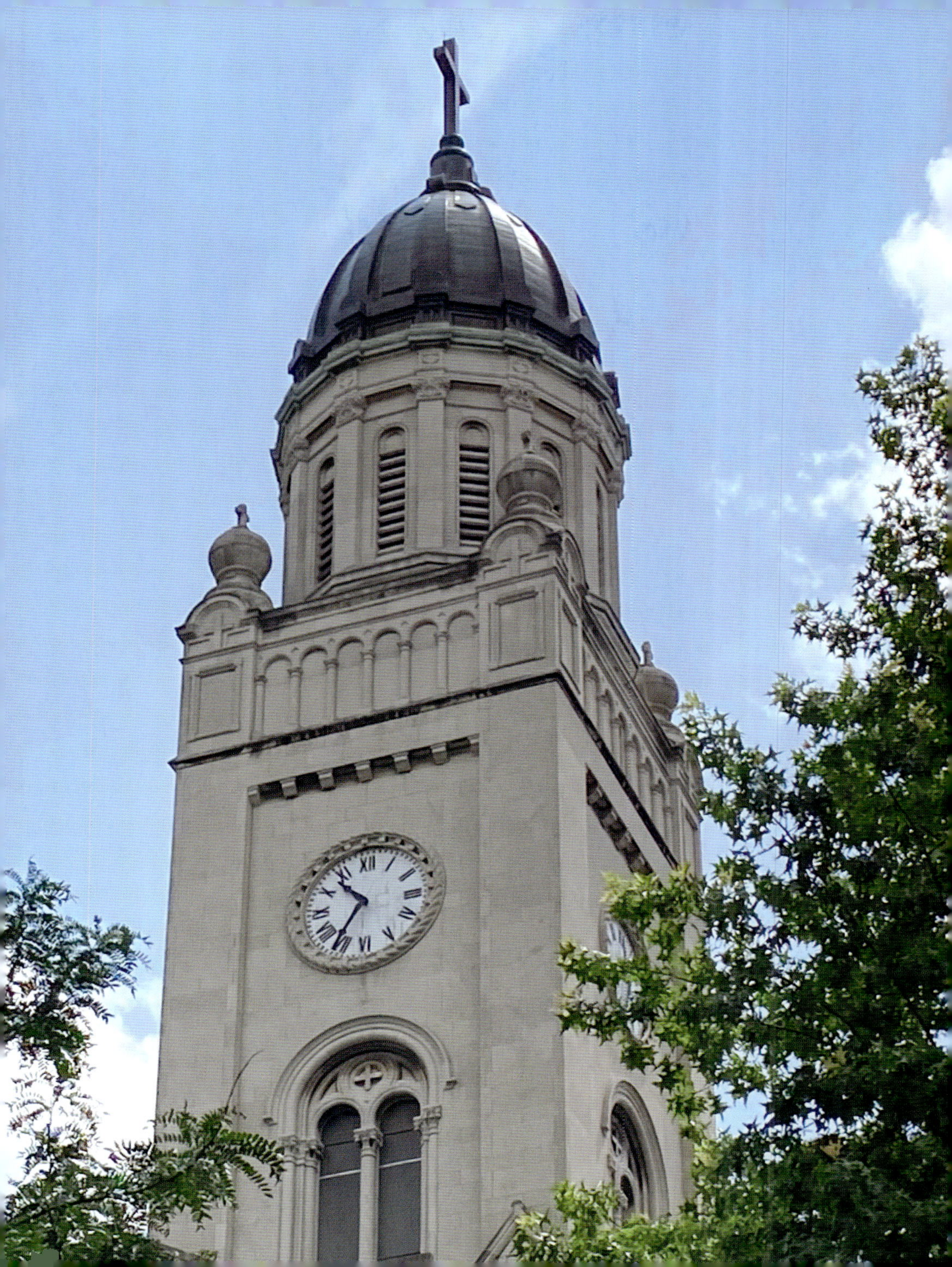

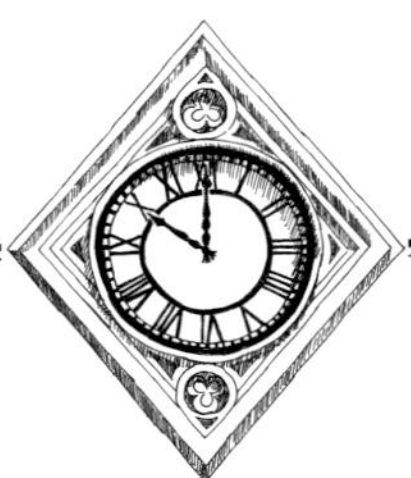

MARBLE COLLEGIATE
CHURCH
1 WEST 29TH STREET
1854

Built between 1851 and 1854 at the corner of Fifth Avenue and 29th Street, the Marble Collegiate Church was designed by Samuel A. Warner. The structure blends Romanesque and Gothic details on a restrained and elegant facade of marble brought down the Hudson River from a quarry at Hastings-on-Hudson. While the building is nineteenth century, the church itself was founded in 1628, making it the oldest continuous Protestant congregation in the United States. The spire from ground to peak measures 215 feet tall, highlighting the four round clockfaces set within diamond-shaped frames. The original clockworks were described by the *New York Times* as "a massive mechanism" and were hand-wound for over a century. The workings were replaced with an electric mechanism by Seth Thomas Clock Company in 1957.

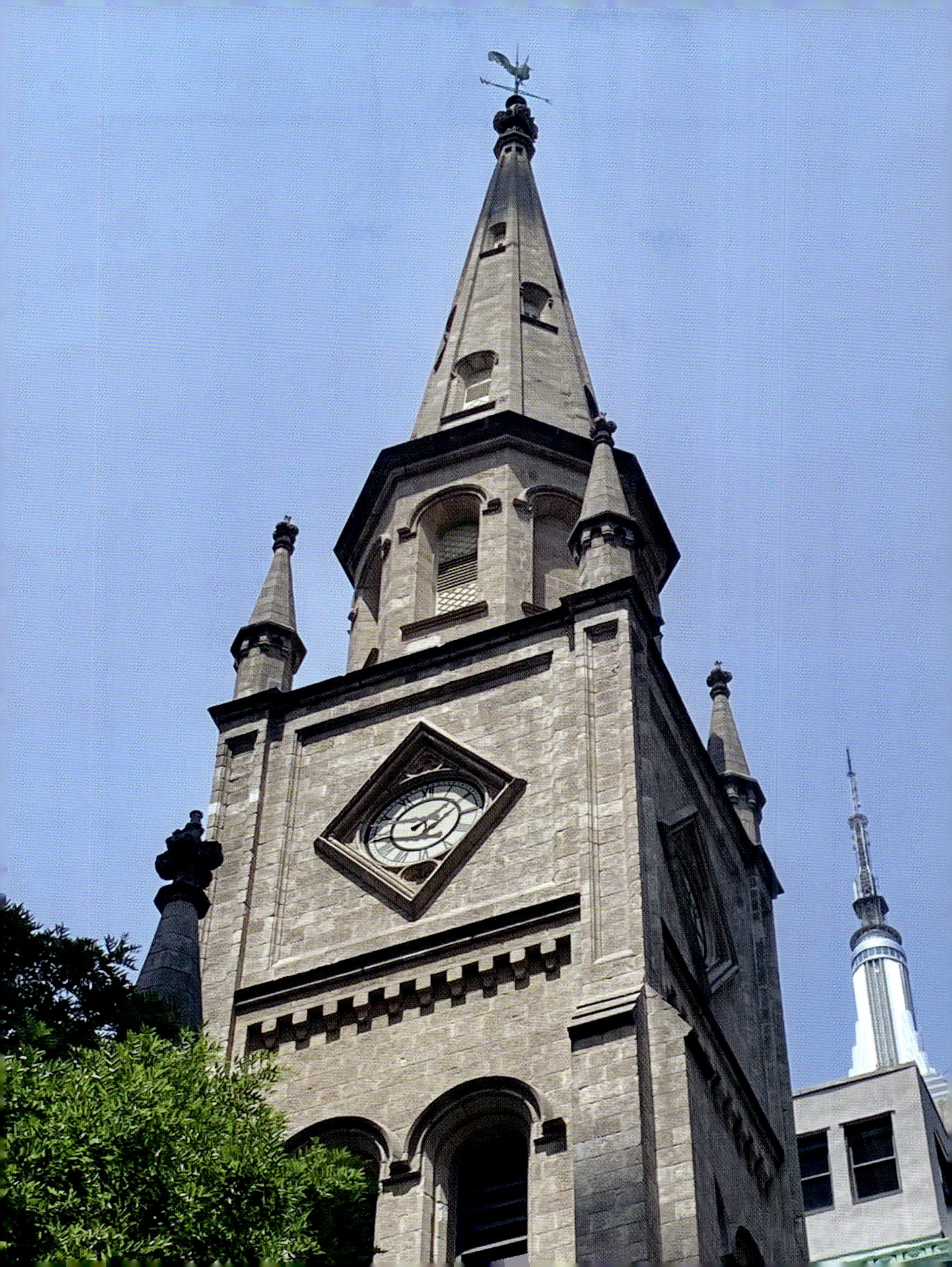

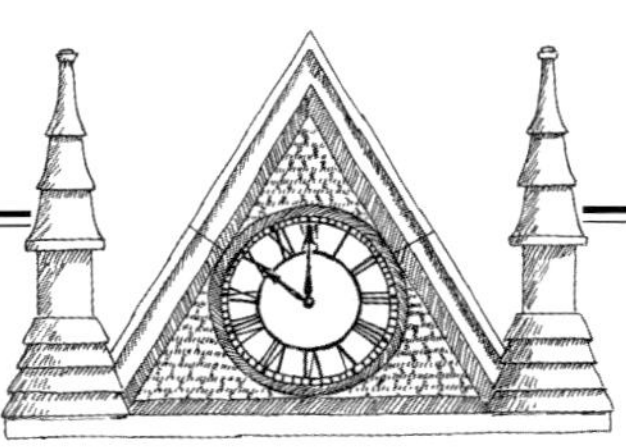

CHURCH OF
ST. ANTHONY–ST. ALPHONSUS
862 MANHATTAN AVENUE
1874

Architect Patrick Keely is perhaps the ultimate example of a New Yorker who never wasted a minute. In 1842, Keely, then in his twenties, immigrated to New York City, one of two million of his countrymen to escape the tragic Irish potato famine. He worked as a carpenter at first, moving on to design six hundred churches, including six cathedrals for the growing population of American Catholics. He settled in Brooklyn, where this church still stands in a charming part of Greenpoint. The 240-foot spire with a four-faced clock was fully visible among the surrounding townhouses and shops in the late nineteenth century. Besides the six hundred churches, Keely and his wife, Sarah Farmer, had seventeen children, ten of whom survived into adulthood.

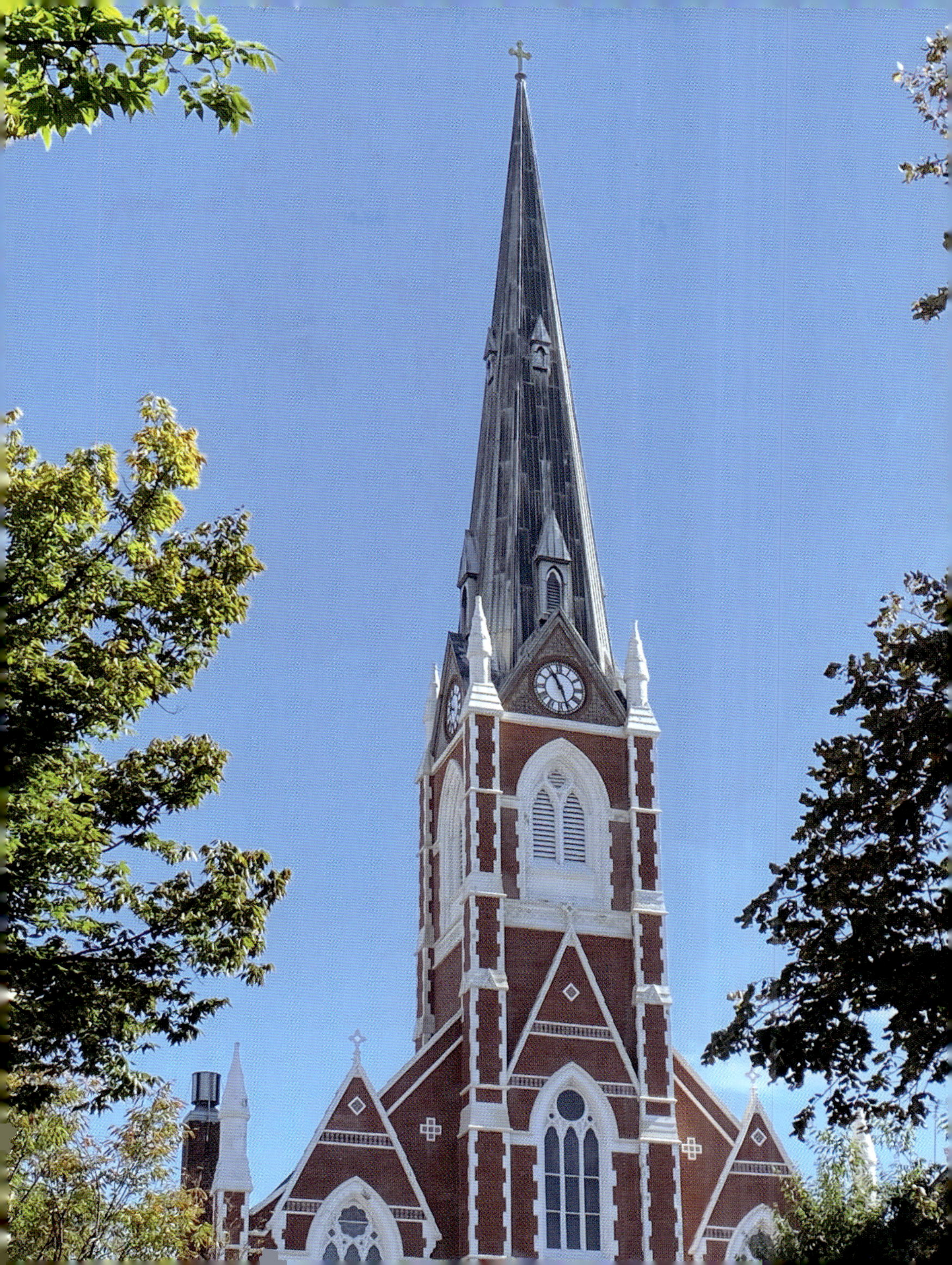

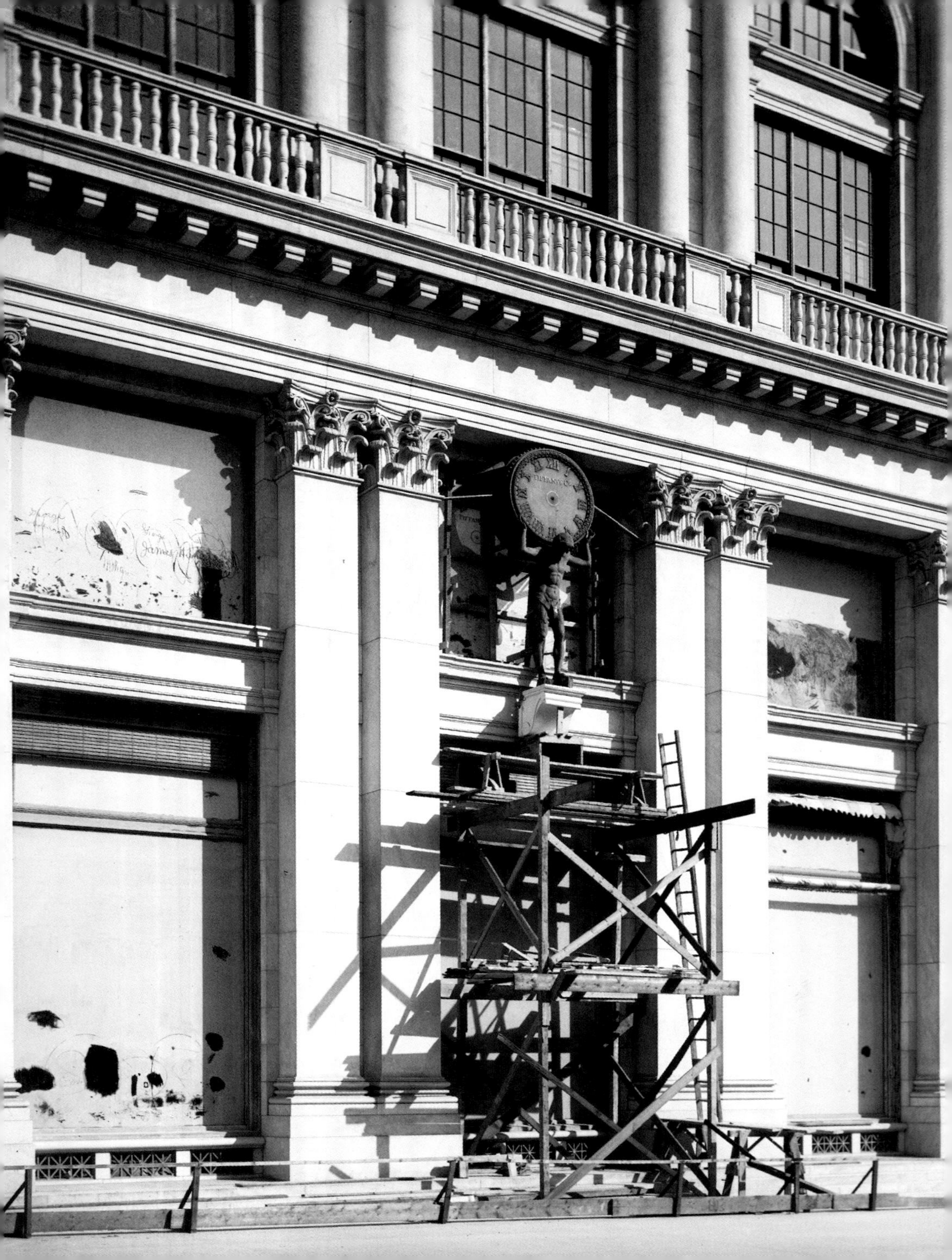

BUYING TIME

STORE CLOCKS

One of the great pleasures of New York City is its stores. You may walk and discover a small boutique or take the subway to a revered department store, and along the way you rediscover another urban perk: people watching. A packed subway car can hold close to two hundred people, meaning rubbing elbows with city dwellers of every age, race, background, and income bracket is a given. Within each subway car exists an unspoken interplay, a shared communion with your fellow humans. In those jostling subterranean moments, I often experience something profound, occasionally hilarious, endlessly entertaining, and almost always beautiful.

As you reach your stop and climb the stairs to street level, that fragile bubble of humanity pops and disperses into a proper parade with you as one of its marchers. Part of the fun of people watching is the clothes. New York street style has an innate savviness, and it runs the gamut. On one side, you'll pass highly curated shop windows with fashionable clothing, which can be exciting enough, but on the other, you blend into the urban runway yourself and become a spectatorial contributor to the human spectrum of style.

New Yorkers and New York stores know how to put on a show,

TIFFANY & CO. BUILDING, built 1905, Fifth Avenue and 37th Street, c. 1903–6

Tiffany's famous Atlas clock is shown being installed on its new building decades before moving farther uptown.

and I feel sure they always did. Pioneering department stores, new and established fashion designers, peacocks, fashion girls, design students, drag queens, window dressers, style editors, and a legion of regular New Yorkers contribute to the spectacle. One can't talk about this without mentioning the beloved chronicler, Bill Cunningham. He started his storied career as a street photographer in 1978, when I was studying ballet here, and he continued until 2016, the year of his death. If because of some tragic blind spot, you are unaware of Cunningham's thirty-eight years of documenting street style in his *New York Times* series *On the Street*, fix that. Cunningham, who devoted every waking minute to his work, was in many ways the best of New York, while also being the kindest, dearest man.

Now, let's get back to those stores . . .

Department stores in New York pushed the boundaries of retail spectacle, creating fierce competition within the city and setting trends across the nation. In the late nineteenth century, John Wanamaker, a major retailer from Philadelphia, threw his hat in the New York ring by opening a branch of his department store in Manhattan with a massive building that took up a full city block. In the early twentieth century, he expanded Wanamaker's to another building across the street, connecting the two with an enclosed pedestrian bridge with an elegant clock perfectly positioned to catch the eyes of those walking below. With the store having more than thirty acres of shopping space, an auditorium, and a massive restaurant, the "bridge of progress" was not only a connector but a visual reminder to the public that it's always a good time to shop.

Many New York retailers used clocks for brand promotion just as other businesses did, but they approached advertising clocks as if they were jewelry, a sort of fashion accessory for their buildings. Creative retailers commissioned public timepieces

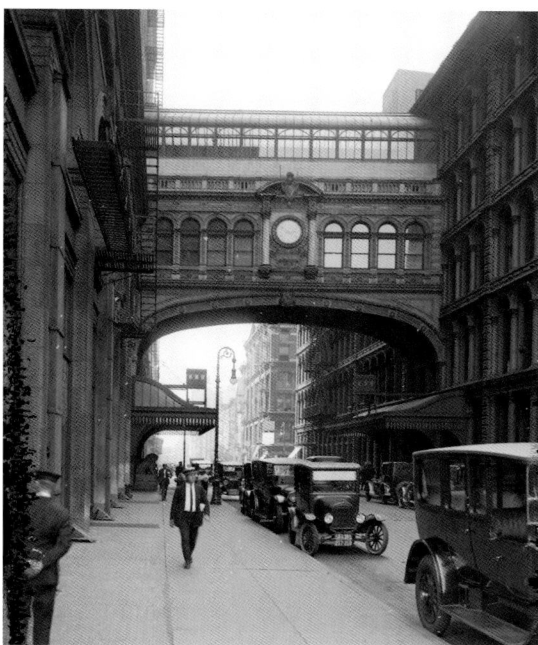

to express their unique sense of style. Some became iconic. The Tiffany & Co. Atlas clock first appeared on the store in the 1850s and was relocated to each of the three following buildings as the company grew and moved farther uptown. The Tiffany clock has remained a constant image of this luxury jewelry store for 175 years.

The clocks that follow still beckon us from the sidewalks. And let's be honest, isn't it a lovely idea to get offline and take in a moment of retail therapy, assisted by an actual person amid thoughtfully prepared displays of the most enticing products? Maybe even take a break and have lunch upstairs to rest your weary well-shod feet? Before you hit the street, remember this is New York; change your internet-scrolling sweats for something that makes you a contributing member of the sidewalk runway. Ready? Time to shop.

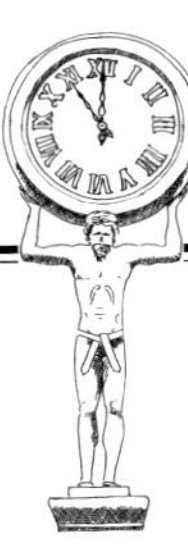

TIFFANY & CO.

727 FIFTH AVENUE
1853

The iconic Atlas clock on the Tiffany & Co. flagship store at the corner of Fifth Avenue and 57th Street has been the branding symbol of this historic New York company since 1853. The nine-foot-tall figural clock was sculpted in wood by Henry F. Metzler, a carver of ship figureheads. Painted to look like bronze, the striking timepiece was first installed above the Tiffany entrance at 550 Broadway. It made two more stops before moving uptown to its present location in 1940. In 1905, after one of its earlier moves, the *New York Times* described the store exterior this way: "The only mark of Tiffany about the new building is the great clock outside of the third story on the shoulders of a giant Atlas. This ornament was taken from the Union Square store." It is the oldest public clock still in use by a New York store.

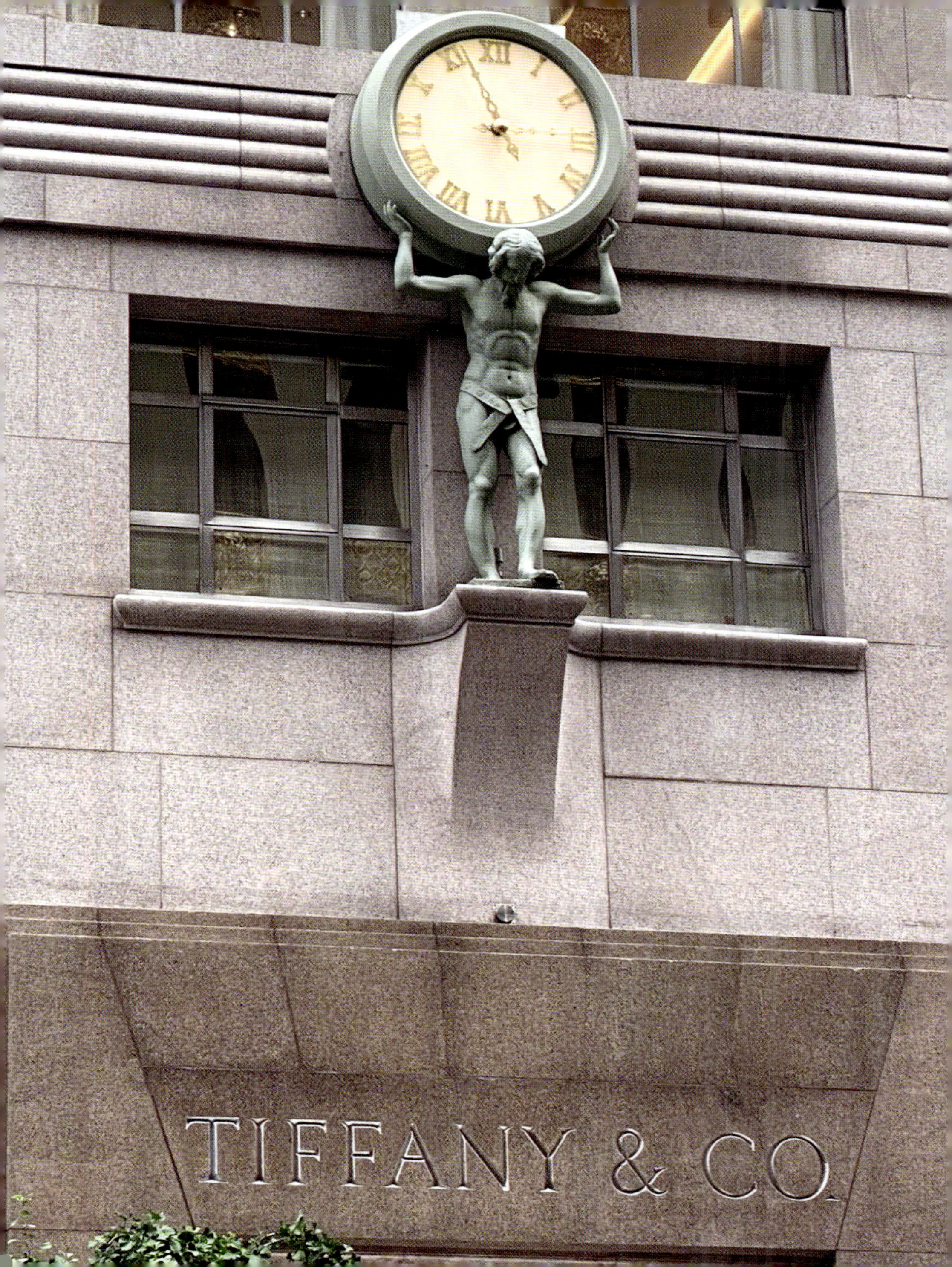
TIFFANY & CO.

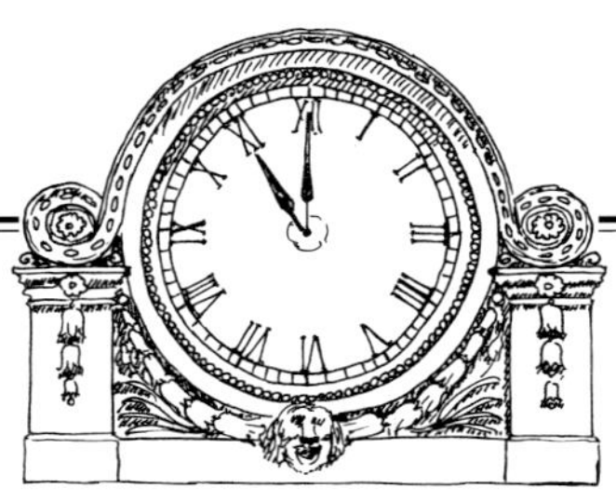

MACY'S HERALD SQUARE

151 WEST 34TH STREET
1902

Designed by De Lemos & Cordes, Macy's covers an entire city block and remains the largest department store in the United States, an honor the store has held since it was built in 1902. The monumental 34th Street entrance is typical of the architects' highly decorative work, taking inspiration from Greek and Roman design but filtered through a turn-of-the-nineteenth-century lens. The granite, almost triumphal arch entrance on 34th Street is flanked by elaborate metalwork that continues to the jewel-like clock above, appropriately fitted with Roman numerals. The highly detailed clock is nestled into the architectural scheme like a gem in a precise setting. It is flanked by four maidens created by sculptor J. Massey Rhind, referencing the Acropolis caryatids in Athens.

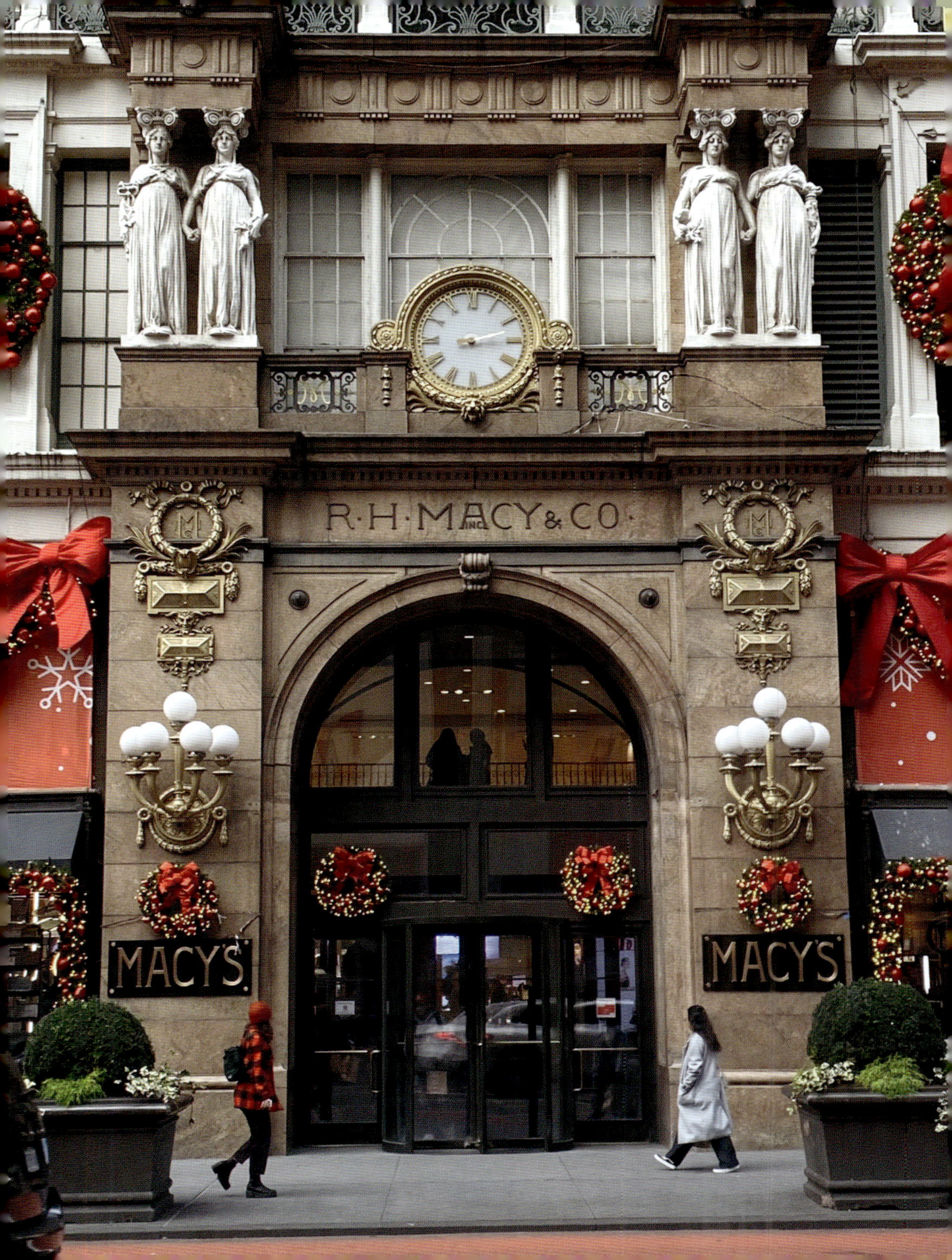

R·H·MACY&CO
INC
MACY'S
MACY'S

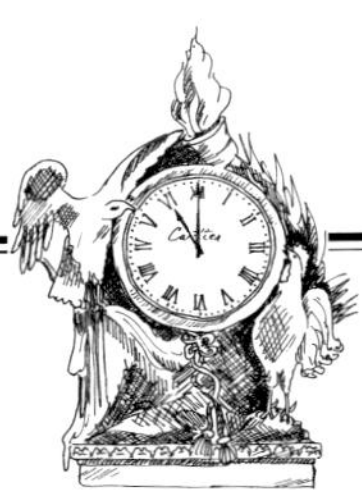

CARTIER FIFTH AVENUE
653 FIFTH AVENUE
1919

The rather exuberant Baroque-inspired bronze clock on the third-floor facade of the Fifth Avenue Cartier mansion was commissioned by Pierre Cartier—once the owner of the fabled Hope Diamond—and installed in 1919. Created by the Brooklyn-based sculptor R. Bonet, the clock casing features an American eagle and a French rooster, symbolizing the United States and France, respectively. Cartier explained the symbolism this way: "I have used my best efforts to promote and develop, through Franco-American organizations, the closest economic and cultural relations between the United States and France. To me France and America are sister countries, and they will always remain so." The building was originally designed by Robert W. Gibson and completed in 1905. It is one of the few remaining mansions on Fifth Avenue.

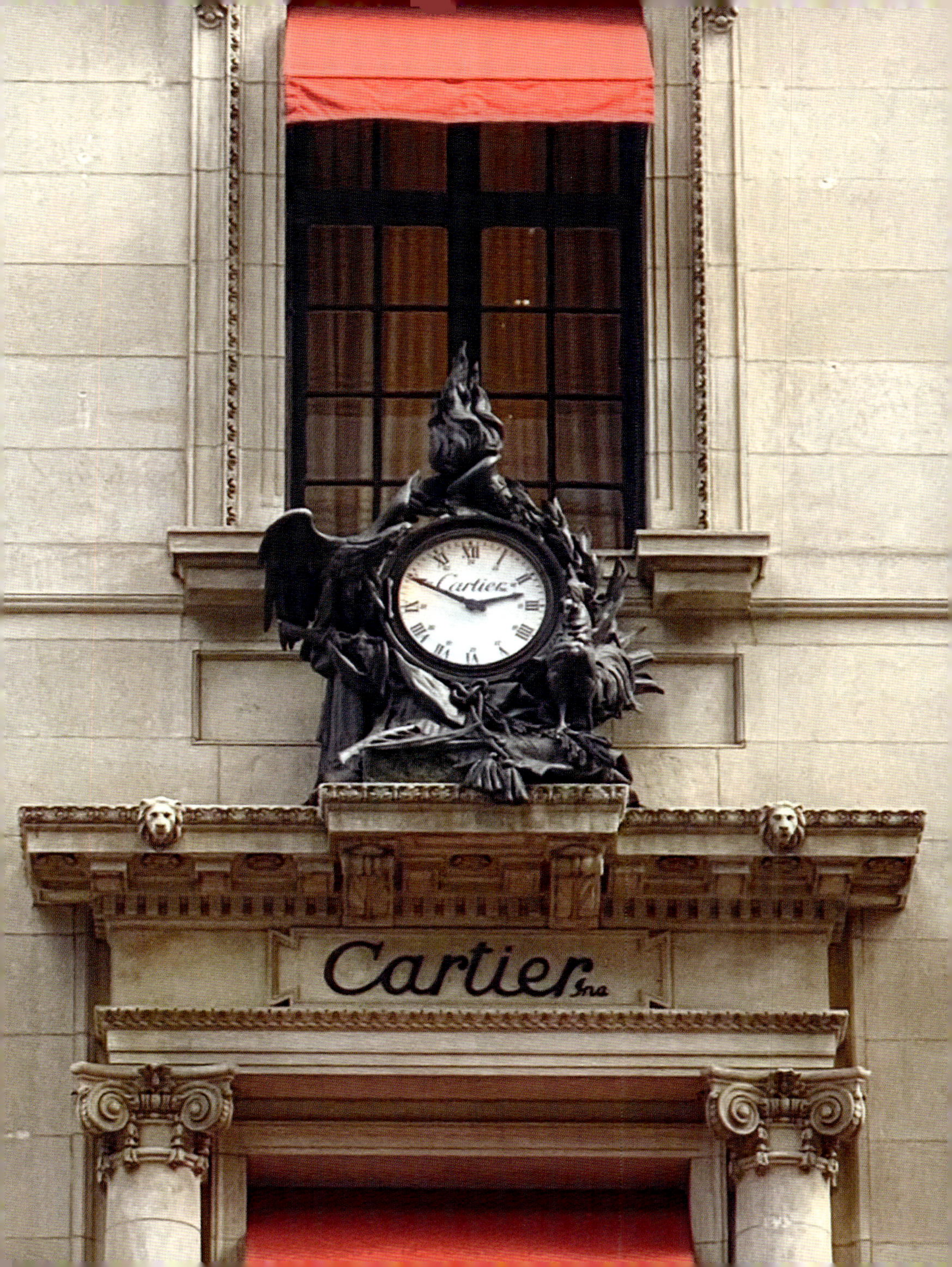
Cartier
Cartier Inc

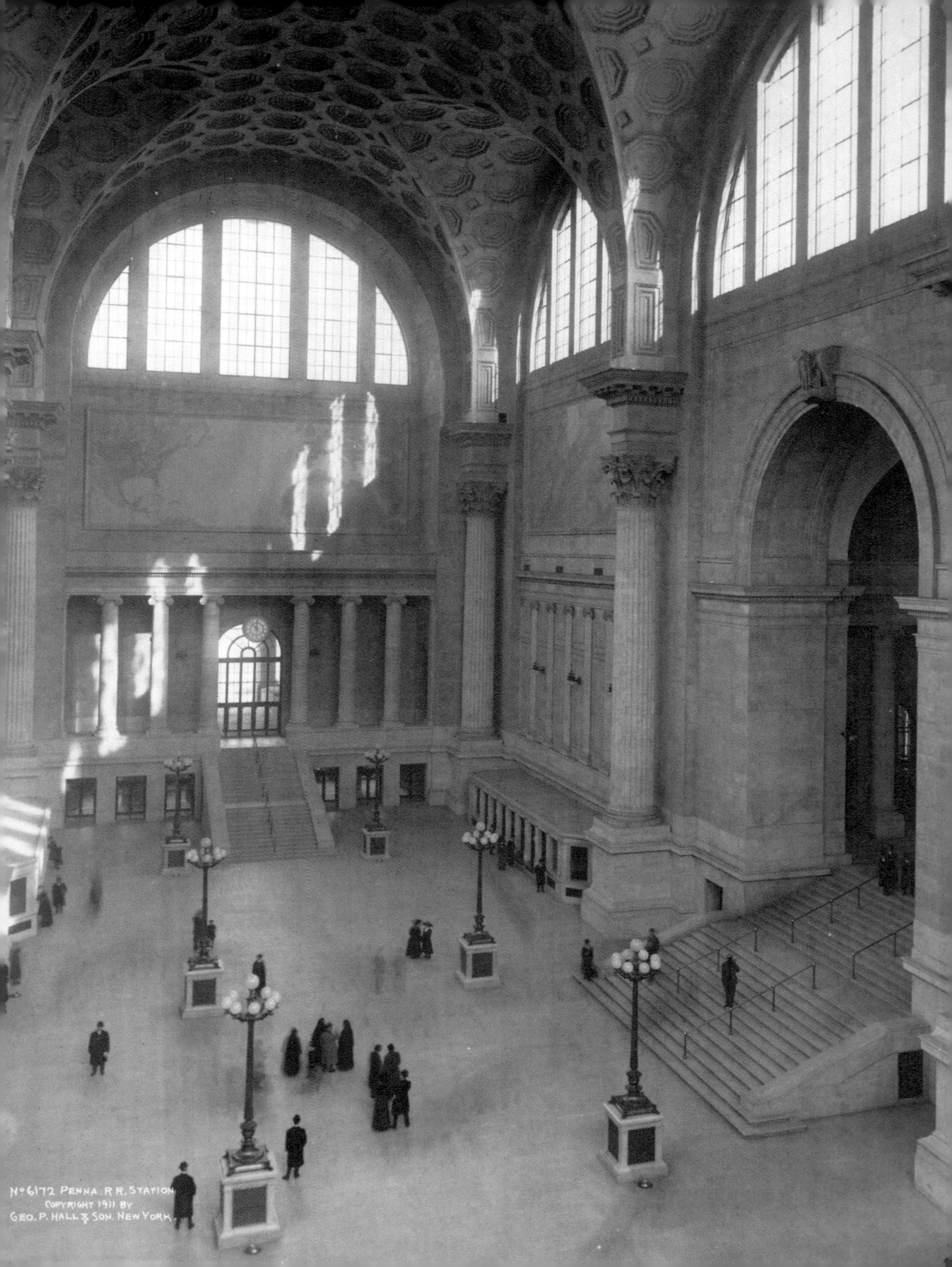

Nº 6172 Penna. R.R. Station
Copyright 1911 By
Geo. P. Hall & Son, New York.

ONCE UPON A TIME

PENNSYLVANIA STATION
CLOCKS

Once upon a time there were *two* glorious train stations in Manhattan, both expressing the aspirations of a great city. Grand Central Terminal (discussed in chapter 1) still exists, but there was another of equal (some say greater) magnificence that does not—the old Pennsylvania Station. Considered a monumental masterpiece and a life-enhancing structure in its time, the old Penn Station was designed by McKim, Mead & White and completed in 1910. It was destroyed in 1963 because of shortsightedness and the total disregard for the vision it took to create this masterpiece and how it could still contribute to the city. And what replaced it? The new Madison Square Garden that squashes down on a claustrophobic "new" Penn Station. The station's low ceilings, cramped public spaces, and narrow staircases make a has-been suburban shopping mall look far more appealing. This mid-century development remains a dismal excuse of a building that is as ugly as it is soul crushing to use as a commuter. None of the clocks from the replacement station will be shared here. Instead, let's take a moment to see what was taken from us, and, on a brighter note, how this great loss birthed a movement that helped other historic buildings survive and thrive.

Given the room's enormous size, the clocks seem much smaller than they were. These timepieces, located at entry and exit points, were perfectly situated for rushing travelers.

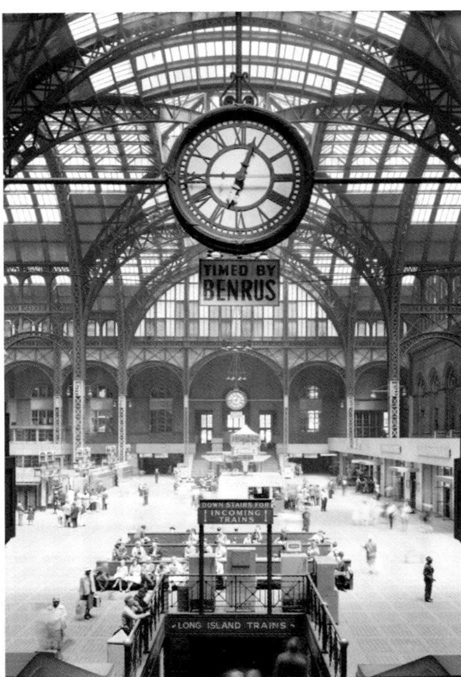

PENNSYLVANIA STATION, interior, 1962

This glass roof supported by iron trusses created a light-filled space in which to board the trains. The clocks pictured here are likely original, but the "BENRUS" sign advertised a wristwatch company in the 1960s.

Alexander Cassatt (the older brother of the Impressionist painter Mary Cassatt) was the president of Pennsylvania Railroad. Cassatt had the bold vision to create a monumental structure using the Gare du Quai d'Orsay in Paris as inspiration, but with the goal of topping that magnificent building to create a world landmark in New York. Key to erecting the new station was digging tunnels under the Hudson River, an engineering feat that had never been attempted on such a scale. Charles Jacobs was the chief engineer on the project. In 1902, Cassatt reached out to Charles McKim to design a train station inspired by ancient Rome and the Baths of Caracalla. However, McKim and Cassatt both did not live to see the completion of their largest life project.

Opening to the public in 1910, Pennsylvania Station made access to New York City by rail from the south possible for the

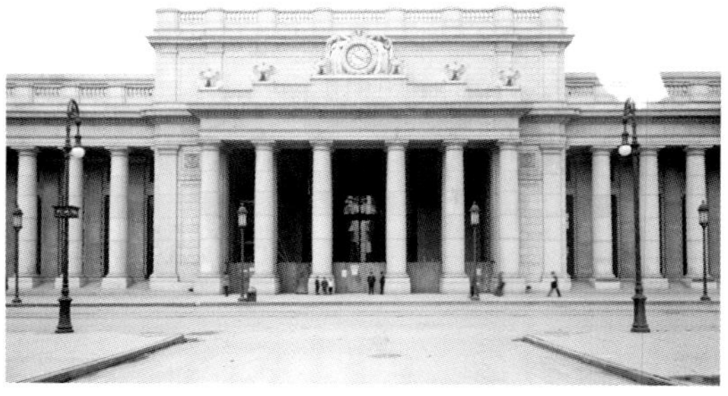

Pennsylvania Station was an architectural masterpiece and deeply mourned gift to New York. The clock, (detail below) flanked by female allegorical figures of Day and Night, represented the nearly constant use of this monumental building.

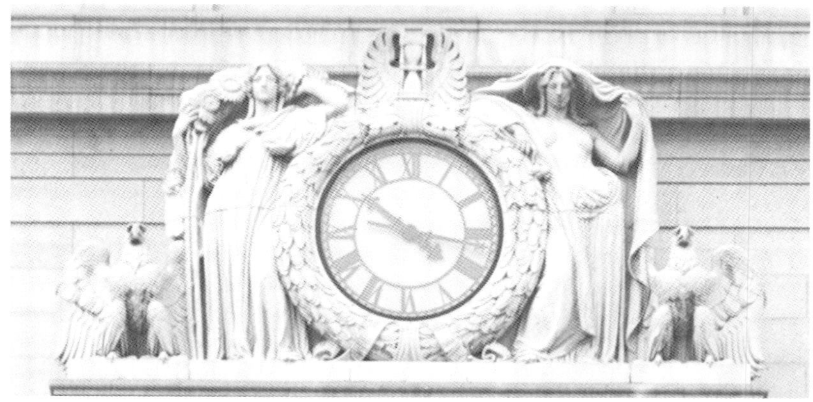

first time, bringing an expanding and ennobled workforce to the city, who marveled at the station's Roman-inspired magnificence. Centered on each of the four exterior elevations was a nearly symmetrical stone sculpture grouping, consisting of two goddess-like figures leaning on large clocks flanked by a pair of eagles. These were known as the "Day and Night" clocks, with the woman on the left representing "Day," as she holds a crown of sunflowers like a halo behind her head, while "Night" is depicted bare-breasted, pulling a mantle over her head, symbolizing the coming darkness of nightfall. The seven-foot wreath-framed clock they lean upon is surmounted by an hourglass flanked by wings, representing the speedy passing of time. On each side of the women are eagles, which are repeated elsewhere on the

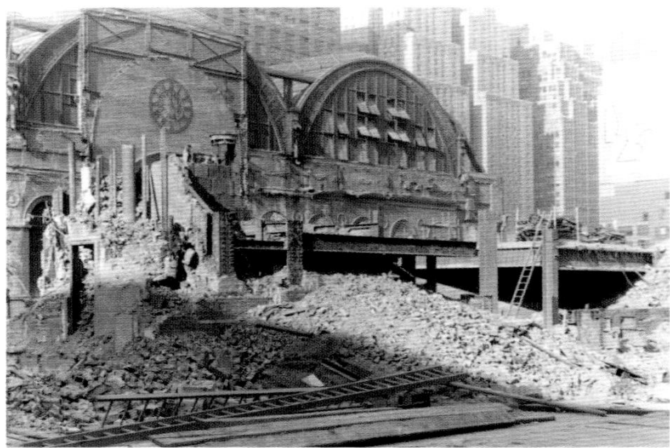

entablature. These clocks were positioned on each facade so regardless of the side one entered the station, the time was always visible.

Much has been written about the tragic loss of Penn Station and the fight by Jacqueline Kennedy Onassis and others to make sure the same fate did not fall upon Grand Central Terminal. There were attempts to save Penn Station, but the demolition plan was kept from the public until the last moment, so very little organizing could take place. In the 1950s and '60s, there was little public interest or awareness of the value of historic preservation. This was a new issue for most Americans. New York's mayor at the time, Robert Wagner, saw the need and established the Committee for the Preservation of Structures and Esthetic Importance—but it was too late for Penn Station.

Beloved Yale art historian Vincent Scully was a harsh critic of the demolition of Penn Station, and after it was replaced with Madison Square Garden, he famously wrote about the former magnificence of this New York gateway: "One entered the city like a god; one scuttles in now like a rat." Pulitzer Prize–winning Ada Louise Huxtable, the first full-time architectural critic of the *New York Times*, wrote on October 30, 1963: "It is the

shame of New York, of its financial and cultural communities, its politicians, philanthropists and planners, and of the public as well, that no serious effort was made. . . . We will probably be judged not by the monuments we build but by those we have destroyed."

The historic photographs on the previous pages remind us of what we have lost and how, in so many ways, the replacement building has extended our mourning. Beautiful spaces created for the public are life-affirming because they were designed to do just that. Buildings erected solely for harsh financial realities almost always fall short because they are designed to be serviceable until they are demolished, which usually isn't soon enough. A civilized society understands there is value in the creation of beauty meant to last, and that it should be preserved for many generations. It's also better for the planet. For me, the old Penn Station was the perfect example of a building that inspired and expanded the view of human potential. I believe experiencing greatness inspires greatness—living with mediocrity does not.

Efforts have been in the works for many years to right this terrible wrong, and headway was recently made to create a transportation space in the magnificent old post office (called the James A. Farley Building) directly west of Penn Station. This building was also designed by McKim, Mead & White, bringing a lovely symmetry to the effort. The new Moynihan Train Hall opened in 2021, with a glass-covered train hall where the main mail-sorting room used to be. Suspended from that crystal ceiling is the only contemporary clock in this book. This twenty-first-century timepiece is an object of use and beauty in the spirit of the historic clocks I've shared here. I feel it joins hands with the others in the spirit of civic pride, practical use, and good design, intentionally created to inspire and feed the soul. You'll find it on the next page.

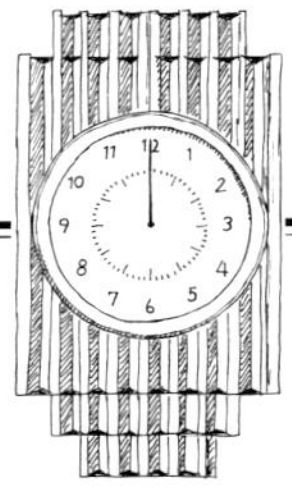

MOYNIHAN TRAIN HALL

350 WEST 33RD STREET
2021

Peter Pennoyer Architects designed this twenty-first-century clock in a nod to the Art Deco period, a style that Pennoyer refers to as "modern classicism." The twelve-foot-tall, four-sided clock hangs like a meticulous, fluted pendant that embraces a machine-age aesthetic appropriate for a twenty-first-century train station housed within a historic building; it suspends from iron trusses in the beautifully repurposed neo-classical post office building. The numerals on the clock are part of a typeface designed in 1936 specifically for road and railroad signage, and yet it pays homage to public clocks in New York City dating back to the eighteenth century. Proving that the City Beautiful movement can still exist when there is a will and responsible understanding that the population deserves good design in its public spaces, this impeccable clock reminds us that we stand in the now.

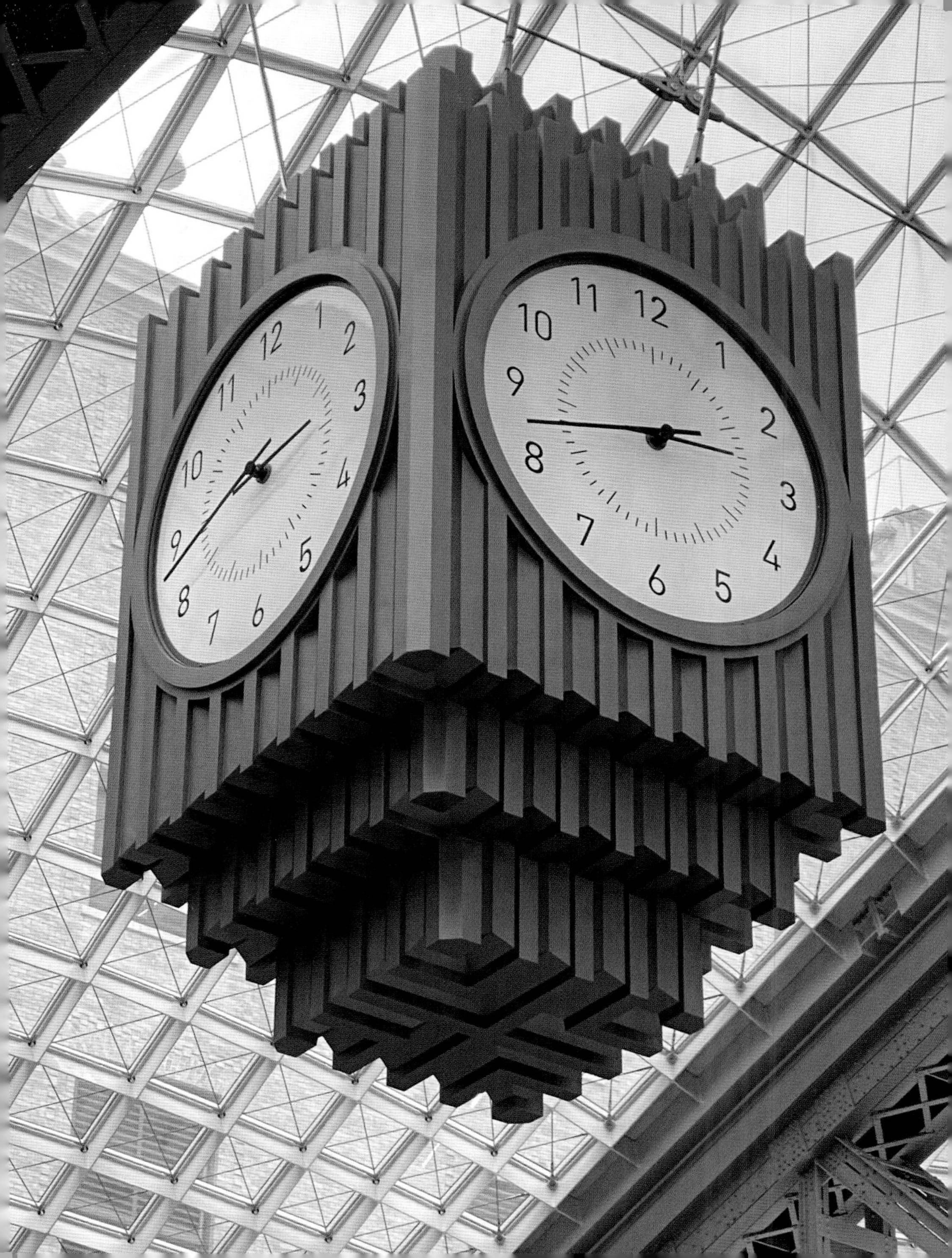

AFTERWORD
ODD CLOCKS IN

I've spent decades arranging things: my body into ballet positions, interiors, collections, gardens, shops—and now the clocks in this book. Everything has an ideal place, and I've always sought to find order and put things, and myself, precisely where they belong. That hyperawareness of place, of home really, came to me after I realized I was born very much out of place in Texas, a location and a culture that never felt right or even safe for someone like me. I was fortunate that my path led me to New York City, and grateful I had the chutzpah to make the leap, not fully realizing I was the first in my family to do so (or to use a Yiddish word in a sentence).

Arranging things was a skill not necessarily related to my Texas experience, but could be more correctly blamed on my obsessive fussiness about such things. While organizing the clocks in this book, I found a few beauties that didn't fit into my very specific categories. Could it be that I had created outsider clocks? Perish the thought.

One of these timepieces is a singularly handsome, neoclassical clock in Harlem ornamenting the facade on, of all things, a fireproof storage facility. Designed for the templelike facade of Lee Brothers Storage Warehouse near Riverside Drive and

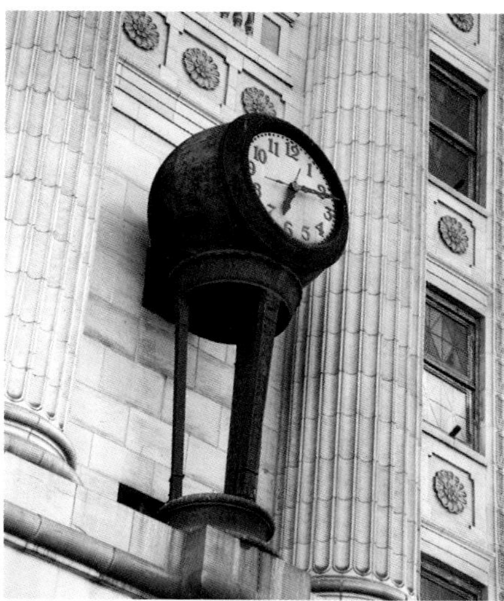

A clock on the neoclassical facade of this warehouse stands tall in Harlem. The clock and the facade it resides in are an extraordinary style statement for a building that has such a basic purpose: storage. It shows the desire for New York businesses to be seen as players in the urban, man-made landscape.

134th Street in Harlem, this bronze, globe-shaped clock on a tripod base suggests an ancient Greek brazier. The *New York Times* wrote in October 1998: "The beautifully detailed, classically inspired building, erected in 1929, was designed as a furniture warehouse and has remained just that." It was rumored to have been built for the Astor family, though that could have just been a way to promote the business. Designed by George S. Kingsley, who created other classically inspired warehouses, the building still stands, though the clock no longer remains.

The second is a sundial, tucked away inside Central Park's 72nd Street eastside entrance. The sundial is part of an extraordinary granite bench known as the Waldo Hutchins Bench, erected in 1932. Waldo Hutchins was an attorney, congressman, and member of the original Board of Commissioners of Central Park, serving from 1857 to 1869 and again from 1888 until his death in 1891. The designer of the granite bench commemorating Hutchins was architect and interior designer Eric Gugler, who among other things designed the Oval Office commissioned by FDR following a fire. The bench and sundial were fabricated by the

Piccirilli Brothers, a firm created by an Italian immigrant family. (The Piccirilli Brothers were well-known as the most prominent stone-carving studio in the United States, creating many iconic monuments, such as the Lincoln Memorial in Washington, DC, designed by Daniel Chester French.) A footed sundial sits centered on the top edge of the bench. The sundial's gnomon, or shadow-casting element, is a bronze female figure by sculptor Paul Howard Manship, who created the Prometheus statue at Rockefeller Center. Chiseled on the inside curve of the sundial is the Latin phrase "Ne Diruatur Fuga Temporum," which translates to: "Let it not be destroyed by the passage of time."

Because this sundial is a surviving oddball, I decided to have my portrait taken with it, hoping it would find a place in this book. It was only when I mentioned this to my brilliant friend Margaret Roach that I realized, or more accurately, she made me realize, I had something in common with this clock—we were both outsiders in a city of outsiders.

As my picture was being taken on a perfect "Autumn in New York" day, Marlo Thomas walked into the park wearing a jogging suit. She passed behind my good friend and photographer Stephen Mack as he was shooting, and sat at the far end of the long, curved bench. Celebrity sightings are never a surprise in Manhattan, and following proper New York etiquette, none of us disturbed her. Such disruptions are usually selfish, and besides, who has time for that?

Being that close to *the* Marlo Thomas, I was instantly transported to the 1960s when as a child I fell head over heels in love with the woman and her groundbreaking sitcom *That Girl*. I'd almost forgotten about its personal impact on my preteen self, or that it was my first introduction to New York, a city I didn't yet know existed. After finishing the shoot, I hailed a cab on Fifth Avenue to head home. In the cab, I took a moment to reflect on the

once-outrageous storyline of a young, single woman moving to the city alone to pursue her dreams. Not her father's dreams, not her husband's. Hers. Marlo Thomas was the first woman in television history to do this. Sounds silly today, but it was a very big deal back then. That "girl" at the end of Waldo Hutchins Bench made it possible for many, including this sissy boy, to dream big and get out of Dodge. Bless her heart (and I don't mean that in the Texas way).

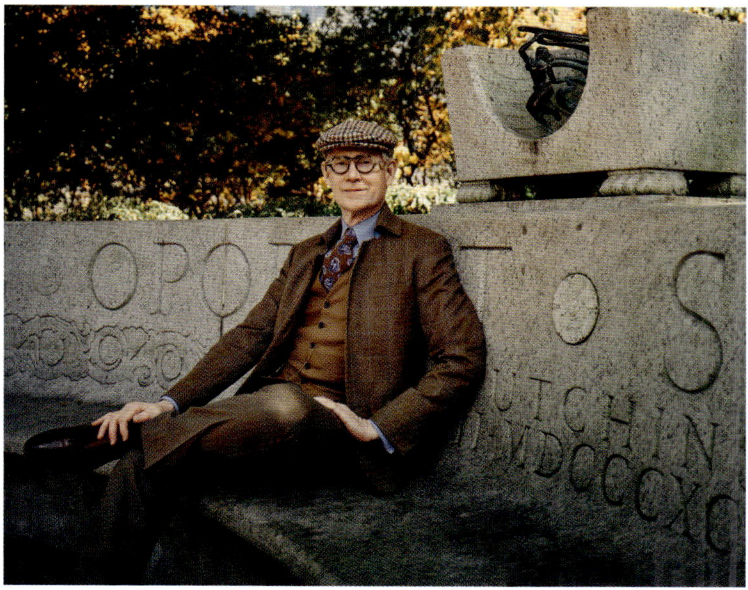

Waldo Hutchins Bench, 1932, Central Park

The author seated beside a granite and bronze sun-dial on the Waldo Hutchins Bench in Central Park.

ACKNOWLEDGMENTS

Time for gratitude: These beautiful people, and those I mistakenly failed to mention, make (and in some cases made) the world a better place.

To each one I say thank you.

Eternal gratitude to my own Thomas Schumacher.

A ballet bow to my generous friend, and ultimate New Yorker, Wendy Goodman.

Mentors and supporters in life, dance, art and design: Mom and Dad, Millicent Lahm, Neil and Camille Hess, Melissa Hayden, Willy Burmann, Edwin Anthony and Tony Greco, Elly Nordskog, John Loring, Suzanne Slesin, Margaret Russell, Paige Rense, Jason Kontos, Dan Shaw, and Randi MacColl.

Deep appreciation to those with lovely things to say: Doug Wright, Joel Grey, Michael Henry Adams, and David Rockwell.

The ever supportive and talented White Webb team: Frank Webb and Kacie DeMaio.

Dear friends who helped and encouraged: Margaret Roach, Rick Miramontez, Charles Tolbert, and Aubrey Lynch.

Patient, gifted, and generous bookmakers: Lauren Orthey, David Fabricant, Stephanie Baker, Misha Beletsky, Louise Kurtz, and the whole team at Abbeville Press.

FURTHER READING

Barnett, Jo Ellen. *Time's Pendulum: From Sundials to Atomic Clocks, the Fascinating History of Timekeeping and How Our Discoveries Changed the World.* New York: Harcourt Brace, 1999.

DeSantis, Chris. *Clocks of New York: An Illustrated History.* Jefferson, North Carolina: McFarland & Company, 2006.

Diamonstein-Spielvogel, Barbaralee. *The Landmarks of New York: An Illustrated, Comprehensive Record of New York City's Historic Buildings.* 6th ed. New York: Washington Mews Books, 2016.

Diehl, Lorraine B. *The Late, Great Pennsylvania Station.* New York: Four Walls Eight Windows, 1985.

Dolkart, Andrew S. *Morningside Heights: A History of Its Architecture and Development.* New York: Columbia University Press, 1998.

Gray, Christopher. *New York Streetscapes: Tales of Manhattan's Significant Buildings and Landmarks.* New York: Harry N. Abrams, 2003.

Homberger, Eric. *The Historical Atlas of New York City: A Visual Celebration of 400 Years of New York City's History.* 3rd ed. New York: St. Martin's Griffin, 2016.

Kaplan, Paul M. *New York's Original Penn Station: The Rise and Tragic Fall of an American Landmark.* Charleston, South Carolina: History Press, 2019.

Landes, David S. *Revolution in Time: Clocks and the Making of the Modern World.* 2nd ed. Cambridge, Massachusetts: Belknap Press of Harvard University Press, 2000.

Lowe, David Garrard. *Stanford White's New York.* New York: Watson-Guptill, 1999.

New York City Landmarks Preservation Commission. *Guide to New York City Landmarks.* 3rd ed. Hoboken, New Jersey: John Wiley & Sons, 2003.

Norcross, Frank W. *A History of the New York Swamp.* New York: Chiswick Press, 1901.

Silver, Nathan. *Lost New York.* Boston: Houghton Mifflin, 1967.

White, Norval, Elliot Willensky, and Fran Leadon. *AIA Guide to New York City.* 5th ed. New York: Oxford University Press, 2010.

ILLUSTRATION CREDITS

Alamy: p. 126 (Heritage Image Partnership Ltd.). *Art Resource (Museum of the City of New York)*: pp. 24 (Byron Company), 26 (Byron Company), 28 (Byron Company), 88 (Heliotype Printing Co.), 90 (bottom: Byron Company), 91 (Wurts Bros.), 112 (Irving Underhill), 124 (Wurts Bros.), 127 (Byron Company), 166, 169 (Wurts Bros.), 185 (Edmund Vincent Gillon). *Getty Images*: p. 64 (Erika Stone). *Library of Congress*: pp. 16 (top: A.P. Yates, Syracuse; bottom: William Henry Jackson), 17 (Keystone View Company), 40 (John Feulner), 42 (Detroit Publishing Co.), 44 (Alfred S. Campbell), 74 (Detroit Publishing Co.), 76 (right), 140 (Detroit Publishing Co.), 143 (Detroit Publishing Co.), 178 (Cervin Robinson), 179 (Detroit Publishing Co.). *Stephen Mack*: p. 188. *Neal Boenzi/The New York Times/Redux*: p. 20 (right). *New York Historical*: pp. 11, 14 (Irving Browning), 29 (Courtesy of New York Transit Museum), 43 (George P. Hall & Son), 62 (Irving Browning), 90 (top: Irving Browning), 110 (Robert L. Bracklow), 153 (Courtesy of New York Transit Museum), 176 (George P. Hall & Son), 180 (Alexander Hatos), 184 (Irving Browning). *New York Public Library*: pp. 65 (Berenice Abbott), 76 (left: Mail & Express), 150 (William D. Smith). *Matthew White*: front and back cover, pp. 6, 8, 18–19, 20 (left), 21, 23, 31, 33, 35, 37, 39, 47, 49, 51, 53, 55, 57, 59, 61, 67, 69, 71, 73, 79, 81, 83, 85, 87, 95, 97, 99, 101, 103, 105, 107, 109, 115, 117, 119, 121, 123, 131, 133, 135, 137, 139, 145, 147, 149, 155, 157, 159, 161, 163, 165, 171, 173, 175, 183

INDEX

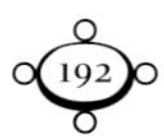

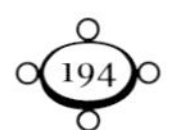

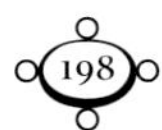

MATTHEW WHITE is a former ballet dancer and a noted interior designer, author, antiquarian, and preservationist. An emeritus board member and former chairman of Save Venice Inc., he currently lives in the Hudson Valley with his husband and two dachshunds while running a historic general store and working to revitalize the historic hamlet of Hillsdale, New York. It was New York City that pulled him out of the Texas panhandle, and it was New York City that saved him from a life that stood still. His first book, *Italy of My Dreams: The Story of an American Designer's Real-Life Passion for Italian Style*, was published by Pointed Leaf Press.

WENDY GOODMAN is the design editor of *New York* magazine and *Curbed*. She has written two books, *The World of Gloria Vanderbilt* and *May I Come In? Discovering the World in Other People's Houses*, and she is the co-author of *Tony Duquette* with Hutton Wilkinson, all published by Abrams Books. She is a born and raised New Yorker, a devoted subway rider, and stopped wearing a watch years ago.

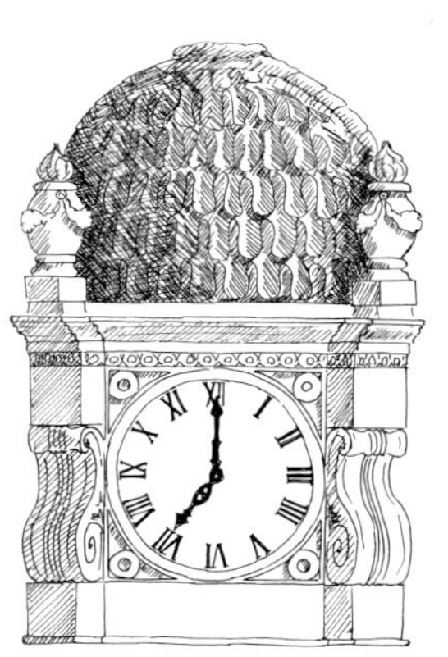

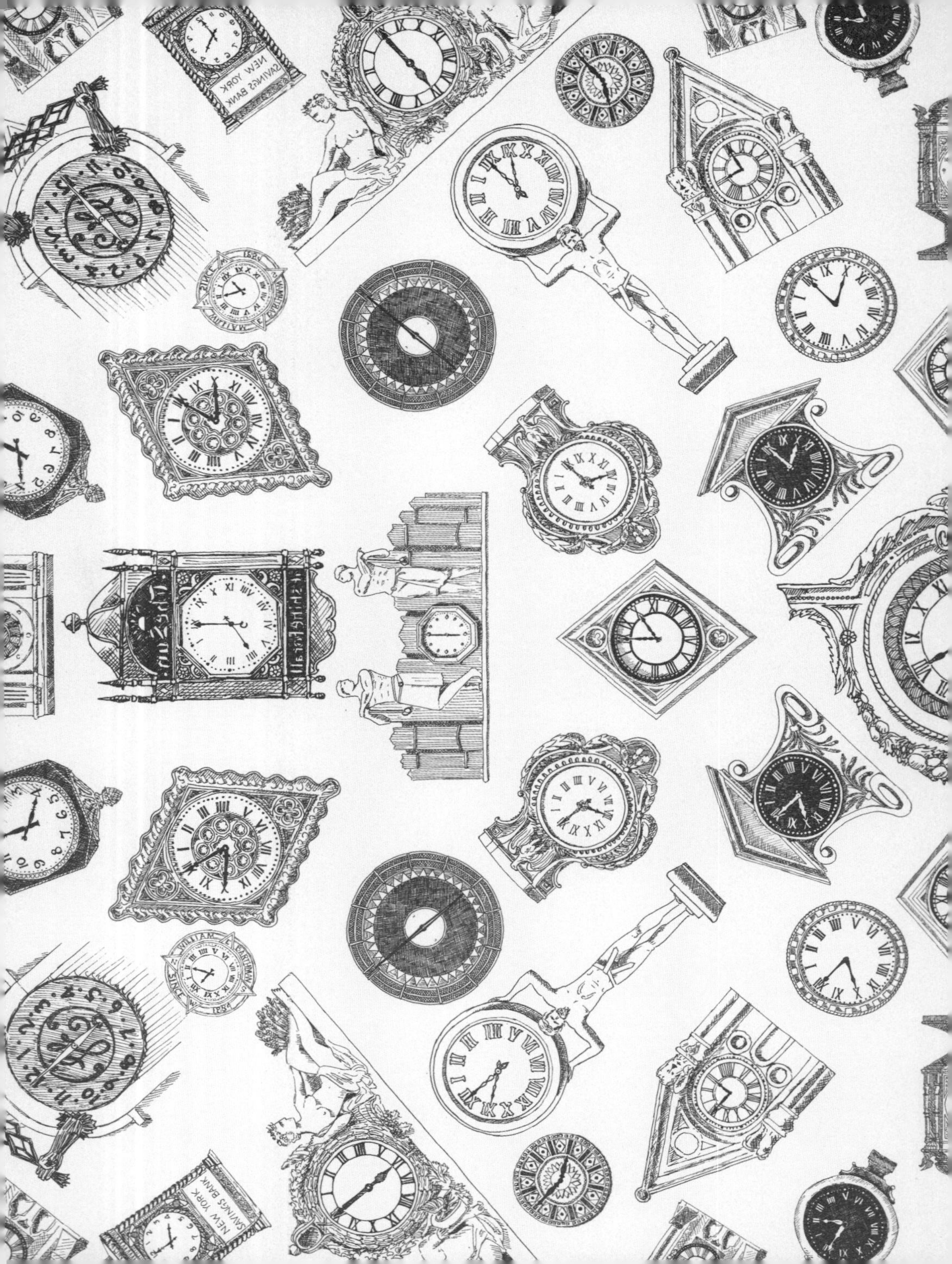